Affectionately,
to Lionel Carley,
Author, Linguist, Scholar, Archivist,
from the "young man"
of pp. 82/99

Felix Aprahamian

more than half-a-century later

26·iv·1988

THE
PROMS

The Proms, 1980 (*cartoon by Peter Brookes, courtesy of* Radio Times)

THE
PROMS
and the men who made them

Barrie Hall

London
GEORGE ALLEN & UNWIN
Boston   Sydney

First published in 1981

GEORGE ALLEN & UNWIN LTD
40 Museum Street, London WC1A 1LU

© Barrie Hall, 1981

British Library Cataloguing in Publication Data

Hall, Barrie
   The Proms.
   1. Concerts–England–London–History
   I. Title
   785'.07'3   ML4   2.L7 80–41895

ISBN 0-0-04-780024-0

Set in 11 on 12 point Baskerville
by King's English Typesetters Limited, Cambridge
Produced in association with Book Production Consultants,
Cambridge
and printed in Great Britain
at the University Press, Cambridge.

for Jean

Contents

	page
Introduction	15
Eighteen Ninety-Five	19
Robert Newman's Promenade Concerts	26
The Vanishing Band	36
'This Brat Wood'	42
In the Midst of Life	51
The Great War	59
Different Drummers	70
Diary of a Young Man	82
Sir Henry Wood's Jubilee	100
Beyond the Call of Duty	108
Jubilee of the Proms	112
The King is Dead	120
Sargent: The Golden Years	130
Checkmate: Sir William Glock	146
'This man will ruin the Proms'	165
Towards the Eighties	179
'Summer would not be summer without the Proms'	196
Promenade	210
Continuity . . .	214
Acknowledgments	218
Index of Events	220
Index of Performers Mentioned	222
Index of Works	227

List of Illustrations

Frontispiece: The Proms, 1980 (*cartoon by Peter Brookes*)

1. Sir Henry Wood (about 1900) — *page* 33
2. Dr Peter Skeggs with a steam engine made by Sir Henry Wood's father — 44
3. Dame Eva Turner in *Le Nozze di Figaro* (about 1930) — 57
4. At Appletree Farm (1924) — 73
5. Dame Myra Hess rehearsing with Jelly d'Aranyi (1928) — 74
6. Queen's Hall and Broadcasting House (1932) — 77
7. Sir Henry Wood intent on carpentry — 83
8. Harriet Cohen and Eileen Joyce — 90
9. Sir Henry Wood (1938) — 103
10. Sir William Walton at a wartime Prom — 110
11. Solomon playing cards with Moiseiwitsch — 115
12. Basil Cameron — 123
13. Sir Malcolm Sargent conducting — 134
14. Larry Adler with Sir Malcolm Sargent — 138
15. Ursula and Dr Ralph Vaughan Williams with Sir Malcolm Sargent — 141
16. John Ogdon — 144
17. Sir William Glock with Peter Maxwell Davies at Dartington Hall — 147
18. Sir Clifford Curzon at a rehearsal — 152
19. Sidonie Goossens OBE — 155
20. Gillian Weir — 157
21. Leopold Stokowski conducting at the 1963 Proms — 160
22. Benjamin Britten conducting Bach's *St John Passion* (1967) — 163
23. Sir Colin Davis — 166
24. Dame Janet Baker and Sir Adrian Boult — 170
25. Jacqueline du Pré — 173
26. Pierre Boulez — 174
27. Karlheinz Stockhausen — 177

28. Bernard Haitink   181
29. Jessye Norman – an unplanned First Night (1980)   183
30. Kyung-Wha Chung   186
31. Jill Gomez   187
32. Emma Kirkby   191
33. Simon Rattle   192
34. An unusual group   194
35. Distinguished pickets (1980)   198
36. An impromptu concert (1980)   199
37. Gennadi Rozhdestvensky with his wife, Victoria
    Postnikova   207
38. Some Promenaders   211
39. Waiting for the doors to open (1980)   213
40. Richard Baker interviewing Promenaders (1975)   215

'The man that hath no music in himself,
Nor is not mov'd with concord of sweet sounds,
Is fit for treasons, stratagems, and spoils;
The motions of his spirit are dull as night,
And his affections dark as Erebus:
Let no such man be trusted.'

Shakespeare, *The Merchant of Venice*; set by Vaughan Williams in
Serenade to Music, a superb tribute from one musician to another.

Introduction

There is no sound quite like it anywhere else in the world. A chorus of over seven thousand voices, all standing up and letting their lungs fill the vast spaces of the Royal Albert Hall. It makes the hairs tingle at the back of your neck, a prickle creep along your spine. It is a sound looked forward to, and heard, by about a hundred million people every year.

In mid-September, in the second half of the Last Night of the Proms, and part-way through Elgar's orchestral *Pomp and Circumstance March No. 1*, the whole audience rises to its feet to sing 'Land of Hope and Glory' to that great tune in the middle. At that moment a fresh excitement grips everyone, whether singing in the hall, listening on the radio, or watching on television. If anyone stopped to think about it, the words are hopelessly outdated, the sentiment embarrassingly jingoistic. Thinking about the words is not the point. For a few brief moments, in that brilliant throng, sweltering in motley dress and waving banners under the hot television lights, it feels very good to be alive, and especially good to be in England. The words they sing may no longer ring true, but there is still a pride in singing them; this is still the finest country in the world to live in. *God, who made thee mighty, make thee mightier yet!*

For eighty-five years the Henry Wood Promenade Concerts were successfully given in almost uninterrupted sequence, over a couple of months during the summer and autumn. They withstood the recurring threat of financial ruin. They emerged intact from two world wars. They survived the destruction of their original home in Queen's Hall at the height of the blitz on London in 1941. Never, until 1980, did they fail to start on the date advertised.

A hostile group, ironically enough based at Queen's Hall, once vigorously opposed these concerts being broadcast. They were convinced that if the newly-formed BBC was allowed to bring public performances into the home by radio, this would be the death of concert-going. By a strange twist of fate and a reversal of fortunes, this same group was soon afterwards obliged to approach the BBC cap in hand, asking them to save the Proms from extinction. They were considerately received; but the price was to broadcast from the Proms in return for accepting financial responsibility. In spite of earlier fears, this did not empty Queen's Hall. On the contrary, to broadcast an event has generally tended, over the years, to sharpen the public's interest in it. The BBC has been organising and developing the Proms for over half a century; until 1980 their future looked secure for as long as there was radio and television.

The conjunction of the Proms and the BBC made a substantial part of the classical repertoire available every year to an audience far larger than Queen's Hall could have held. The world outside came to know the Proms first by radio and then by television, which now between them largely account for that huge audience of a hundred million.

Three men evolved the Proms as we know them, Robert Newman, Dr George Cathcart, and the best remembered, Henry J. Wood. The idea of concerts where people could walk about was not itself new. What Henry Wood did, with a foresight amounting to genius, was to lay down a set of principles for his very first season which were so successful right from the start that they have not had to be altered except in minor details for almost ninety years. In that time the Proms have grown from an orchestral series into what the Press have called 'The Biggest Music Festival in the World'.

The spreading fame and success of the Proms has encouraged others to try a similar formula. Many British cities outside London now enjoy their own two- or three-week series. They have been tried elsewhere in Europe, notably in Holland, where a faithful audience watches our own Last Night each year via Eurovision. The famous Boston Pops owe something to the Promenade concept; while for New York's short-lived experiment in the genre, another notable Proms figure, Sir Malcolm Sargent, was brought over from England to conduct and to lend authentic atmosphere. His American audience was even allowed to dine at tables during the performances.

One of the hidden strengths of the 'original' Henry Wood Promenade Concerts was that final responsibility for them remained in the hands of one man. Sir Henry J. Wood is the only man to have borne single-handed the combined tasks of planning the programmes, and doing all the conducting as well. Even before his death in 1944 the double task had become too great a burden. Not only would the conducting and the planning in future be undertaken by different people; even the conducting was shared from 1940 onwards. This book is the story of the men who have guided the Proms for nearly ninety years, starting with their energetic Founder. It is also the story of the other music-makers, of the many struggles and crises, and some often dramatic changes of fortune.

I have been blessed with a sympathetic ear and a considerable number of very good friends. With the one I have listened attentively to the other. In this way combined memories of the Proms, going back to well before the Second World War, have brought vividly to life for me what was happening in

Queen's Hall in those far-off days when my father was trying to interest me, as a very small boy, in his newly-acquired crystal set. Later on at the site of the Proms themselves, many conversations in the long watches kept me aware of what had gone on in the past and what was then taking place. Much of this with the passing of time has turned into open secret or common knowledge. I have tried here to reproduce for the reader some sense of the atmosphere of these concerts at various periods in their history.

From professional experience I know that people are interested in what goes on behind the scenes, though such things should never be allowed to distract from an audience's unruffled enjoyment of a concert. Talking to a music club audience, or with friends at dinner, or face to face with just one enthusiast, a few background sketches are always highly appreciated. This book does not try to keep up with every first performance, or debut of artists, though some of these things are mentioned from time to time. It sets out to chronicle the broad developments of nearly ninety years, and to give some of the reasons behind the struggles and changes at the time they were happening. If these things prove interesting to music-lovers, and a good read, then the object of this book will have been achieved.

If it is possible to discover any of the secrets which may have contributed to the long and vigorous life of these concerts, their roots are probably to be found in the very first season. With hindsight we can look at that beginning and draw all kinds of conclusions from it, congratulating ourselves on our powers of analysis. A thorough familiarity with the first year does provide many of the clues to what followed, which is why we shall spend some time considering it; but this is still not where the Proms were conceived. To discover how that happened, we must travel even further back in time, into the void before the Big Bang of the first opening night, a void where such a concept as a whole summer season of Promenade Concerts might at the time have seemed unthinkable; back to the more spacious, leisurely Victorian days at the beginning of the year 1895.

Eighteen Ninety-Five

Early in the spring of 1895 my grandfather stood waiting to hail a cab at the corner of Oxford Circus, looking prosperous, well-groomed, and almost unbearably smug. It would not have taken him all that much longer to walk; there were few people about, and even less traffic, at this time of the evening. One good reason for not walking was the amount of smut in the air; enough for you to need a wash on arrival. Besides, he could well afford the cab.

It struck him as he waited that when you came to think of it, this part of London was rather like a large village. There were places beyond Regent's Park you didn't know much about. It was that fellow Beau Brummel, surely, who had never left the fashionable area bounded by Bond Street, the Mall, Park Lane, and that end of Oxford Street? Which made this the next village to Beau Brummel's. A local doctor lived around Harley Street, where the distinguished and the merely rapacious might share the same surgery. Then there were all those village stores along Oxford Street whose owners lived above the shop. This reminded him that someone had mentioned a fine scale reproduction of the Great Northern Railway's 4–2–2 Stirling 'single'* engine in that excellent model shop; he must find time to look at it one midday. There was even a new Village Hall next to the church; just north of him stood the Queen's Hall into which, until recently, you might have glimpsed the beard of George Bernard Shaw disappearing. A pity he left *The World* when its editor died last year; whatever his musical skill, Shaw had written most entertaining reviews.

Deliberately lifting from a brocade waistcoat pocket his half-hunter by its gold chain, he flicked it open to reassure himself that there was still comfortable time. A selfish chap, really, Beau Brummel, he thought; *he* would

---

* Having only one pair of driving wheels.

never have supported advancement for the working classes. Now Prince Albert – he stroked his moustaches in subconscious tribute to Queen Victoria's long lamented Consort – the good prince had given the nation such a splendid lead, not only in the arts and sciences, but also in self-improvement of all kinds. Everything reasonable was now being done so that people could learn to lead fuller lives. The better-off were paying. *He* was paying. His conscience was clear. What a time to be alive! The glorious Empire. Solid. The ground felt firm beneath his feet.

There was the sound of horses' hooves rounding a corner. A cab; at last. A word to the driver as he removed his hat and climbed in: 'St James's Theatre.' The new Wilde comedy *The Importance of Being Earnest* was playing to packed houses. Everyone said it had to be seen. He had finally managed to obtain tickets.

The spirited crunching of the cab wheels' iron treads on the cobbled road at once plunged him into the midst of his evening's enjoyment. Sunblinds were out over the shop windows down Regent Street against the late afternoon sun. Not the Music-Hall this week, he thought, as the cab passed the Pavilion; though that young Marie Lloyd had shown great promise when he'd last seen her. No; tonight, the Play. His dear wife would be joining him there from her Charity; wasn't it today they were voting on whether to work with that rabble-rousing Salvation Army? Not much further to go. He suddenly realised that this cab was passing his tailor, his shoemaker, and his hatter, in that order. The thought amused and pleased him.

He tipped the driver carefully; perhaps a trifle generously. He could already feel that this was going to be a very good evening. He entered the plush foyer of St James's Theatre, where the soft low hiss of the bright gas mantles welcomed him in to warmth and comfort.

My grandfather might have been mildly surprised, whilst watching Algernon Moncrieff on the stage before him consuming the cucumber sandwiches intended for Lady Bracknell, had he known that away behind him in Queen's Hall the manager was at that moment in his office, sitting in his leather armchair, feet on the desk, hands clasped behind his head, eyes closed, deep in thought and a haze of cigar smoke. The manager was Robert Newman, letting his mind roam once more among the options open to him.

He was grappling with a problem that has vexed all impresarios in all ages. It worried the Greeks in their theatres, and it worried the Romans in theirs. It had been Shakespeare's problem; and it is the concern of all actor-managers and concert societies everywhere. By what new stratagem do you ensure that the seats are filled, not just for one event, but every night? Not that things were going too badly at Queen's Hall. An orchestra sounded better there than in any other hall in London. The curiously boat-shaped smaller concert room upstairs was satisfactorily booked for recitals. But the time seemed ripe to take a big leap forward in this new hall; and Newman felt it was up to him to come out with some infallible master-stroke to astonish the bourgeoisie. Every manager hopes for the brilliant idea that will strike gold. The trouble is, he soon realises that all the brilliant ideas have already been tried.

As a matter of fact, Newman had been toying vaguely with one of them for some time. Nearly half a century ago, an unknown Frenchman had taken London by storm with a new idea he had brought with him to Covent Garden; Promenade Concerts where, true to the title, some of the audience could indeed walk about, seeing and being seen. What concerts those had been! Hundreds of performers; orchestras and military bands together. The very latest quadrilles and polkas. Soloists galore. Attracting huge audiences in all their finery, out for a good time and knowing they would not be disappointed. People in the business of putting on concerts still remembered them to this day.

Indeed they had never quite disappeared from the London concert scene. They had been tried again from time to time, at the Haymarket and other places. Newman had run them at Her Majesty's, and quite recently in Queen's Hall itself. There was the snag. They had been tried, yes; but never with quite the same degree of success. They had lacked the intensely magnetic attraction of their original central figure, the dazzling, the irresistible personality of that prince of showman conductors, Louis Jullien. He had gone back to Paris after making and losing several fortunes with his novel concerts here. To put on a show such as he had done involved a large investment, and that money was at risk if the concerts failed to catch on. Nevertheless, the feeling persisted that now was the right moment to be leading audiences forward with more concerts of even better music – if they could be persuaded to come. Newman had already made his choice of conductor. He intended to put the whole weight of his experience behind one young man, whose reputation would grow along with that of the new concerts. The trouble, as always, was money. The young man had none of his own to put up, that much was certain. Newman could not for the moment see where the necessary financial backing might be found, should he decide to try the Jullien formula once more in this new place. He again shelved the idea for the time being; then quietly let himself into his private box, to hear the rest of the Bach Choir's sure-fire success in his hall that evening, the *Mass in B minor* with Brahms's old friend Joseph Joachim playing the violin obbligatos, and Charles Villiers Stanford conducting.

Less than a quarter of a mile away, in Upper Wimpole Street, a doctor with a sizeable practice treating ailments of the ear, nose and throat, was pouring out a glass of claret for a friend. The friend was a tolerably good bass singer, a Scot called W. A. Peterkin, who had often had cause to consult Dr Cathcart about those sinus troubles with which all singers seem to be plagued. Peterkin was taking singing lessons with a young coach, recommended to him by his friend Cathcart, a young man already marked out for a successful career with singers, who only last year had been rehearsing with Nellie Melba at her home in Great Cumberland Place. As it happened, he would be having a lesson the very next day. Would Dr Cathcart like to sit in once again on the lesson, to judge for himself how things were progressing? The young man knew a great deal concerning the human voice, so it was always quite interesting, as George Cathcart also dedicated part of his life to those same vocal organs, if from a rather different standpoint. And so it was agreed.

In his own private rooms above his father's model shop in Oxford Street, the young man whose work was known to both Robert Newman and Dr Cathcart independently, wrenched himself with difficulty away from the 3½ inch gauge model steam railway running all round the second-floor room which served him as workshop, laboratory and playroom. His father's scale models were a great joy, some of the best locomotives available. It needed a real effort of will to douse the little spirit lamp underneath the boiler. Strength of will was one of the young man's characteristics, fortunately for his destiny. In a life already crowded with pursuits, all of them highly interesting and enjoyable, his time had to be strictly apportioned. He took painting lessons at the St John's Wood Art School, as befitted a man who had met John Ruskin in the Lake District whilst directing Mary Wakefield's famous Music Festival. He gave singing lessons. He played piano and organ accompaniments. He was becoming quite well-known as a coach and a conductor of opera; a three-month tour with the Carl Rosa Company had just ended. There was something new in the air at Queen's Hall too. Nothing wrong with a chap being keen on model railways, of course; but a living had to be earned as well. There were scores to be studied, lessons to be prepared. This particular young man's reputation was already such that he could ask half-a-guinea for the hour's coaching, a sum not to be sneezed at. He descended the stairs to the drawing-room, now given over to him as a music-room by his parents – *they* lived in a cottage in the garden behind the shop. Selecting a vocal score from the shelves, he sat down at his Broadwood grand piano and began to refresh his memory of one particularly difficult bass aria, for the lesson he had to give next day.

When Peterkin and Dr Cathcart entered young Henry Wood's large music-room the next day, Cathcart slipped unobtrusively into his accustomed corner seat furthest away from the piano. The first time Peterkin took him along to observe a lesson, there had been no formal introductions; just 'You don't mind if my friend sits in?' from Peterkin; since when, Cathcart had sat anonymously in the shadows, a discerning, silent audience of one. Henry Wood paid him no attention at all beyond a 'good morning'; always brisk, he wasted no time on preliminaries, but launched Peterkin immediately into the vocal exercises he had written out for him.

At one point in this memorable lesson early in 1895, Peterkin began to find that Henry Wood's zeal to improve his singing was putting a strain on his voice. It was a fiendishly difficult bass aria he was tackling; Wood knew all its problems thoroughly; but it was Peterkin who had to sing it. Wood suggested a break, and began chatting to Peterkin about Queen's Hall.

'Can you imagine what an opportunity this would be?' he was saying. Only a week or so ago, the new manager of the Queen's Hall had asked Wood to pass by, and put to him the idea of giving a season of Promenade Concerts there. Wood, aware of Robert Newman's reputation, said that if anyone could organise and run them, it was Newman. The orchestra and soloists would be supremely important, of course; but yes, it might work very well. Newman, every bit as brisk as Wood, took him out to lunch at Pagani's Restaurant, that gathering-place and hatchery of new schemes until it was consumed in the holocaust which was to destroy Queen's Hall in 1941. There he had greatly impressed Wood with his musical knowledge and ideals, as well as his head for the business side. Here was a manager who wanted the public to hear more good music than was at present available. He proposed to lead them gently from polkas and quadrilles to the symphonies of Beethoven. If he could achieve this, Queen's Hall would become the best-known venue for music in the country. He asked Wood if he was willing to conduct a permanent Queen's Hall Orchestra for ten weeks of Promenade Concerts.

Wood had been thrilled and flabbergasted. 'But you've never seen me conduct.' To Wood's surprise, Newman had seen him conduct, and not only in London. He also knew talent when he saw it, a quality essential to the successful impresario. He was prepared to back Wood with all the managerial skill at his command. But who would back the concerts? He thought two or three thousand pounds might be needed. Wood had to confess that he had no means of obtaining such a sum; nor could he think of anyone who might have the means.* There the project had to be left for the time being, though Wood came out of Pagani's, as may be imagined, his head teeming with fresh, exciting ideas. What a chance for him, if only the money could be found!

Peterkin and Wood remained quiet for a moment, thinking. Then a voice broke unexpectedly into the silence. They had forgotten Dr Cathcart. 'Please tell me more about this project, Mr Wood.'

Now for the first time Peterkin formally introduced his friend to Henry Wood, whose alert mind at once began ordering the details into coherence. Dr Cathcart, a successful consultant: presumably a man of substance. A music-lover; one who loved singing and the human voice. A private patron? It seemed unlikely. Perhaps he had wealthy friends.

Now it came out that Cathcart also knew a good deal more about Henry Wood than Wood could ever have suspected. That he had been following his career, in the opera house, on the concert platform, and as a teacher. That it was he who had sent Peterkin to him for lessons in the first place. He asked Henry Wood to arrange a meeting with Robert Newman as soon as possible, to discuss the project further. He liked the sound of it. He also liked Henry Wood, and had faith in his future. He intended to help things along if he could. Dr Cathcart also had a couple of hobby-horses of his own; such a

---

* A realistic comparison for 1981 would be about £60,000.

fortunate opportunity to give them rein might never again present itself.

Wagner was one of them. He told Wood how quite recently at the German Club, home of the London Wagner Society, he had a brush with Carl Armbruster, who said English conductors didn't understand Wagner. Cathcart, thinking of Henry Wood, contradicted him, and was shouted down amid a great deal of jeering. According to them, no Englishman was capable of conducting Wagner. Cathcart hoped Wood might find a place for Wagner, if ever these Promenade Concerts materialised, to confound that self-opinionated lot at the German Club.

All this had a familiar ring. Wood had dared to criticise to his face the distinguished German conductor Carl Muck in that same club, for a shoddy performance of *The Flying Dutchman* at Covent Garden. Muck had contemptuously replied that anything was good enough for England, as nobody could tell the difference. Wood could tell the difference. He was furious.

Robert Newman expressed complete agreement with the idea of letting Wood conduct Wagner, when the three men finally met for lunch; but he had misgivings about the other hobby-horse. Dr Cathcart also wanted to change the pitch at which music had always been performed in this country.

It is difficult to understand, more than eighty-five years on, just what a revolution in this country's musical life was brought about in 1895 by an unknown doctor from Upper Wimpole Street. A little explanation may help. Pitch is a question of the number of vibrations per second. If you vibrate a wire by plucking it, a taut membrane by striking it, or a column of air by blowing it, the number of vibrations per second determines the pitch of the resulting sound. When you sing a note, a column of air vibrates your vocal chords. You can vary the pitch of the sound you make, up or down, sharp or flat to the original note. In the evolution of the orchestra a standard pitch had to be established, so that instruments would not sound sharp or flat against each other, and thus out of tune when they were played simultaneously. Unfortunately, not all countries adopted the same standard. France settled on 435 vibrations per second for the note 'A' on the oboe to which orchestras tune before a concert begins. The London Philharmonic Society settled on 452.5 vibrations, giving an 'A' sounding nearly a semitone higher, the distance between any two adjacent notes on a piano. This may not seem a great distance, but it puts a tremendous strain on the voice to have to *sing* everything nearly a semitone higher, as any singer will tell you.

Dr Cathcart was now proposing that Britain should adopt the 'continental' pitch of France and other countries, nearly a semitone lower. His objective, as a throat specialist, was simply to relieve the considerable strain on the whole of a singer's vocal equipment when forced to sing at the higher pitch. Henry Wood was naturally on the side of the singers, who had until then been fighting their own unsuccessful battle for a lower standard of pitch. Newman, however, preferred things the way they were. He perhaps also foresaw a further difficulty.

Violins, and all other members of the string family, present no problem in being tuned to a higher or lower pitch. The player simply tightens up or loosens the strings. Brass and woodwind instruments, including the organ, have almost no room for manoeuvre, their pitch being determined by the bore and length of their pipes. To change from English high pitch to continental low pitch, as Cathcart wished, meant all brass and woodwind players having new instruments, and all organs being tuned down, a costly business. Dr Cathcart found himself faced with a big obstacle right at the start; and there was only one way round it. To have his own way over pitch, he would have to buy all those new instruments himself; to put his money where his mouth was, in the vulgar but singularly apt expression.

It cost him dear. Years later Cathcart admitted that he had not foreseen how much. All this had taken place in his youth, a time when everything seems possible. His judgment was soon vindicated though, for the players bought their instruments from him at the end of the first season of concerts. This explains why you may occasionally find an apparently cheap instrument such as a bassoon in a second-hand shop. Beware; it will be at the old, higher Philharmonic Pitch, and quite unplayable with any ensemble today.

The overall loss which Robert Newman had foreseen, that gap of some few thousand pounds between what the concerts cost to put on and how much money they took at the Box Office, Cathcart also underwrote, and continued to do so for many more years. He never complained, and he never regretted it.

Since 1945, the bust of Sir Henry Wood has looked benevolently out at the audience from behind the platform at the Promenade Concerts, and rightly so. But we shall do well to remember here that it was Robert Newman, manager of Queen's Hall, who originally had the vision and courage to propose the concerts, and the skill and tenacity to run them. That it was Dr George Cathcart who enthusiastically shared the vision, providing the necessary money for many years; and that it was he who finally established low pitch in this country. One further thing these two pioneers had in common. They were both absolutely determined that the new Promenade Concerts should be conducted by young Henry Wood.

Robert Newman's Promenade Concerts

If a man did have an infallible formula for filling a concert hall, he could easily make himself a fortune. Unfortunately, there is no such thing as an infallible formula. As the violinist Isaac Stern once wittily remarked, at a luncheon given in his honour in London's Royal Festival Hall, 'If people are not coming to your concert, nothing will stop them.'

'Robert Newman's Promenade Concerts' was the style in which the first season of Proms was advertised, making it clear that there existed a public which could be expected to respond to the guarantees implicit in the name of Robert Newman. Similar guarantees are before us today, in 'Val Parnell Presents' or 'Festival Director, Ian Hunter'. Before a page of the prospectus is turned, the reader already has a pretty good idea of what to expect. When the season opened, not more than a handful of people could ever have heard of Henry Wood, as he was always the first to acknowledge. By the end of that season, he had emerged as a pathfinder, the first English conductor decisively to break the foreigners' domination of our concert halls and opera houses.

The opening was fixed for Saturday 10 August 1895; though there is an enchanting paragraph in the *Illustrated London News* for 3 August, only a week before they were due to start, stating that a series of Promenade Concerts would *probably* begin at Queen's Hall the following Saturday. It conveys the flavour of an altogether different, more leisurely, tolerant, and perhaps unpredictable age. Such uncertainty would be quite impossible today, except for those operas and concerts abroad, in Italy and Spain particularly, which are always apt to start an hour or two later than the time advertised.

Henry Wood had submitted his draft programmes for the new concerts to Robert Newman only four months earlier. They had gone over them together very carefully indeed, with more than a passing glance at the Box Office. It was absolutely essential to make every evening as attractive as possible. The costing of the concerts left very little margin for error. Both men were finely tuned to the shades and subtleties of public taste at that precise moment; both could gauge what might be tried out in comparative safety, and what constituted too great a risk. Where there was room for doubt between them, Wood bowed to the older man's greater experience, always to good effect.

Just as in the 1980s it is sound business to put on a Mahler symphony, or a concert of Early Music played on sackbuts and shawms, whereas twenty-five years before you could hardly have sold a ticket for either, so in the late nineteenth century there were things both Newman and Wood knew they could rely on to fill their hall. Mahler was not among them. The thirty-five-year-old Austrian was thought of, when he was thought of at all, as conductor of the Hamburg Opera's London season three years before, which had included Wagner's *Ring* cycle and *Tristan*. Wood had been present. For Wagner, even in concert performance, there was certainly an audience. On 28 March 1895 George Henschel had given his annual Wagner concert which was followed, on 25 April, by a short Wagner series in the capital conducted by the composer's son Siegfried Wagner, Felix Mottl, and Hermann Levi. The boost had come forty years earlier with Wagner's personal appearance here, invited to conduct by the London Philharmonic Society in 1855 when he was half-way through *Die Walküre*. Small wonder, then, that the first sound heard at the new Promenade Concerts was that stirring trumpet crescendo on A which begins the Overture to *Rienzi*. (On the first page of the orchestral score he used on that opening night is this comment from Wood's determined pen: '*The Timpani part for this Overture is hopeless and wants rewriting.*' Of course he was right; and he rewrote it. No doubt Muck and Mottl stuck obstinately to Wagner's original.)

Interest in Wagner was just one symptom of the wider availability of music since the death of Beethoven in 1827, when European musical performance was still substantially under princely patronage, and beyond the reach of most people. A Royal Academy of Music had then been in existence here for five years. In the succeeding half-century, the London Philharmonic Society (made Royal in 1912) and the London Bach Society were founded; while from 1883 our capacity to train young musicians was just about doubled with the further establishment of a Royal College of Music.

There was also an audience for symphony concerts and recitals, especially those featuring soloists of distinction. Henry Wood conducted for the pianist Emil Sauer's first concerto performance at Queen's Hall on 28 March, the very night of Henschel's annual Wagner Concert. Not only that; Adelina de Lara, who had studied with Clara Schumann, gave a recital in the Steinway Hall the same evening. Unfortunate clashes we might think today; but there was an audience for all three events.

There was also an enthusiastic following for the popular operettas of W. S.

Gilbert and Arthur Sullivan. Songs and duets from *The Mikado, Iolanthe, The Gondoliers* were not beyond the accomplished amateur at home, after supper, perhaps before a small, indulgent audience. There was no television, no radio, no recording even; people entertained themselves. It was socially very acceptable to be able to play, or to sing. Versions of the Savoy operettas with fairly easy piano accompaniment sold well.

People also stayed in to perform the Music-Hall songs and popular Ballads, whose paths rarely crossed. The Music-Hall song, cosy with synthetic sentiment, was often saucy; the Ballad could be just as cosy, but was always proper. Compare 'A Little of What You Fancy' with 'She Wandered Down the Mountainside'. Mendelssohn's mannerisms, but not his elegance, were all-pervading. Even at the Music-Hall, 'Isn't it a Pity that the Likes of Her'* was set to the opening of his *Spring Song*. This repertoire was probably first heard outside the home, at the Ballad Concert or Collins's Music-Hall. There seemed to be an inexhaustible audience for Ballads. Night after night such concerts were advertised, the songs alternating with cornet solos and the like in a long programme, cheap to put on as it required only a supporting pianoforte. A taste for cornet, clarinet, trombone, and other instrumental solos was acquired through the Operatic Selection which featured members of the brass or military bands. A band concert might be as close as many people would ever get to *Carmen* or *Faust*.

All kinds of music of this sort, for entertainment, or for uplift, were available somewhere, at some time or other. Even assembling elements from each to make up a programme having the widest possible appeal was not new; that idea had often been used successfully in the past. What was bold and daring about Robert Newman's plan was the sheer size of it. He was proposing to steal ten weeks out of London's richly varied musical life, or one-fifth of the calendar in a solid slab. Promenade Concerts would be available at Queen's Hall for sixty consecutive evenings, Sundays excluded, surely a monotonous diet. The hall held just over 3,000; where did he think 180,000 people might be found who had nights to spare for a Promenade Concert among all their other activities? What kind of music-lover had he in mind? We have read of the exceptional person who does not miss a single performance of some play, or who attends every concert by a favoured soloist, no matter where; but that is only two people. How many might have enough spare cash for the self-indulgence of going night after night to Queen's Hall? Could Newman and Wood between them alter a public's tastes and habits to such an extent as that? To look back at their first season with the benefit of historical perspective is to admire their skill and daring, to share in their optimism, and to feel their increasing confidence as it became clear that they were winning.

One discipline imposed itself on programmes right at the start. Works

---

* From 'It's a Great Big Shame'.

needing the full orchestra had to be strictly rationed; the finances did not allow enough rehearsal time. There would have to be plenty of instrumental and vocal solos with piano accompaniment to fill out the evenings. Even so, there might be eight hours of orchestral music in a week, to be rehearsed in six hours. What luck that Wood was also a superb organiser, able to make the fullest use of every scrap of rehearsal time available. Even so, such limitations would still present problems more than thirty years later.

There was no Prospectus. The whole season was not disclosed at the outset. Newman and Wood left their options open, monitoring strengths and weaknesses as they occurred, ready to adjust if necessary, or to repeat a proven success later in the season. The amount of repetition seems curious to us now; it was one way to conserve the precious rehearsals. Auber's Overture *The Bronze Horse* was played twice in three days, a couple of Dvorak's *Slavonic Dances* on three successive evenings. Mendelssohn's *Italian Symphony* was performed in full at the second Wednesday 'Classical Night', just its *Saltarello* being given again in a programme three weeks later. Such repeats would happen before a substantially different audience; the few season-ticket holders would not have to mind. A qualifying 'By desire' (by request) sometimes appeared against a work being repeated. By whose, was never disclosed.

In the printed programmes the Dvorak pieces first appeared as *Sclavic Dances*, 'Sclavic' being an obsolete form of 'Slavonic' even then. Someone must have pointed out that the unfamiliar 'Sclavic' might put people off; they would know the *Slavonic Dances* from Dvorak's original piano duets. The title was changed at once, for the next night. It shows the care with which Newman and Wood cherished their customers. (The programme-note beneath the title was not changed though; it retained 'Sclavic' throughout the season.)

The matter of how much orchestral music to include on any night having perforce resolved itself, a whole evening could take shape around it. For some time the basic pattern did not change, except in details. The concerts began with a substantial piece from the orchestra. They remained on the platform to accompany an aria, to play a few light items, and to end the first half with another fairly hefty work. In between their contributions came the songs, and the solos on flute, clarinet, or other instruments, all with piano accompaniment. On Wednesdays, called 'Classical Night', the first half would include something like Schubert's *Unfinished Symphony*, that *Italian Symphony* by Mendelssohn, his G minor Piano Concerto, or Niels Gade's Symphony No. 4 in B flat.*

After the Interval, the audience reassembled to hear one of many Operatic Selections, *Carmen*, *Il Trovatore*, *Cavalleria Rusticana*, and so forth, which featured solos on violin, cello, flute, oboe, bassoon, horn, euphonium,

---

*Danish composer, one of the first 'nationalists'. He became deputy conductor to Mendelssohn at the Leipzig Gewandhaus, and gave early encouragement to Carl Nielsen.

providing a rousing start to the unashamedly popular second half. These Selections were also rotated throughout the season. After this came more songs and instrumental solos with piano, in particular one for the cornet. Wood has told us that he was originally indifferent about including a cornet solo, but Newman insisted. There was a cornet solo almost every evening; and many years afterwards Wood paid tribute to the virtuosity of England's greatest cornet player, Howard Reynolds, who rapidly became an institution at these early concerts.

The orchestra also provided an overture or some short descriptive piece, and a resounding finale to send the audience home in an excellent mood to tell their friends what a grand time they'd had. At the very first Prom this final item was a 'First Performance', of a Grand March *Les Enfants de la Garde* by Schloesser, a German-born teacher at the Royal Academy of Music; this was one of two 'firsts', even on the very opening night. The introduction of new pieces was an inbuilt feature of the Proms from the word go. Wood referred to such items as 'Novelties', a palatable euphemism for the unfamiliar, calculated to draw in your average listener, rather than to scare him off, as 'New Music' might have done. In the same spirit Sir Thomas Beecham later used the term 'Lollipops' for those light but perhaps not well-known items he used to slip in as encores. 'Lollipops', as the name indicates, would startle no one. Wood's 'Novelties' on occasion startled people very much, as we shall discover.

The programme order just outlined is still a reliable permutation today, for variety theatres, pier pavilions, church hall concerts and the like. Each half must start well and end better; the best performer is given the best placing, at the Top of the Bill. Here is a typical programme from early in the first Proms season, showing how the music from various sources was deployed:

1.	Slavonic Dances Nos 1 & 4	Dvorak
2.	Song 'Thou'rt Passing Hence'	Sullivan
3.	Chromatic Concert Valses from the opera 'Eulenspiegel'	Kistler
4.	Cavatina 'O Mio Fernando'	Donizetti
5.	Overture 'Mignon'	Thomas
6.	Air 'Cielo e Mar'	Ponchielli
7.	Overture 'Fra Diavolo'	Auber
8.	Three Intermezzi from 'Carmen'	Bizet
9.	Military March (orchestrated)	Schubert

interval 15 minutes

10.	Grand Selection 'Faust'	Gounod
11.	Song 'Molly Bawn'	Lover
12.	Solo Cornet 'Killarney'	Balfe

13.	Nocturne in E flat (orchestrated)	Chopin
14.	Song 'Fisher Song'	J. L. Pease
15.	Overture 'Mirella'	Gounod
16.	Song 'The Flower Song' (Carmen)	Bizet
17.	Valse 'Amoretten Tänze'	Gungl
18.	March 'Tannhäuser'	Wagner

Items 2, 11, 12 and 14 came from the Ballad Concert repertoire, and did not require the orchestra. Perversely,

Items 9 and 13, which were originally solo piano pieces, and as such could have saved a bit more rehearsal time, were actually played by the orchestra.

Item 3 was a repeat from the First Night, where it had been a 'First Performance in England'. Every single item in this programme was repeated elsewhere during the first season, at one time or another.

As everyone has pointed out, starting with Henry Wood himself in later years, it would be hard to find an audience to fill a hall for such concerts today. Newman and Wood created them from separate components which gradually went out of fashion, but are now enjoying their individual revivals. The BBC's International Festival of Light Music features the orchestral and vocal items; it has been filling the Royal Festival Hall for years. Old-Tyme Music-Hall has never been more popular than now; almost every village in the land makes money from it; while *The Good Old Days* on BBC television has a huge following. After forty years of neglect, the Ballads too are returning to fashion. Tenor Robert Tear and baritone Benjamin Luxon have had great success with their complete programmes of Ballads and duets, many of them now on records, with André Previn at the piano.

There is perhaps now no exact equivalent for Newman's plan to tempt people with 'polkas and quadrilles' into hearing a little Wagner or Beethoven, except the Proms themselves, today luring people with Wagner and Beethoven into hearing something by Berio or Stockhausen. The nearest equivalent exists when a film like *Elvira Madigan* introduces millions to the miraculous slow movement of a Mozart piano concerto (even DGG used a still from the film on the record sleeve), when the Swingle Singers or Jacques Loussier popularise Bach, or when the Apollo moon missions on BBC television open people's ears to *Also sprach Zarathustra* by Richard Strauss, an idea borrowed from Stanley Kubrick's film *2001*. (How many people bought a record as a result, and lost interest after the bit at the start they knew?) Incidentally, *2001* also gave many people their first taste of Ligeti. This kind of introduction to music through an entirely different medium or experience can be multiplied a hundredfold today.

For the Proms to have survived intact for over eighty years implies tremendous resilience, and a chameleon-like ability to change with changing tastes. The more closely one looks, the more amazing it is that they ever began at all. Only a month beforehand, the Nikisch Orchestral Concerts had taken place in Queen's Hall with lots of Wagner in the programmes. That had about the same effect as a week with Herbert von Karajan and the Berlin Philharmonic would have on the London concert scene today. There were the rival attractions of the Queen's Harpist, John Thomas, and his Band of Eight Harps at St James's Hall, followed the next evening with a piano recital by Artur de Greef, as famous then as Shura Cherkassky is now. But that was not all, by any means. Eduard Strauss, the Waltz King's youngest brother, brought the full Strauss Orchestra over from Vienna around the same time, for concerts at the Imperial Institute spanning nearly a whole month. They were advertised every day in the newspapers, with special price reductions in Bank Holiday Week. A whole series of Viennese Evenings; it is hard to imagine anything more popular. Yet Bank Holiday at the Crystal Palace also drew crowds, with bands, balloon ascents, variety, illuminations, fireworks, and ending with a Military Promenade Concert featuring Jullien's British Army Quadrilles by the massed bands, drummers, fifers and pipers.

Eduard Strauss was still in London on Wednesday 6 August, when the first modest advertisement for Robert Newman's Promenade Concerts appeared. Strauss gave his final afternoon and evening concerts on 9 August, the very day before the Proms were due to open. It is a marvel that anyone had any money left. The new Proms were not devised for a different audience; Newman was aiming for the widest cross-section, those who had attended the Nikisch concerts, those who had gone out of curiosity to hear eight harpists, those who had packed the Viennese Evenings. No wonder he and Wood threw in everything they had, the songs, the selections, the cornet solos, the endless popular overtures. Who shall blame them; and who shall blame the audiences for thronging back again to enjoy such thundering good tunes?

Throng back they did; but not just because of those small advertisements. They were modest; Robert Newman was not. He was a seasoned impresario, with the necessary gift for public relations; and everything was working for him. He and Wood had been talking for months about their new Proms. An orchestra of eighty players had been chosen and engaged, likewise a whole parade of soloists. The time for assembling all these may seem short by today's standards; but this was long before the aeroplane. Players and soloists were never far away. All these preparations had also come to the notice of the Press. Before the Proms opened, any music-lover in London worthy of the name knew that something big was afoot at Queen's Hall.

The doors finally opened at 7 p.m. on Saturday 10 August, but a crowd had begun to gather on the pavements outside long before then. Those attracted by Newman's main advertising point – *Admission One Shilling* – poured down into the Promenade, where all seats had been removed. Two shillings paid meant rushing up flights of stairs to the Balcony for a grandstand view. For

---

1. Sir Henry Wood, about 1900 (*BBC Hulton Picture Library*)

three or five shillings there were no stairs to climb, entrances leading straight into the Grand Circle. A few, not so many at first, who knew a bargain when they saw one and had the necessary guineas, came provided with a Season Ticket – Robert Newman's idea, offering huge savings in all parts of the hall. On the way in everyone took note of the ample refreshment and smoking rooms provided, in the Entrance Hall and the Grand Salon; a Supper Room for 100 off the vestibule at the top of the stairs, an American Bar in the corridor, seating for 500 in the Small Hall above, and for another 200 in the small Conservatory leading out of it. A moving picture show was provided by David Devant during the interval, in the small Queen's Hall. For an extra sixpence the audience could see a forerunner of the newsreel. This sideshow continued until 1903.

The first thing to catch the eye inside was the unusual arrangement of the Promenade itself, with a flower-bordered fountain at the centre, and three small booths round about selling Horton's Ices, cigars and flowers. The fountain was Dr Cathcart's idea; he thought it might keep the atmosphere humid, and help to divide the mass of bodies. There were blocks of ice in the water to begin with, and some rather cool goldfish. Cathcart would have seen similar fountains at the Crystal Palace and the various Exhibitions. It gave him a certain satisfaction as he took his seat next to Newman's. Across the aisle in the Grand Circle sat my grandfather, and not just to be seen with his wife at this opening night; he would not have missed it for anything. A love of music was inherited from his own prosperous father who, as a young man, had known the excitement of attending the first London performance of a Ninth Symphony by the German composer Beethoven, to whom in 1824 the Philharmonic Society had sent a generous fee for the privilege. A young girl in the Promenade, Agnes Nicholls, noticed two people in particular who stood near the rostrum, a man in a grey frock coat, and a small spare lady in a round bonnet, both awaiting the conductor's arrival with keen interest – they were his parents. After the concert, when the lights had been lowered, they were the last to leave, proud and thrilled with their son. Agnes Nicholls became a soloist in many later Proms seasons, and eventually married Sir Hamilton Harty.

It was intended to provide a real night out for the audience, and a true *promenade*; supper would be served at any time during the evening in the Balcony Supper Room for anyone wanting it; they could come and go at will. A printed programme at two pence showed what music lay ahead. It contained explanatory notes by Edgar Jacques, but not about every piece, plus advertisements for Erard pianos, Pagani's Restaurant, bespoke tailoring; and this triumphant declaration about the low French Pitch: '*Mr Newman is glad to say that it will also be adopted in future by the Philharmonic Society, the Bach Choir, the London Symphony, Mottl, and Nikisch Concerts, and on concerts under his direction: i.e. the Queen's Hall Choir, and the Sunday Afternoon Concerts which begin on October 6th.*' Game, set, and match; even a small plug for his next venture. The

July number of Kingston's penny *Pathfinder* was also on sale; unsold copies, evidently. It gave sports fixtures, with special insurance for foot-ballers, transport times, a diary of events, portraits of Dr W. G. Grace and Mr H. J. Wood, and it promised to feature other soloists in future issues, including Wood's pupil W. A. Peterkin.

Downstairs the public milled around expectantly, dressed to cut a dash, even to flirt a little if the opportunity arose. How do people know when something is in the wind? Do they generate the fever themselves, before ever a note has been heard? Certainly they were keyed up; the whole of Queen's Hall was coming alive with the feel of it. As orchestral players began appearing in twos and threes on the platform everyone could see that it was going to be a satisfyingly large orchestra; eighty players in fact, a permanent orchestra in London for the whole eight-week season, with a good body of strings as Wood had insisted.

A piercing oboe sound was followed immediately by strident orchestral hubbub; and then, without asking, by a sudden hush. Everything went quiet. The moment had come. Henry Wood strode purposefully out past his First Violins and briskly mounted the rostrum to face his audience.

It was a thrill he would never forget. A young man, with a beard and a baton, he stood there briefly, and bowed. The applause left him in no doubt. Conductors have been known to admit that the gift of holding an audience is God-given. It takes but seconds for a crowd collectively to decide if it will take part in the ritual about to be performed, according to the personality and magnetism of the high priest. Wood scored high, and he knew it, as an actor senses instantly that an audience is eating out of his hand. He turned smartly round, his long white baton pointing directly at the First Trumpet, and with its three crescendos and the big tune in Wagner's *Rienzi* Overture the most astonishing event in the whole history of public concert-giving blazed into life.

The Vanishing Band

N o one could possibly begrudge the bass singer W. A. Peterkin his many appearances during the first season. He had been the catalyst bringing Robert Newman, Dr Cathcart and Henry Wood together. But for Peterkin's lessons with Wood they might have continued to pass each other by in the street. He sang on the First and Last Nights and several times in between, a just reward. Henry Wood rarely let friendship influence his judgment, and usually regretted it when he did; but Peterkin was not only his pupil, he was a good singer as well.

We may imagine those three conspirators carefully scrutinising the course of the first season as it inched forward. It is always exciting to be on the brink of something; they could hardly have known how big, but they must have had hopes. They began by playing very safe indeed, gradually settling into a weekly pattern, soon to crystallise into a basic shape which lasted for many years; traces of it still remain, even today.

The first 'week' was actually of eight days. A Promenade Concert season always began on a Saturday, because Saturday is a night out. Monday is often a night in, after the weekend's excesses. Each week ended with another night out, another festive programme. The First Night of all gave very good value, even though it would surely have drawn a full house anyway. Peterkin sang some Gounod, and 'The Soldier's Song'. There were three other vocalists, including two American ladies; flute, cornet and bassoon solos; and music by Chopin, Chabrier, Bizet, Haydn, Saint-Saëns, Leoncavallo, Liszt, Schubert, Rossini, and others long forgotten. There was also, even at this first concert, a 'First Performance in England' and a 'First Performance', which nowadays we inflate into a 'World Première'.

A definite statement was made about the first Wednesday evening with the label 'Classical Night', meaning a symphony or concerto in the first half, and no Ballads or bassoon solos until the second half. The first week ended with a piece calculated to carry lively memories of these concerts safely over Sunday into the following week, Koenig's *Post Horn Galop*, which has never lost its power to stimulate an audience. It was so effective that Wood repeated it the next Saturday, again three weeks later, and a fourth time to bring the whole season to a rousing finish.

In the third week, one-composer nights were tried for the first time. Sullivan Night on Monday offered no great risk, unlike Wagner on Tuesday, whose music 'only a few years ago was considered devoid of melody, chaotic in structure, and generally lacking in beauty and coherence' (programme note by Edgar Jacques). The first piano concerto played at a Prom was Mendelssohn's in G minor during the Wednesday Classical Night. At the same concert Wood performed a *New Suite in Four Movements* by the twenty-five-year-old Percy Pitt, a name which will crop up again at a crucial point in the story of these Proms. There was a Gounod Night on Friday and a Strauss Night – today's popular Viennese Evening, so long ago! – to end that week.

The printed programmes show two nice printing errors, announcing a cornet solo, Mattei's *Non ever* (for *Non è ver* – It's not true) and the Mendelssohn concerto to be taken *Molto allegro con fuoro* (for *con fuoco*). Anyone who has been responsible for producing concert programmes will know the feeling well.

The way the Proms were advertised seems modest by today's standards. Even on the day they began, the Leeds Music Festival took a much larger space in *The Times* than Robert Newman felt was necessary (or could afford?) for his new venture. Perhaps Leeds was a long way to go, even with Sir Arthur Sullivan conducting. Newman put some faith in the low price of admission to Queen's Hall for his concerts (a shilling). Later he included the names of soloists, but no composers or works. Not until the Proms had been going for a fortnight was a full programme advertised. After that, brief details of a future week, or full details of a second concert, might be included in the curious newspaper advertisements of those days, occupying the space of three separate insertions, ruled lines and all.

Wood and Newman might have been found, after a concert or a rehearsal, having a meal in Pagani's and comparing notes. The Dvorak *Slavonic Dances* had twice gone down well; they could be done again. No harm in repeating Tosti's 'Goodbye' either, or a movement from the *Unfinished Symphony*. How the audience had clapped the cornet solo! Robert had been right about that; it must stay: and why don't we have a Military Prom as they do at Crystal Palace? So they did, on Friday of the fourth week, which began with a Wagner Night on Monday, a place it was to occupy for years. Tuesday was a spectacular Scottish Night, with the Pipers of Her Majesty's Scots Guards, Hamish MacCunn's *Land of the Mountain and the Flood*, Macfarren, Mackenzie, 'John Anderson, my Jo', Strathspey Reels, and 'Ye Banks and Braes of Bonnie Doon'. Wednesday's Classical Night included Weber's *Concertstück* plus piano solos, and the whole of Schubert's 'Great' C major Symphony, only twenty-eight years after Arthur Sullivan unearthed the manuscript in Vienna; this sublime work can hardly have had time to become as popular as it is now.

Thursday brought Irish Night, with predictably 'The Minstrel Boy', Wallace, Balfe, 'Come Back to Erin'; but there was even a recitation as well. There was another the following evening, Tennyson's 'The Defence of Lucknow' for the Military Prom, which also paid an apt tribute to Louis Jullien by including his British Army Quadrilles, first put on at his own Covent Garden Proms half a century earlier, as that Frenchman's tribute to us.

By the time they arrived at the half-way mark, our three conspirators must have been feeling much more confident. They entered the fifth week with two certainties, Wagner on Monday and Classics on Wednesday. To these they now added a third, Beethoven on Friday, though only once in this season. The exceptions were that on the seventh Monday, the last but one, Wagner was displaced by 'MR SIMS REEVES', a concert featuring the greatest tenor of the day; and that on the final Wednesday, Newman and Wood put on a whole evening of First Performances, proof enough that they felt victory to be securely in their grasp.

A performance of Mendelssohn's Violin Concerto gave annotator Edgar Jacques the opportunity to rebuke *The Saturday Review* for having recently referred to the composer as 'that shallow Jew'. The last two Fridays were respectively a Mendelssohn Night and another 'MR SIMS REEVES WILL SING and The Grand Orchestra Will Play'; clearly the reputation of Sims Reeves could be counted on to pack them in a second time. The problems were not over yet, though. On Monday of the final week a tremendous shock awaited Henry Wood when he walked into his rehearsal at Queen's Hall. He found himself facing an entirely different orchestra.

Where had all the players gone? Where was his Leader? Henry Wood knew all too well as a matter of fact, and had immediate confirmation from his Deputy Leader, one of the few players remaining from his original orchestra. All the others had gone to 'a certain Festival' (Leeds); what was worse, they would be away for most of the week. For the first time in the season Wood had fallen victim to the dreadful Deputies System. There had been the occasional unaccustomed face at some earlier rehearsals, but nothing on this scale. The sensation must have been rather like going to the Royal Festival Hall today expecting to hear the London Symphony Orchestra, and finding most of its players replaced by music students.

In the nineteenth century an orchestra could be kept together only by consent of its players. They were paid by the concert; they had no contract and no permanent employment. If any player agreed to do a rehearsal and concert at some future date, and in the meantime a more lucrative offer came along, he was perfectly entitled to send a deputy to do the first date. The player collected both fees, paying the deputy as little as possible. He could do this for several engagements in a row, without explanation or fear of recrimination. 'Pernicious, mercenary, and inexcusable proceedings' was how *The World* critic had referred to them some years earlier.

How ever did conductors put up with it? In 1895 they had very little choice in the matter. Musicians in British orchestras have always been justly proud of, and universally renowned for, their enviable ability to read at sight any music put in front of them, *and* to keep one eye on the conductor at the same time. Consequently, players held the opinion that a rehearsal was for the conductor's benefit, rather than for theirs. This was not arrogance; mature and experienced masters of their instruments, they knew it would be perfectly all right on the night. Well, almost perfect. A performance of sorts is possible if someone merely beats time and the players follow. A *good* performance of a work is unlikely in this case; and a conductor's individual interpretation of it is out of the question. Allowance must of course be made for a conductor of such personal magnetism that the whole orchestra is swept along by the intensity of his vision; but on the whole, performances under the circumstances described must have been workmanlike, even perfunctory.

It was a bitter disappointment to Henry Wood in his final week. He knew that interpretations bearing his stamp were possible only from a disciplined orchestra with whom he had built up a personal relationship over a period. Except for an occasional deputy, this new Proms band* had been with him for seven weeks, giving him enough confidence to schedule a concert of what might nowadays be called contemporary music, which began to look more risky with untried players. Wood had the assurance which comes from being fully aware of your own potential. He wanted things played his way, and did not propose to tolerate obstacles. He liked everything to be as well organised as he was himself. Those players he did have at that final Monday rehearsal could not possibly have known it, but they were looking at the very man who would break the Deputies System in this country for ever. It was to take him nine long years; and the London Symphony Orchestra would be born out of the final confrontation.

For the moment there was very little Wood could do but grin and bear it. He had already complained (chiefly to Newman) of the tremendous problems involved in putting on at least fifteen hours of music a week with only nine hours of orchestral rehearsal. This orchestra had not played, in previous weeks, those works Wood was hoping to repeat without further rehearsal in order to get through; and the strain upon him was becoming almost unbearable. Quite naturally, he felt badly let down by his Leader, and immediately ended his association with these concerts, promoting the Deputy Leader for his fidelity. That was how in 1895 the Proms began with an orchestra led by W. Frye Parker and ended with one led by Arthur Payne, a

---

* 'Band' is affectionate usage for 'orchestra' among professionals. So is 'Who's carving?' of conductors.

man whose performance of Mendelssohn's Violin Concerto had greatly impressed Wood at a concert some time before on Llandudno pier to which, in 1902, Payne returned as Musical Director.

With Arthur Payne's talents as Leader, and Henry Wood's considerable flair and organising ability, they got through the final week with credit. It is doubtful if many of the audience noticed anything amiss, which is as it should be. All the work had been done, all the problems solved, at rehearsal. Even Thursday's Novelty Night passed without incident. What nerve, what supreme confidence Newman and Wood must have had to put on such a concert! Consisting exclusively of First Performances, it would be enough to put an audience off even today. Operatic Preludes to *Guntram* by Richard Strauss and Scharwenka's *Mataswintha;* Halvorsen's *Boyards' March*; 'Eugene Aram', a recitation with music by Mackenzie; Tchaikovsky's *Marche Solennelle* and Massenet's *Phèdre* Overture; individually either unexciting or unfamiliar; fairly daunting when all heaped together. The reader may quite well object that those pieces consist only of agreeable tunes, simply harmonised; that there is nothing to compare with the splintered music of Webern, the concussion of *The Rite of Spring*, or the alien din of Stockhausen's *Kontakte*. This is because we listen to nineteenth-century music with twentieth-century ears. In 1895 your average music-lover took the same unknown risks with Richard Strauss that his counterpart today takes with Krzysztof Penderecki.

The second successful Sims Reeves concert on that final Friday gave added stature in the public's consciousness to the Proms as they arrived at the crowning climax of the Last Night. This was declared a Benefit Concert for Robert Newman, a gesture we are more accustomed to see in the worlds of cricket or football. It paid proper tribute to his unflagging support and shrewd management in successfully promoting the first season, and netted him £400 (about £8,000 at today's values).

W. A. Peterkin sang twice, as did several others. There were two recitations, Edgar Allan Poe's 'The Bells' being one of them, with music by Stanley Hawley; it was to be better served eighteen years later by Rachmaninoff. There was an unaccompanied *March* for solo flute, other solos for cello, piano, cornet – the redoubtable Howard Reynolds playing three, one in the by now customary Operatic Selection. With orchestral pieces by Wagner, Grieg, Paderewski, the evening progressed towards the ultimate excitement of *The Post Horn Galop*. We can only imagine how that must have sent the audience scurrying out into the night, bubbling and chattering, talking for weeks to come about the marvellous new Promenade Concerts at Queen's Hall. The very next day, Grand Orchestral Concerts started off the winter season there, with W. Frye Parker back at the Leader's desk; but that was because Alberto Randegger was conducting, not Henry Wood.

Truly 1895 had been an eventful year. The first season of Proms had come and gone, unfolding into a pattern which proved a winner to withstand the tests of time. Henry Wood had begun the season relatively unknown outside a fairly tight circle and ended it with his reputation made, just as Robert Newman had planned. Strange as it may seem to us today, in that bicentenary year of the death of our greatest composer not a note of Henry Purcell's music was played. His day had not yet come; nor were the Proms yet the obvious place they later became for such anniversaries. But there was a notable birth. At his home not far from the Albert Hall in the High Street of the lovely stone-built town of Stamford in Lincolnshire, Harry Sargent, coal merchant and church organist, learned that his wife Agnes had been prematurely delivered of a son whilst staying with friends in Kent. She returned home three weeks later and they christened him Harold Malcolm Watts.

'This Brat Wood'
1896–1899

The undiscovered genius working alone in some garret is a romantic figure, more likely to occur in fiction than in fact. Exceptional talent is difficult to hide; someone is almost sure to recognise it before long. Mediocrity born to over-ambitious parents is far more probable. Henry Wood was born with great gifts, God-given or hereditary according to your standpoint; but not for one moment did those enormous talents blush unseen.

His father prospered selling those beautiful model steam engines. Conductor Michael Costa once urged him to sing professionally; but he chose to keep music as a hobby and love, giving his son every opportunity to develop clearly precocious musical skills, first discovered when his mother gave him piano lessons. Leading performers filled the home with good talk; he was taken to plays, opera, concerts, exhibitions; and late at night studied scores by the light of candles bought out of his own pocket money. At ten he was allowed to practise on the organ of the Church of the Holy Sepulchre without Newgate, where now a stained glass window honours his memory. Through his years at the Royal Academy of Music he accompanied opera classes on the piano, studied composition with Ebeneezer Prout, took lessons from every available professor of singing, and heard every vocalist of the day. His father paid for him to study with the best organists; and, before he left the Academy, plenty of people were aware of him, as always happens with a really promising student.

He emerged a musician of parts, with second interests in painting and science. In 1912, when he was forty-two, fifty of his oils were exhibited at Piccadilly Arcade, the proceeds benefiting fellow musicians. Early experiments with Leyden jars brought him the unusual luxury of electric light for his Bord pianette. Lectures at the Royal Institute gave him an hour's peace as counterbalance to the intensity of his later conducting activities. Particular interest in the human voice resulted in a four-volume gradus ad parnassum *The Art of Singing*, which is still a daunting challenge. His father also paid for him to hear the Boston Symphony Orchestra in America, quite a voyage at that time. Professional life began to burgeon in several directions simultaneously, as accompanist and coach to singers, as organist, as conductor of more and less successful touring opera ventures; and soon he returned to the Royal Academy of Music as a teacher. Always some of the profit was ploughed back in the shape of still more scores for his personal library.

He was exceptionally aware from the start of his career; ready to question much of what others took for granted, even the competence of his teachers. He knew a bad piece when he heard one, and begrudged time wasted rehearsing rubbish. Little escaped him; Busoni's exemplary pedalling, Ysaÿe's violin bow positions, Sevcik's system of fingering; and he vividly retained every detail of Artur Nikisch conducting. He also argued that Mozart concerts, using smaller orchestras, were a sinister fashion which put musicians out of work; but this seems an ephemeral judgment, as curious now as his eagerness to score Chopin piano pieces for full orchestra.

In 1890 Sir Arthur Sullivan invited Wood to train the cast for the first production of *Ivanhoe*. Sullivan even sought his advice before conducting Bach's *Mass in B minor*, ample tribute to Wood's increasing authority. The Imperial Opera of St Petersburg wrote offering him second-in-command to Luigi Arditi (of 'Il bacio' fame) directing then unknown Tchaikovsky operas on a British tour. As a guest at the famous Concerts Lamoureux in Paris his youth astonished everyone. George Bernard Shaw wrote glowingly in *The World* about his interpretations. Wood's steadily advancing stature as a conductor was no accident. He had decided in his own mind to begin at the top and to stay there. He knew all the tricks of his trade, including those which orchestral players will try on a novice. He stopped the percussion section slipping out for a drink by getting Robert Newman to lock the doors.* Every instrument had to be tuned beforehand to his complete satisfaction; he even kept a special silver tuning reed for absolute accuracy. Sectional rehearsals were held, greatly improving the final ensemble; at some provincial festivals, with brass players from local theatres, Wood complained that through two hours of rehearsal he never heard a single chord played dead in tune. In Queen's Hall he would go up into the Grand Tier while the orchestra went on playing, to hear how it sounded, bringing them to a halt with a little handbell whenever he had something to say. In due course he put his foot down once and for all about players sending in deputies. Robert Newman supported him, brusquely telling the Queen's Hall Orchestra before a rehearsal, 'Gentlemen, in future there will be *no* deputies; good morning.'

---

* Later he installed an electric bell in the bar of the 'Glue Pot' pub in Mortimer Street. It could be rung from the conductor's rostrum to recall the players.

2. Dr Peter Skeggs, son of Sir Henry Wood's physician and nicknamed 'Gerontius', with a model steam engine made at Wood's father's shop in

Forty players resigned immediately and were as swiftly replaced. They formed themselves into a rival London Symphony Orchestra from 1904 with Hans Richter as their conductor.

Musicians tend to regard this kind of thing as high-handed until they get used to it. In 1896 Henry Wood's considerable library of scores and orchestral parts was housed near to Queen's Hall in the care of W. H. Tabb (later of Goodwin and Tabb, the famous hire firm.) There, during a rehearsal interval Wood, unobserved, chanced to overhear two old hands from the orchestra discussing his unpleasant habits. No longer could they wander in at half-past ten. Wood was up on the rostrum at ten sharp, looking at his watch. For the benefit of every player who did arrive late, he would go right back to the beginning and start the rehearsal all over again, a nasty trick which everyone hated; but one which cunningly forced those who had arrived on time to discipline their own colleagues. Nor did Wood dispense with rehearsing the old war-horses and let the band off early; rather did he squeeze the maximum out of every minute. It is hardly surprising that those two old-timers were grumbling. 'Damn these youngsters, I say! I wonder where Newman picked up this brat Wood?'

How revealing that Sir Henry should choose to recount this unintentional compliment in his autobiography. Evidently it gave him some satisfaction to learn that his methods were beginning to bite. Had there been no more to him than this, players would never have grown so fond of him as they did in later years. His musicianship they very quickly respected; it could hardly have been faulted. He also fought the management year after year to have their pay increased, gradually raising it by 400 per cent before the BBC took over in 1927. He worked them hard, and demanded discipline; but they were always foremost in his thoughts.

There is a sense in which one may have authority only by consent of others; Henry Wood commanded it effortlessly. Hardly tall enough to be physically imposing, the fire and purpose within him showed in an erect head, the jut of his beard, and above all in his eyes. Each player felt they were upon him the whole time; Wood never missed a thing. He made a virtue of not having the last refinements of speech; grammar and syntax were apt to be lost in haste to get his points across. These were the more vigorously made precisely because of the pithy vernacular in which they sprang to life. He spoke with a marked London – not to put too fine a point on it, a Cockney – accent. Though he said less at rehearsal than many conductors (in itself a virtue) what he did say stuck in the mind. '*Every eye!*' focused attention for his downbeat as the rehearsal started. '*Two sorrow-laden crotchets!*' as the Prelude to *Tristan* unfolded

---

Oxford Street. When Sir Henry died, he lay in young Peter's bedroom, where people came to pay their last respects (*Nicholas Hall*)

saved explanation and time. *'What are you a-doing of, sawing away regardless?'* brought the string section to heel.

He was not at all conceited, as Dame Maggie Teyte has pointed out; and he would never embarrass a soloist at rehearsal. Even if a student made a mistake running through a concerto with the Royal Academy Orchestra (which Wood always made room in his busy schedule to conduct) there would be a hand-written note to his Professor gently pointing out the fault. Wood wrote innumerable letters in his own hand; it is often the busiest people who will spare the time. Dame Myra Hess treasured all her life a personal note of apology from him after a concert where he had failed to bring in the orchestra exactly at the end of the third movement cadenza in Beethoven's Fourth Piano Concerto. Otto Klemperer's daughter Lotte once admitted privately, during a young conductors' contest where that notoriously treacherous passage was among the test-pieces, 'Even Daddy sometimes misses that'.

Little attention was paid to the 1895 debut of Wood's Promenade Concerts by *The Times* of London, busy reporting at great length remote festivals like Leeds and Cheltenham. There was grudging praise for an 'extremely well played'* *Unfinished Symphony*, but Wagner Nights were considered to be 'made up of excerpts perfectly familiar to amateurs'. *The Times* also rather loftily looked down its privileged nose at 'the extraordinary preponderance of the lighter forms of music'. Well, the second season offered no less than *five* solo cornets every evening except the last, the ever-popular Howard Reynolds and a quartet called The Park Sisters. Never again would a group of soloists have the luck to be engaged for every concert but one during a season. Henry Wood went up into the organ loft on one occasion, to play in Sullivan's 'The Lost Chord'; a violinist played only the first movement of Beethoven's concerto on another evening; while the second halves of all concerts continued to be just as popular as ever. There are some grounds for considering that the season was just a touch less lowbrow overall. There were several performances of Dvorak's three-year-old *New World Symphony* ('Founded on Old Negro and American Indian Melodies' said the programme, helpfully). Schumann Night included not only the Piano Concerto but the Fourth Symphony, which took years to earn a place in the repertoire. Wood even tried out Beethoven's *Battle Symphony* and gave Mendelssohn's *Hymn of Praise* at a concert designed to show 'Musical Development During the Reign of H.M. The Queen'; altruistic and impartial of him for, as he wrote, 'in those early days of my conducting, Mendelssohn was not a great favourite of mine'. For the same concert Robert Newman commissioned a *Coronation March* from Percy Pitt who had become official accompanist to the series. After five weeks the orchestra was increased to ninety players 'in consequence of generous support given by the public and press'; and the *Post Horn Galop* once again brought the season to an end.

---

* To save space, quotations in this book are not always identified. It should be clear from their context whether they are from conversations, documents, or Press reports.

In February 1896, before the season began, Henry Wood's mother, deeply-loved counsellor and confidante, and source of the strength he drew from his home life, died suddenly of bronchitis. For some time he and his father struggled along with a succession of avaricious housekeepers. Six years previously, during the *Ivanhoe* rehearsals, a mysterious Cornish tenor (mysterious because no one ever discovered how he came to be in the cast) had brought a Russian Princess Olga Ouroussoff to Wood for singing lessons. She now re-entered his life through helping to manage the Wood household economically. They were married in July 1898 and spent their honeymoon in Braemar. On returning they moved from Langham Place to Norfolk Crescent, and Wood's father went to live with friends.

With the greatest courage Olga surmounted recurring bouts of ill-health resulting from an earlier severe operation, betraying no sign even when singing in pain. Wood thoroughly enjoyed playing piano accompaniments for her occasional recitals in London and the provinces. In 1899 they went on a busman's holiday to Bayreuth, where Wood was a frequent visitor to the Wagner Festivals; and in 1901 Olga made a most successful Proms debut singing Elisabeth's Prayer from *Tannhäuser*.

There is a huge old leather-bound ledger proudly guarded by the BBC's Music Division. It records alphabetically every work performed at the Proms between 1895 and 1927 when the BBC took over – at a rough guess, ten thousand entries giving dates of performance and the time taken to play each one. Nothing more immediately illustrates the awe-inspiring organisation and attention to detail Wood and Newman brought to their task right from the start. Then there is the great library of Wood's scores and orchestral parts housed at the Royal Academy of Music, all marked up with phrasings, bowings, annotations, improvements here and there to the scoring, so that nothing should be left to chance at rehearsal or performance. Librarian Edgar Johnson says that some of the material is now unobtainable elsewhere. (Wood also kept meticulous notes on every soloist he auditioned.) When it suited him, Wood protested that he had no head for business; but the investment in orchestral material provided additional income all his life, for he hired out the score and parts of any work for half-a-guinea the performance, even at his own Proms. If he had one fault, it was predictability. Whenever he made jokes whilst rehearsing, he scribbled reminders in the margin, and they are still there. Next time he rehearsed a piece, up would come the same joke, at the same place. His players awaited it indulgently, as an audience waits for a favourite comedian's inevitable catch-phrase, and still laughs.

The audience was invited to plan its own Proms in 1897. On three separate occasions voting papers and ballot boxes were available in the vestibules a fortnight beforehand. There were three Plebiscite Concerts based on the results. Beethoven's Fifth, *Peer Gynt*, the Mendelssohn Violin Concerto, were all predictable winners; but who voted in Frances Allitsen's *Song of Thanks-*

giving? There was a change in the weekly pattern, Tuesdays, Thursdays and Saturdays all becoming Popular Nights; and from 20 September it was announced that Leader Arthur Payne would be 'Principal Violin and Conductor of the Second Part' at each concert, a rest for Henry Wood. From 4 to 8 October there was the first mini-festival, five consecutive evenings of Wagner, with an orchestra further increased to 103 players from then onwards.

A 'Wonderful Child Pianist', Bruno Steindel made his British debut at the Proms, playing Beethoven's Fourth Piano Concerto on a specially requested Rud. Ibach Sohn piano instead of the Queen's Hall's Erard, with poppa Steindel from Gladbach conducting. The boy was immediately booked to appear four nights later, and again on 15 October, on each occasion playing piano pieces by Schubert, Chopin, Raff and Sapellnikoff, bang in the middle of a Wagner Prom. Nobody seemed to mind. Ten days after the season ended, this 'Wonder Child of the Diamond Jubilee Year' gave his first London recital, which included a *Fantaisiestück* of his own composition. Clara Butt was relegated to a supporting role in the same concert. A critic of *The Daily Telegraph*, having heard him privately, testified in advance to his extraordinary gifts. However, Henry Wood later recalled that 'his power, technique and musical intelligence were remarkable; but, like so many prodigies, he did not fulfil the promise of his seven years'.

A special Prom to celebrate the 'Record Reign' of Queen Victoria was given on 23 September, the programme pointing out that when she ascended the throne in 1837, only Exeter Hall was available for big concerts.* Now the longest reign in British history was being properly celebrated in a hall named after Her Majesty. Successful concerts attract advertising; revenue came in that season from whisky, beer and mineral water firms; from purveyors of poultry, game, cakes, chocolates and 'fluid beef'; and from those who could offer High Class Sanitation and Decoration, or a Resort 'for school treats and outings'. Some distraction must have been experienced in the last season from the Promenade itself; henceforth all programmes carried the legend: *Gentlemen are politely requested to refrain from striking matches during the performance of the various items.*

At the end of this season came an accolade; a royal command for Henry Wood and the Queen's Hall Orchestra to play at Windsor Castle before Her Majesty and sixty guests. Scrupulous preparations included Wood (no mean carpenter himself) advising Windsor about a special orchestral platform. On such gala occasions something generally goes wrong; a librarian failed to wake up at the Windsor terminus, so he and the music gently travelled all the way back to Paddington on the train. Wood was not pleased to find he was required to wear white kid gloves ('like a seaside bandmaster'); but he was

---

* Two London concert halls were replaced by hotels, Exeter Hall by the Strand Palace, Queen's Hall by St George's.

delighted with Newman's ruse for smuggling in Dr Cathcart as an extra triangle player. Newman for his part was upset at not being presented to the Queen (*Managers* are *never* presented); but there was an inscribed baton for Henry, and a good supper for everyone, perhaps less stodgy than Her Majesty's choice of music: Wagner, Saint-Saëns, Tchaikovsky, Humperdinck, and more Wagner.

Another prodigy appeared in 1898, the 'marvellous child pianist' Wolodia Roujitzky, who played only the first two movements of Beethoven's Third Piano Concerto, and the wrong way round at that, presenting programme annotator Edgar Jacques with a nice problem. We can almost see him putting the tips of his fingers together as, without the flicker of an eyelid, he explained that 'The two movements given this evening are presented in reverse order, the second movement of the concerto being used as an opening section.' This is the purest joy to read now; but it was all taken quite seriously at the time.

Newman and Wood did not cease trying out variations on their precious formula, some small, some significant. Two-composer nights were tried in 1898: Weber and Dvorak; Grieg and Massenet; Beethoven and Schumann; Tchaikovsky and Berlioz; Brahms and Tchaikovsky; Wagner and Liszt (never alas Brahms and Liszt). In 1899 Wagner held on to Mondays as usual; but all the other nights were a mixed bag, of slightly higher class. In 1898 the 'Austrian National Hymn' movement from Haydn's *Emperor Quartet* was played in memory of the Empress of Austria. In 1899 came the first anniversary tribute, fantasias on *Il Trovatore* and *Aida* on Verdi's eighty-sixth birthday. The age manifested a distinct taste for solo quartets; The Park Sisters on cornets, and four trombonists in 1896; a quartet of clarinets and another of flutes in 1898; even a *Concertstück* for four horns by Heinrich Hübler (principal horn at Dresden), now totally forgotten in the popularity of Schumann's radiant work. This was fertile soil for Elgar to write in 1905 perhaps the greatest of all, *Introduction and Allegro* for string quartet and orchestra.

Two first prize winners from the Paris Conservatoire were each given an 1898 Prom date by Newman and Wood, one a pianist, the other a fiddler. The programme for 5 October 1899 stated that the winner of the North Atlantic yacht race for the America's Cup, between Sir Thomas Lipton's *Shamrock* and Mr Iselin's *Columbia*, would be announced at the earliest possible moment during the concert. There was also a tendency to do things to death. In 1898 J. M. Coward conducted his *Vocal Waltz*, which then had twenty consecutive performances, including the Last Night. Frederick Godfrey's *Reminiscences of England* (ending with 'Rule, Britannia') were played every night for a week, and again on Trafalgar Day, the Last Night of 1899. That was still six years away from the centenary of Nelson's great victory, and the première of Wood's own *Fantasia on British Sea-Songs*.

The only time Wood lost his temper with Newman was during 1898. Newman had him conducting Sunday Afternoon Concerts four weeks before the Proms ended, and then over-reached himself by putting on Sunday Evening Choral Concerts as well, a total of eight concerts a week. No conductor would stand for it today, and Wood did not stand for it then. Newman was obliged to find someone else to conduct on Sunday evenings.

The Proms had been established long enough in 1899 for Wood to complain of 'the old, old story; as soon as novelties appear, box-office receipts disappear'. (Things have not changed.) The end of the century also marked the end of an era; with the retirement of Howard Reynolds there would be no more cornet solos.

In the Midst of Life
1900–1910

It is improbable that the Promenade Concerts will enter their 106th season without some special high jinks, a Royal First Night perhaps, BBC-commissioned works for the year 2000, this kind of thing. There is no evidence that the Proms acknowledged the arrival of the present century with anything like that; by 25 August 1900 it was no doubt already stale news. The first decade manifested its own significant changes. These lifted the Proms from trying to please everyone into pleasing themselves, and thus to pleasing an audience they were themselves creating. When other forms of music-making such as Ballad Concerts came to the end of their useful life, they were simply replaced by something else. The Proms in 1900 were about to reveal a capacity to move with the times, to survive, even to be a pathfinder. It all depends on finding the right path, as the dinosaurs proved.

The change now most obvious to the eye may well have been all but imperceptible to the audience then. Wood and Newman sensed a possible improvement and decided to take a risk. Two-thirds of the way through the 1904 season they quietly began to dismantle the Grand Operatic Selection, which for ten years had been a corner-stone to start the second part of every concert. They were very careful how they did this. On 28 September they substituted Weber's *Invitation to the Waltz*, then carried on with the Selections for two weeks as if nothing had happened. Nothing did happen, so they tried *Capriccio Espagnol* and *Till Eulenspiegel*, following those two evenings with another week of Operatic Selections. Still there was no reaction, which is surprising when you think what violent public outcry greeted a proposal many years later to abandon 'Land of Hope and Glory'. Emboldened, Newman and Wood slipped in *Don Juan*, *Till Eulenspiegel* again and *Zampa*, one after the other. By now they were confident their judgment had been correct; that public taste at the Proms had advanced beyond the Grand Operatic Selection. From the 1905 season they discarded it for ever.

This may seem a small thing now; but to jettison such a well-proved favourite was a big step to take at the time. It shows Wood and Newman with their finger accurately on the public's pulse. It shows adaptability, which the dinosaurs did not have; and it proved to be an essential step forward, opening the way to providing a better standard of music after the interval.

The Proms encountered their first real crisis early in the century. Soon after the 1901 season Robert Newman, for all his ingenuity and skill, his tireless energy and careful management, found himself getting into financial difficulty at Queen's Hall, and finally went bankrupt. This was not due to some fatal lapse, otherwise he would not have been kept on under a new regime, but rather to the remorseless rise in the economics of concert promotion. With care, an impresario may take a profit from a single concert, even today; but no one makes a profit on a long season. In 1901 the gap between the swings and the roundabouts was widening to a point where hard work and inventive planning were no longer enough to prevent the accounts going into the red. Would Newman be forced to give up? Would the Promenade Concerts, the longest series at his hall and the most expensive to run, have to be sacrificed? Dr Cathcart was still backing them loyally, but he could hardly be expected to bear the whole financial burden of Queen's Hall. Some other way out would have to be found if disaster was to be averted. There was no shortage of alternatives; several bodies were anxious to take over, as Wood notes in his memoirs. Where financial help is offered, there are often unpalatable conditions attached. A publishing house might want to push its own composers, for instance, depriving Wood of his autonomy. They would have to choose very carefully.

Whether by good luck or good judgment, Henry Wood was singularly fortunate in his choice of Madame von Stosch as his first soloist of the century. A pupil of the world-famous Belgian violinist Eugène Ysaÿe, she played the *Rondo Capriccioso* by Saint-Saëns on the First Night, and made such a splendid impression that she was booked to appear another five times during the 1900 season. As a direct result, Wood and Newman came to know her husband very well, Sir Edgar Speyer, an extremely rich financier who numbered among his closest friends the singer and conductor George Henschel, Richard Strauss, pianist Emil Sauer, Georges Enesco, and a host of other prominent musicians. He and his wife maintained an elegant London house with a delightful Italian garden at 46 Grosvenor Street. There was a suite of rooms at the disposal of visitors such as Edvard Grieg and Claude Debussy, who both came to London originally at Speyer's invitation. Following the crisis of 1901 Sir Edgar formed Queen's Hall Orchestra Ltd, a syndicate influential enough to ensure financial stability, with himself as Chairman and retaining the valued services of Robert Newman as manager. Wood estimated that Speyer's personal contribution to music in Britain over the next twelve years amounted to the equivalent of a quarter of a million pounds at today's values.

There may have been a final despairing effort in 1901 to cut costs before the crash. The last week's printed programmes that season were exceptionally full of advertising, leaving room for only the titles of works; the lengthy notes were omitted, so the sheet had to be given away free. Shortly after the syndicate was formed, the programme cover was for the first time printed in two colours; Sir Edgar Speyer is there shown becoming first a baronet in 1906, and finally the Rt Hon Sir Edgar Speyer Bart in 1910. Alas, for all his philanthropy his days were numbered, like those of the German Club in London.

It was very much the custom at this time to offer several dates during a season to certain soloists like Madame von Stosch. The distinguished Sims Reeves, who sang in the first year, or Kirkby Lunn, who seems to have sung in all the others so frequently does her name appear, brought top-ranking artists before the Proms public. Kirkby Lunn had been the first British singer to star in both the grand season at Covent Garden and the Metropolitan Opera of New York. Her greatest triumph was as Delilah at the Royal Opera House. She considered the English very serious, complaining: 'Everyone wants to pin a Suffragette button on me'. The 1901 Proms debuts of two young keyboard lions Wilhelm Backhaus (seventeen) and Mark Hambourg (twenty-two) symbolise the Proms role in discovering, as well as offering, great talent. Young unknowns will increasingly be given a first big chance on this platform; a tradition is in the making.

But what debuts those two made! In the first half of the 1901 season Backhaus played Mendelssohn's G minor Concerto, the Brahms *Paganini Variations* solo on another evening, the Grieg concerto, more solos four nights later, the Schumann, Tchaikovsky First, and Beethoven Fourth Concertos, and two more concerts of solos to round off his first London appearance. Immediately afterwards came Mark Hambourg playing in quick succession Rubinstein's Fourth Concerto, Beethoven 3, Saint-Saëns 4, the Schumann again, Liszt 1, Chopin 1, Liszt's *Hungarian Fantasia*, and with splendid symmetry the Mendelssohn G minor to end his Proms debut.

Here at a 1903 Prom is a remarkable pianist who knew Brahms, studied with Clara Schumann, and played all over Europe with Joachim, Gervase Elwes, and Pablo Casals; Fanny Davies, giving her superlative performance of Beethoven's Fourth Concerto, which fifteen years earlier she had played in Leipzig at a concert where Tchaikovsky conducted his own Fourth Symphony. 'Who's on viola?' Casals used to ask when invited for private music-making; if it was Lionel Tertis, Casals would play quartets. Tertis was twenty-seven in 1903; a soloist then in Mozart's *Sinfonia Concertante*, he was at Promenade Concerts during the next forty years. This doyen of viola players lived for thirty years after that, to the grand age of ninety-nine. Percy Grainger (of *Molly on the Shore*, *Handel in the Strand*) played Tchaikovsky's First Concerto in 1904, the Grieg in 1909; there is a piano roll of his Grieg. Pianist

Egon Petri and baritone Peter Dawson both appeared for the first time in 1904, the year Donald Francis Tovey (of the indestructible *Essays in Musical Analysis*) played a Mozart concerto and the First Book of Brahms's *Paganini Variations* at the same concert. Wilhelm Backhaus had found the *Variations* enough for one night, but not Tovey. When Wood suggested a quick encore, Tovey (who was apt to lose track of the time when playing) sat down and launched into the Second Book. At ten past eleven Wood sent the band home, telling Percy Pitt to play 'The King' on the organ when Tovey finished. Every programme did carry a warning that demands for encores might lead to omitting some items! Next season the eighteen-year-old Myra Hess made her Proms debut playing Liszt's E flat Piano Concerto.

The Scots baritone W. A. Peterkin was still going strong in 1909; a tribute must be paid to the durability of Sullivan's ballad 'Thou'rt Passing Hence' which rotated between Peterkin and others several times a season for over fifteen years. A young contralto was given ten dates in 1900 and sang frequently afterwards, Jessie Goldsack, another of Wood's many pupils, of whom there will be a great deal more to tell. As she stood beside him on the platform in Queen's Hall, did she perhaps fall a little under the spell of the handsome and popular young conductor?

Henry Wood shouldered all the conducting for the first seven years, but that is only half of it. He coached the singers, and he went through concertos at the piano, there being insufficient orchestral rehearsal time. He was ready to play organ or piano solos; and he must have spent hours and hours studying full scores. many of them new to everyone. To convey these to his players he had to be note-perfect. The terrific strain took its toll; the last forty-two concerts in 1902 were conducted by the Leader Arthur Payne. Dr Cathcart packed Wood off to Morocco on his own for a complete rest. While he was there, Olga cabled the sad news of his father's sudden illness and death.

This decade is the dawn of great discoveries; of Wood as Christopher Columbus. The British première of Rachmaninoff's First Piano Concerto was at a 1900 Prom. A proud list of novelties was published in the 1902 programme, including Mahler, Fauré, Tchaikovsky – how well Wood served him – and Sibelius, with work after work brought before the public, the symphonies, *En Saga*, the Violin Concerto, *Swan White*. In 1902 the audience first heard 'Land of Hope and Glory', Elgar's *Pomp and Circumstance March* – at that time, the only one – set to embarrassing doggerel in his *Coronation Ode*, which he conducted himself, its projected Covent Garden première having been cancelled owing to the King's illness. Four vocalists and a full chorus being required, Wood seized his chance and put on the first complete Proms performance of Beethoven's *Choral Symphony* (not in 1929, as every other reference book states) but, owing to his illness, it was Arthur Payne who conducted.

Elgar was ever championed at the Proms; the *Enigma Variations* and three

performances of his *New Symphony in A flat* were given during the 1909 season.*
His *Pomp and Circumstance* marches were played almost as the ink dried; the
Introduction and Allegro in 1905, six months after its première. It always
appeared in programmes with the subtitle 'A smiling with a sigh' from
Shakespeare's *Cymbeline*. The first sounds of Mahler ever heard in this country
were those of his First Symphony, in 1902; Wood also did Bruckner's Seventh
in 1903 and Liszt's enormous *Dante Symphony* the following season. How
delighted they were to announce the 'Third performance in England' of
Symphonia Domestica by Strauss in 1905. 'The four saxophones and oboe
d'amore', said a footnote, 'were specially made for this performance, the
saxophones in London, the oboe in Paris.' (How odd, when Adolphe Sax had
flourished in Paris.) Now the names begin to unfurl; Claude Debussy's *Faune*
in 1904 opened the way to *La Mer, Images*, even *Le Martyre de St Sébastien* later
on in 1915. Ralph Vaughan Williams enters with the premières of *Norfolk
Rhapsody* in 1906 and *Fantasia on English Folk Songs* in 1910. There was the
Delius Piano Concerto in 1907, the same year as Havergal Brian's *New English
Suite* and *New Overture, for Valour*, and Ravel's *Rapsodie Espagnole*. The names of
Granville Bantock, Reger, Arensky, Coleridge-Taylor, are also beginning to
crop up.

Not that Wood looked only forward. Where at that time could you hear any
Bach? The *Mass in B minor*, certainly; but the *Brandenburg Concertos?* Concerted
works for two violins and other combinations, for two and four keyboards
(Henry Wood playing one of them), the Orchestral Suites, the cantatas
'Amore Traditore' and 'Ich will den Kreuzstab'? Wood had scheduled all of
them by 1910, and the *Toccata and Fugue in D minor* for organ solo. Arthur
Catterall, who became Leader in 1909, had even played the great *Chaconne* for
unaccompanied violin. Another tradition in the making; by the thirties
Wood's Bach Nights sold out immediately. There was quite a bit of chamber
music at the Proms in those early days. Beethoven's *Septet* was given in 1906,
the first three movements on 28 September, the last three on 5 October, not to
bore the customers with too much at a time. Max Reger's long *Serenade* was
given the same treatment the following year.

To mark special occasions is a minor function of a major concern, but some
measure of its standing. The century began well, a Thanksgiving Concert on
28 August celebrating the relief of Mafeking and victories of our Imperial
troops in the continuing Boer War, with a special choir of 250 voices for
Mendelssohn's *Hymn of Praise*. There was a concert for Dvorak's fifty-ninth
birthday on 8 September, and a memorial Prom after his death in 1904, the
year Wood had been the first Englishman to conduct the New York
Philharmonic. Queen Victoria's death in 1901 was commemorated with a

---

*This symphony is not listed among the 'important novelties' in the Appendix to Wood's *My
Life of Music*. The second symphony is shown in 1910, whereas Wood did not conduct the
première until May 1911. Perhaps Sir Henry did not compile this Appendix himself.

concert before the Proms season. Siegfried's Funeral March was played two nights running in memoriam William McKinley, late President of the United States. Wood writes that he performed Chopin's Funeral March in homage to only three distinguished musicians, Joachim and Grieg in 1907, and Sarasate the next year, forgetting that he had done it three years earlier for Dvorak.

Then there was the centenary, on 21 October 1905, of Nelson's victory at Trafalgar. For this Wood arranged a *New Fantasia for Orchestra on British Sea-Songs*. Its first performance was at the special matinée put on by Newman that day; but the arranger's identity was not disclosed. Nor was he mentioned when they repeated it to open the second half of the regular Prom that evening. It was next played on the last two Saturdays of the 1908 season, still anonymously. In his arrangement Wood exactly imitated, perhaps from conscience, the favoured orchestral solos of the abandoned Grand Operatic Selection. There were ten in the *Fantasia*: piccolo, flute, oboe, clarinet, horns, trumpet, trombone, euphonium, violin and the lovely 'Tom Bowling' on cello. When the 1909 season began with the *Sea-Songs* Henry Wood's authorship was for the first time publicly acknowledged. Five days later, to show impartiality, he conducted his *Fantasia on Welsh Melodies*, and nine days after that another *Fantasia on Scottish Melodies*. Both were repeated before the Last Night, on which the second half began with the *Scottish Fantasia* and ended – at long last – with the *Sea-Songs*, though that did not at once establish a tradition.

Wood had particular personal connections with the 1909 Last Night; his friend W. A. Peterkin was singing, and so was his wife Olga. He had first presented her to the Promenaders in 1901 when she was proudly billed, then and always, as 'Mrs Henry J. Wood'. Prudently too, for his name had the drawing power; but Dame Eva Turner has confirmed that Olga was a considerable artist, as audiences were about to discover. Over the next nine years she sang a very wide range, arias from *Tannhäuser*, *Eugen Onegin*, *Aida*, *Fidelio*, *Prince Igor*, *Alceste*, *Figaro*; Isolde many times; works by Handel, Mascagni and Bantock; Mahler's Fourth Symphony; songs by Schubert, Schumann, d'Albert, Tchaikovsky, Hahn; new songs by Eric Coates; and, on that Last Night in 1909, two new songs Stanford had specially orchestrated for her. She sang them in great pain. Eight weeks later she was dead.

This was the age of Empire, Elgar, and the stiff upper lip. Wood never wore it on his sleeve, but that great heart surely broke. Olga had been the love of his life. Now he felt there was nothing left to drive him on but work, work, and still more work, with the occasional solace of painting.

Mixing his palette amid the bracken at some favourite beauty spot freed Wood's thoughts to relax him, and his life to heal. His was a receptive, enquiring, scientific mind. He had thought of state support for music forty

3. Dame Eva Turner as the Countess in Mozart's *Le Nozze di Figaro*. Chicago, about 1930 (*Daguerre, Chicago*)

years before it happened. He felt that concerts went on far too long. He dreamed of a subsidised rehearsal hall. He pondered the proportions of theatres in relation to their stages; and he predicted a formally dressed audience such as today attends Glyndebourne. Later, he even foresaw that singers might come to rely too much on the power of microphones and amplification.

As to the hard work, he always made sure of adequate rest after conducting, kept himself in good trim physically, and cleared a path to essential periods of undisturbed concentration and study. He was a perfectionist. For years he broke his journeys to the Norwich Festival so that he could rehearse the four Wagner tuba players who happened to live in Kettering; and he had three harmoniums installed in the Norwich hall, each one tuned four vibrations sharp to its neighbour, so that the distant hidden chorus should sing in tune – an acknowledgment of the Doppler effect.

Fritz Busch once told John Pritchard that looking at masterpieces in the world's galleries enriched a conductor's art. Henry Wood ever sought the company of artists. Over lunch at Pagani's he would have long conversations with the Viennese sculptor and painter Emil Fuchs, who lived in Regent's Park. He even sat for him, the next sitter being Baden-Powell, who founded the Scout movement. Naturally they discussed Sargent, whose *Madame X* had so scandalised Paris in 1884; John Singer Sargent, the most famous portrait painter of the day. Harold Malcolm Watts Sargent was only ten years old at the time, and taking piano lessons with Frances Tinkler in Stamford.

As to what lay beyond 1910, one thing at least was certain. Wood had twice accepted to conduct at the Sheffield Festival while the Proms were on, four nights in 1902 on his own, and a week in 1908 taking the entire Queen's Hall Orchestra with him. On that occasion Eduard Colonne had been brought over from Paris to conduct the New Symphony Orchestra at the Proms. Robert Newman finally put his foot down. Promenade Concert audiences expected to see Henry Wood on the Queen's Hall platform; and Queen's Hall was where in future he ought to be, every night of the season.

The Great War
Proms 1911 – 1926

The twentieth season of Promenade Concerts got off to a false start. It opened only eleven days after Britain declared war on Germany in 1914. Queen's Hall management made certain patriotic moves. They displayed a bust of King George V immediately below Wood's rostrum. They advertised two National Anthems to be sung every evening, 'God Save the King' and 'La Marseillaise.' And they hurriedly substituted a programme of non-German music for the first Wagner Night. It was not done willingly, but their Chairman Sir Edgar Speyer was vulnerable, especially when the German Ambassador to London, Prince Lichnowsky, had just been sent packing. They hid behind their conductor – 'the postponement of Wagner having been rendered necessary by a variety of circumstances, Sir Henry confidently hopes for the continued support of the audience'.

Well there was some straight talking behind the scenes after that; and by Friday British common sense had prevailed. Robert Newman published a letter two nights running, regretting that Monday's decision had been the result of outside pressure brought to bear at the eleventh hour by the Lessees of Queen's Hall (Chappell and Co., the publishers, who may have had government pressure put on them). Newman's directors now wished emphatically to contradict any statement that German music would be boycotted. 'The greatest examples of Music and Art are world possessions and unassailable even by the prejudices and passions of the hour.' Compare this to the Second World War, before which Nazi Germany banned Mendelssohn or any other Jewish music; but during which British audiences applauded German *Lieder* whilst German bombs rained down on them.

National Anthems had not been advertised in the Press before; it fitted the mood, and Sir Henry was busy arranging those of Belgium and Russia. For some time 'The King' opened each concert, and one of the other three closed it in rotation. Then suddenly on a Thursday British justice reversed things; 'La Marseillaise', 'La Brabançonne', or the Russian National Air henceforth began the evening and 'The King' ended it. At one concert they played French composer Florent Schmitt's *New Suite, Reflets d'Allemagne* somewhere between the British and Belgian National Anthems. The programme glossed over M. Florent's inconvenient reflections as 'probably the outcome of holidays spent abroad'.

The Proms had been quietly consolidating since Henry Wood was knighted by George V on 23 February 1911. Olga's untimely death cheated her of that reward and Sir Henry had continued working for dear life. The administration, which first his father undertook, and then Olga, was now in the extremely capable hands of his new secretary, Muriel Greatrex. Inevitably they were often alone at work together. The day when a young girl in a widower's house would cause no comment was still half a century and two world wars away. Victorian attitudes were ingrained; Muriel's father, Major Greatrex, thought it would be better if they married; and in 1911 they did, with advantages on both sides. Wood's business and household affairs were excellently ordered; Muriel immediately became Lady Wood, and later bore him two daughters, Tatiana and Avril. Why Tatiana? A whiff of nostalgia perhaps, for the child he and Olga did not have?

Wood gave the first concert performance here of Wagner's *Ring* cycle at Sheffield, and opened the 1911 London Music Festival with Elgar's *Gerontius*, which he had gone to Düsseldorf specially to hear in 1902, attending a civic banquet with Elgar at which Richard Strauss spoke in praise of the new English genius. How curious that Wood left such a work, or the *St Matthew Passion, Messiah*, or the *Mass in B minor*, out of his Proms; these things did not come in until the 1950s with Sir Malcolm Sargent.*

Reviewers were disappointed at the Proms novelties in 1911; Ravel's *Pavane*, the *Rosenkavalier Waltzes* of Strauss, Debussy's *Children's Corner*, Enesco's *Rumanian Rhapsody No. 1* (soon repeated), and the *Miniature Suite* the twenty-five-year-old Eric Coates dedicated to Sir Henry, but not much else. Many Queen's Hall players were now stepping forward as soloists; one played the Dvorak Cello Concerto. Frank Mullings, a great English Siegfried, made his Proms debut, and The Alexandra Quartet of Lady Singers did Four Songs by Brahms, 'seldom heard in London', as a critic wrote, 'nor is this a matter for surprise'.

Sir George Henschel, whom Wood had seen conducting in Boston, was engaged for the 26 September and 10 October Proms, and again in 1912 for a whole week while Wood was at the Birmingham Festival with Jan Sibelius, Newman having relaxed his ban on Wood absenting himself during a Proms

---

*There is evidence that Sir Henry believed *Messiah* with cuts could be given at a Prom; but even in 1930 when the BBC ran Northern Proms in Manchester, Liverpool and Leeds, including *Gerontius* and *The Damnation of Faust*, the idea was still not extended to the London Proms.

season. Wood was much sought after by music publishers, because of his known eagerness to conduct new works. In 1912 he gave the first performance of *Five Orchestral Pieces* at the Proms, not only the first music by Arnold Schoenberg ever to be heard in Britain, but also a world première. Quite a scoop for Peters Edition – and for Wood! 'The hisses were for the composer, the cheers for Sir Henry and his long-suffering company' was one comment; against which must be set Schoenberg's own compliment to the Queen's Hall Orchestra when he conducted the work himself in January 1914 before a large and appreciative audience: 'There are on the Continent at most two orchestras which could be compared with you – the Amsterdam and the Vienna Philharmonic. It was the first time since Gustav Mahler that I heard such music played as a musician of culture demands'.

Prom attendances in 1912 were large, comments on performances glowing: 'Many of the most famous works in the repertoire were given with a care and general brilliance of effect seldom equalled and never perhaps excelled'. It was the year of the *Titanic* disaster; and of the death of Coleridge-Taylor only a month before Arthur Catterall gave the première of his last work, a violin concerto, at a Prom.

In 1913, whilst rival anthropologists were vying to prove the genuineness of the Piltdown Man skull, Sir Henry Wood was giving the British première of Stravinsky's *Firebird* Suite, which was quickly repeated during a Proms season notable for its enterprise.* Dame Ethel Smyth conducted the Overture to her opera *The Wreckers*, produced in Leipzig in 1906, at Queen's Hall in 1908 (a concert version under Nikisch), and at Her Majesty's Theatre under Beecham in 1909. There was a new Piano Concerto by Glazunov, *The Wasps* Suite by Vaughan Williams, Debussy's *Iberia*, 'which exactly captured the Spanish atmosphere; the performance of this difficult score could hardly have been bettered'; premières from Arnold Bax, Frank Bridge (*The Sea*), Fauré, Reger, Ravel (*Valses Nobles*), Dohnanyi's *New Suite*, and soprano Carrie Tubbs's remarkable performance of the Closing Scene from *Salome* by Strauss.

Attendances broke all records. Night after night there was standing room only by eight o'clock, Wagner, Beethoven and Saturdays being the most popular. It was even suggested that the overflow might fill a smaller hall for a concurrent second series of Proms. 'The public demands nothing more than good music well played, and permission to smoke and move about.'

The Great War changed all that. (It was called the Great War not in retrospect, but right from the start.) As late as 26 June 1914 Queen's Hall Chairman Sir Edgar Speyer had invited his great friend Richard Strauss over to conduct four of his tone-poems, and songs with Elena Gerhardt. With the

---

* The almost obligatory Stravinsky work in any season for nearly forty years. That the Great War's stringencies and a period of Swiss exile had compelled him to write for much smaller ensembles could hardly be guessed from the Proms repertoire until the *Symphony of Psalms* was given in 1949.

declaration of war Speyer's position came under fire from both Press and public. Lady Speyer spoke compassionately to Wood of untrained British youth being sent to face well-disciplined German armies. Before he was despatched ignominiously to his fatherland (in fact he went to America) Speyer presented Wood with title-deeds to the Queen's Hall Orchestra, rather than William Boosey of Chappell and Co., music publishers, who actually took it over. In future it would be known as the New Queen's Hall Orchestra, a device used again half a century later when Walter Legge departed from the Philharmonia Orchestra.

What the Great War was about dawned on the British only gradually, as Harold Nicolson pointed out in a BBC broadcast when a second war broke out between the two nations in 1939. An Austrian archduke had been shot in some remote Balkan city. German armies had invaded Belgium, a place almost as remote to most people; and though the lads in their hundreds were being taken, it was to a green hill, far away. Daily life went on. A few crowds gathered, in straw boaters and wide-brimmed feathery hats. Streets stayed brightly lit, theatres and restaurants crowded. Youth thought of it as adventure. There was a kind of ghastly jollity to sickening songs like 'Goodbye Dolly, I must leave you, though it breaks my heart to go' – and a white feather for anyone who stayed. A slaughterhouse masqueraded as Heroism and Valour. Bit by bit the reality of war was felt, through early Zeppelin raids, German submarine activity, the darkened (but not blacked-out) streets, and food rationing.

The effect was felt at Queen's Hall almost immediately. At the end of the 1914 Proms season the new management referred to the inauspicious circumstances in which it had taken place, with fitful attendances according to good or bad news from the front. 'I cannot say I could look round and find the hall crowded every night as I had formerly done', wrote Wood; but by the end of the season audiences had picked up a little, justifying the courageous decision to carry on. Because of air raids, concerts in 1915 were shortened; and after two 'experimental matinées' on Wednesdays at 3 p.m. to test public reaction, they were subsequently given at 3 p.m. and 8 p.m. on alternate days, though no one could have been sure that the dirigibles would not attack on the late nights, Tuesday, Thursday and Saturday. It helped to soothe public fears, especially as a piece of Queen's Hall ceiling had fallen in front of a bassoonist in mid-solo. Even Sir Henry Wood noticed that. Hearing neither bombs nor anti-aircraft noise, it was only when Promenaders began huddling together for safety under the Grand Circle that he realised a raid was on. Matinées were dropped in 1916 and an earlier 7.30 p.m. start adopted. Queen's Hall was well insulated against outside noise; in both wars it was only our own guns the audience heard. It was excellent inside for sound, too; intentionally designed to resonate like a violin – an orchestra before the bridge, a fine organ behind, and the walls mellowed by music like a well-played fiddle.

Concerts were everywhere given to raise money for various war funds; Adelina Patti sang at one run by Lady Randolph Churchill; Cyril Scott dedicated *Britain's War March* to the Prince of Wales, profits on sheet music sales going to His Royal Highness's National Relief Fund. (It was played at a Prom in 1914.) The Germans erected a forty-foot wooden statue of victorious Field Marshal von Hindenburg into which civilians could drive nails at fifty pfennigs a time for *their* war effort.

Continental soloists finding the journey across the North Sea impracticable, Proms artists were increasingly British, 105 of them in 1914 as against eighty-four the previous year. Wood was grateful to have on hand the young pianist Benno Moiseiwitsch and the even younger Solomon (born Solomon Cutner) only eleven at his Prom debut in Beethoven's Second Concerto. In 1917 a critic asked why, piano concertos no longer being popular, there were eighteen in the season, a piece of bad planning when German grands were unobtainable and good British ones still in the future. It seems a private grouse, though even Wood was by then weary of yet another performance of the Grieg with Artur de Greef. He was bored with conducting National Anthems every evening, too, those of Italy, Serbia, Japan, Canada and Australia having been added in 1915. Two years later they were dropped altogether.

The wartime Proms had begun with Mr Herbert Heyner and the audience singing Elgar's 'Land of Hope and Glory' to end the 1914 First Night. They finished four years later with *Captain* Herbert Heyner doing Iago's 'Credo', and the audience again singing 'Land of Hope' in triumph for victory, on the Last Night in 1918. In between, the Promenaders had welcomed pianist Irene Scharrer, violinist Daniel Melsa, singers Dora Labbette, Walter Glynne (at first without the final 'e'), Vladimir Rosing, the famous twenty-eight-year-old Russian tenor, pupil of Jean de Reszke, who sang here in Tchaikovsky's *Queen of Spades* during the war and went on to launch various opera ventures in America after it, and a host of other soloists. They also had the rare treat of an evening's Lollipops with Mr Thomas Beecham on Saturday 9 October 1915, at which Hamilton Harty conducted *With the Wild Geese*. This was Beecham's first Prom. He conducted only two more, during the Diamond Jubilee season of 1954.

Tuesday became Russian Night because of the war and Henry Wood's natural predilections, amplified by his marriage to Olga. He orchestrated Mussorgsky's *Pictures from an Exhibition* eight years before Ravel, played them at a Prom in 1915, and then gave Touschmalov's even earlier arrangement the following season out of fairness. (It is now available in a recording by the Munich Philharmonic Orchestra.) There was Rachmaninoff's *Isle of Death* (then so called)* and Benno Moiseiwitsch playing a concerto by Nikolai Tchérépnin, the French accents a hangover from Imperial Russia, so recently

---

* Spellings and titles change in this book as they did in fact – Rachmaninoff to Rachmaninov, Wagner's *Dusk of the Gods* to *Twilight of the Gods*, etc.

overthrown. During the war years, as critics often complained, there was little that had not been played before, Bartok and a few lesser composers such as Ireland or César Franck excepted; but there were one or two curiosities, Eric Coates, Wood's principal viola, playing the solo in *The Death of Tintagiles* by Charles Loeffler of the Boston Symphony Orchestra; and 'Chant, Belges, Chant', Elgar's contribution to 'King Albert's Book' published as a tribute to the Belgian people. The poem by Emile Cammaerts was read at Queen's Hall by his wife Tita. Curiously, each programme in the last quarter of the 1917 season was headed by an apt couplet on music from Shelley, Wordsworth, Shakespeare and other poets; just that once, and never again.

How poignant that for the Proms première of *A Shropshire Lad* on 6 September that year the composer should have been 'The late Lieutenant George Butterworth M.C.' killed in action only the previous month. They played *The Banks of Green Willow* two years later. Gustav Holst, the family 'von' prudently dropped from his surname during the war, fared better; on the eve of his departure for Salonika Balfour Gardiner paid for the Queen's Hall Orchestra and Adrian Boult to give two semi-private performances of *The Planets*. The Armistice was signed whilst Holst was en route.

More than forty men from the orchestra saw active service; twelve women had joined its ranks by 1916, and Dora Garland became its first woman Leader in August 1918. That year Sir Henry was sorely tempted by an offer to succeed Carl Muck at the Boston Symphony Orchestra, a post the Foreign Secretary would have liked him to accept, as strengthening diplomatic ties with America; but Wood turned it down. Returning troops and war-weary civilians needed the refreshment of good concerts, and he knew where his duty lay.

Just before the war *The Musical Times* proclaimed 'Wood has 2,500 works in his library, every one of which he has personally edited. He has scored more than 120 arias for the Promenade Concerts. There are some who disapprove of his interpretations; some also disapprove of his programmes. But no one can deny his immense vitality, complete control over his resources, and the great service he has done to music in England by his readiness to secure a hearing of unfamiliar works, and especially of British composers.'

'WHO IS TO BLAME?' thundered *The Times* in September 1918. 'The Proms have fallen from their former estate. As long as they were in Wood's hands, all was well. They have ceased to be in his hands. "A firm of publishers" says they are wholly their concern. So far, the Proms have been a gift, like the Beecham opera. No one succeeded the generous Speyer, so a matter of business took over.'

A little unfair to Chappell and Co., who continued to lose money year by year in support of the Proms. Advertising and performing their Ballads in the second half seems the least possible return; those who disliked the lighter stuff were by this time leaving at the interval anyway. Commendable neutrality, rather than interference, marked the remaining years of their sponsorship. Sir

Henry had a free hand to introduce new works and soloists, and to vary the design of a season in consultation with Robert Newman as before; they set about their task with a will.

For the next two years it looked as if the Novelties might return to a pre-war standard, with first performances in England of Casella's *Le Couvent sur L'Eau*, Prokofiev's Piano Concerto No. 1, and *La Pisanella* by 'Ildebrando Pizzetti di Parma' (in the Italian tradition which led to Giovanni Pierluigi da Palestrina becoming known by the name of his home town). Organ works by Widor were presented, the *Sinfonia Sacra* with orchestra in 1919, the *Allegro* and famous *Toccata* from the Fifth Symphony a month later. How the audience enjoyed hearing that for the first time! Widor played it privately for Wood in Paris the following year. There was a mini-festival of Strauss within the season, *Till Eulenspiegel, Tod und Verklärung, Don Juan, Don Quixote* – Wood's performance of that had authority; Strauss had played it to him on the Speyers' piano one evening before the war. Fauré's *Fantaisie for Piano and Orchestra*, and his *Masques et Bergamasques* were both new to London.

After this, foreign Novelties all but declined, British composer-conductors taking over for the next six years. Although a composer might not obtain the best possible performance, the chance to see him in the flesh more than compensated the audience. They saw Eugene Goossens (Scherzo: *Tam O'Shanter* and many other works), Eric Coates, Vaughan Williams doing his *Tallis Fantasia* and *Pastoral Symphony*, Edward German, Armstrong Gibbs, Edward Elgar with *Falstaff*, Rutland Boughton, Cyril Scott, Frank Bridge conducting *The Sea* for the umpteenth time, Ethel Smyth, Arthur Bliss, Gordon Jacob, Herbert Howells, Mackenzie, Moeran, Dyson, Austin, Carse, Fogg, Julius Harrison – some of them returning time and again. One Promenader was struck by the great contrast between Gustav Holst and *The Planets*, of which for some years only Mars, Saturn and Jupiter were given. Holst looked so frail, was obviously short-sighted, and rather shy. When he waved a hand in the direction of the trombones, he seemed quite shaken by the blast of sound this produced.

Round the back of Queen's Hall ran a corridor with entrances at intervals into the Arena, the doors of which were left open. At the end of a new British work, friends of the composer would rush along this corridor shouting 'Bravo!' through each doorway, to stimulate the audience, and to make their little claque seem bigger than it was, like Aesop's frog.

It cannot have been this period that Henry Wood's biographer had in mind when she wrote, ten years after his death, that he had not approved of composer-conductors except for a real first performance. Another of the young men who conducted his works several times was Malcolm Sargent. He had been obliged to direct his *An Impression on a Windy Day* himself at Leicester in 1921. Sir Henry Wood, who had pleaded lack of enough time to study it, had been impressed by Sargent's handling of an orchestra and put him and his piece into several Promenade seasons. Sargent also conducted at Queen's

Hall his *Nocturne and Scherzo* (A Night with Pan) in 1922, and a *Valsette in A minor* rescued from his Durham University doctorate entry, the year after. (His ballad 'My Heart Has a Quiet Sadness' was sung at a 1925 Prom.) He had been studying the piano in London with Benno Moiseiwitsch and appeared as soloist in Rachmaninoff's Second Concerto, for which he persuaded Adrian Boult into a guest appearance with the recently-formed Leicester Symphony Orchestra, which Sargent was then training. Soon afterwards at Queen's Hall Sargent asked Sir Henry Wood which career he should follow. 'You're a born conductor,' said Sir Henry; and that settled that.*

Three Preludes from Hans Pfitzner's eight-year-old opera *Palestrina* were performed in 1925, the same year as Dohnanyi's *Variations on a Nursery Song* (with pianoforte obbligato, it said then) which was subtitled 'For the joy of the friends of humour and the vexation of the others', a work which fascinated the Promenaders, if sometimes leaving them puzzled as to where the 'Nursery Song' had got to. Ernest Bloch's *Schelomo* brought an interest in that composer's works; and Wood recalled that some of the modern stuff in this period was roundly hissed, proving that far from clapping everything indiscriminately, as was sometimes said, the audience had a mind of its own.

It was a singer, Sims Reeves, who had given a boost to the end of the very first Proms season in 1895; and it was another famous tenor, recommended to him by the Danish Legation, that Wood presented to add lustre to the Proms as they were re-establishing themselves after the war. In five appearances Lauritz Melchior bestrode the 1920 season, singing Lohengrin's 'Narration', the 'Steersman's Song', Tannhäuser's 'Pilgrimage', and Siegfried's 'Forging Songs' from Wagner's operas, and 'Vesti la giubba', from Leoncavallo's *Pagliacci*. There is an old argument about whether opera should be sung in the language of its composition or that of the country in which it is being performed. By objecting that Melchior sang nothing in English, Robert Newman obliquely upheld the latter viewpoint, for Melchior sang everything in his native Danish! He appeared with great success in four consecutive seasons, and did once sing in English when he gave the world première of a Chappell Ballad, 'Gold o' the World' by Edric Cundell, in 1922. A publisher's 'royalty' was paid to every singer who promoted a Ballad; perhaps Melchior did well out of it. That same season the audience heard Hubert Eisdell sing in Greek, 'Hoopoe's Song' from *The Birds of Aristophanes* by Parry.

Sir Henry naturally had an ear for a good singer. He introduced Maggie Teyte on the First Night of 1922; she sang Tatiana's Letter Song from *Eugen Onegin*, and 'I Love the Moon' – she was singing in Chappell's Ballad Concerts at the same time. A very young Bella Baillie first appeared in 1923 (she reverted to Isobel much later). There were others, Florence Austral,

---

* In 1924 Dorothy and Robert Mayer saw him at Queen's Hall and at once engaged him to introduce and conduct their new Children's Concerts at Westminster Central Hall.

Astra Desmond, Frank Titterton, Walter Widdop, Harold Williams, Norman Walker, among the many fine singers regularly performing at these post-war Proms.

Every rule about allowing no encores was thrown to the winds when Myra Hess returned in triumph from her American tour in 1923, to open the season with Rachmaninoff's Second Concerto. So tremendous was the reception that she was forced to play an encore. This was the year Rae Robertson performed solo in the Strauss *Burlesque*; next season his wife Ethel Bartlett was with him in a Bach concerto for two keyboards; they became a popular piano duo. It was also the debut of the Argentine pianist Señor José Iturbi, the first of many appearances, and of a young son of a famous father, pianist Mitja Nikisch. Aubrey H. Brain stepped down from his seat in the orchestra to play a Mozart horn concerto; and there was the British première of *Le Carnaval des Animaux*, the grand zoological fantasy by Saint-Saëns which so intrigued Liszt when he heard of it in Paris in 1886 that he asked for a private performance, and which has gone on delighting audiences everywhere for nearly a century.

The Times commented that the Promenaders, 'packed like a football crowd', could no longer walk about, 'a discipline of the flesh and an education of the spirit' in which 'the Classics have it; the earticklers and pastrycooks do not cut much ice'. There was also a daily column listing 'Broadcasting Today' in London, Birmingham, Cardiff, Manchester, Newcastle and Glasgow. The British Broadcasting Company Ltd was just one year old.

On 15 October 1924 the New Queen's Hall Orchestra changed from black to white ties for the first visit to the Proms of Their Majesties King George V and Queen Mary, attended by Lady Cynthia Colville and the Rt Hon Sir Frederick Ponsonby. On arrival Lady Wood was presented and Tatiana Wood offered a bouquet to Her Majesty. Sir Henry Wood, Sir Edward Elgar, and Frank Bridge were presented to their sovereign at the interval; all three conducted during the concert. The final item was Wood's *Fantasia on British Sea-Songs*; Sir Henry turned round towards its climax to direct a chorus of 3,000 voices, as the whole audience rose to its feet for 'Rule, Britannia'. A triumphant accolade; but there were distant rumblings. It had been rumoured that the 1924 Proms might not take place at all: 'We think of them as our best established musical institution, but they are not ours, nor established. They depend on a private fund which may be withdrawn.' Chappell and Co. hardly helped by asserting: 'We alone have the right to decide whether there shall be a season or not, and under what conditions that season shall be given.' Nor had it escaped notice that programmes were becoming stabilised at the expense of really worthwhile new music: 'Once the programmes become stereotyped into an annual repetition of accepted works their days are numbered' – that *Times* judgment precisely identifies the dilemma; it could also provide a text for the future.

Innovation was not altogether absent. Having returned to the normal eight o'clock start after the war, Wood and Newman went for single-opera Wagner

Nights from 1920, instead of the previous hotchpotch. Excerpts from each of the *Ring* operas (except *Rheingold*, which is seamless), from *Lohengrin*, *Tristan*, *The Mastersingers* and *Parsifal*, plus a kind of *Ring* sampler, were given on certain Mondays over the next four years. Then there was the glorious 1925 season when The English Singers on many evenings sang Madrigals by Weelkes, Gibbons, Wilbye, Byrd, folk songs arranged by Holst and Vaughan Williams, Motets and Canzonets, and wonderful mixed programmes from all three. (There had been a forerunner in 1923, the Halifax Madrigal Society singing music from Palestrina to Holst.) Every Saturday Prom in 1924 included an organ solo (except the Last Night, due to an electrical fault) with G. D. Cunningham, G. W. Alcock, Edward G. Bairstow, Harold E. Darke, Stanley Marchant, Reginald Goss Custard, George Thalben Ball – the roster reads like an organists' roll of honour.

We find it odd today that audiences at this time were asked to refrain from applause between movements of symphonies, but not of concertos. Even more odd that from 1902 to 1929 Beethoven's *Choral Symphony* was always performed without the choral section. Not the three orchestral movements only, but 215 bars into the finale as well, according to that inveterate Promenader Victor Gollancz; right through the great theme and its variations to where the baritone should have declaimed 'O Freunde, nicht diese Töne!' The prohibitive cost of four extra soloists, and rehearsal time with chorus, were the real reasons for what amounted to a musical coitus interruptus. It seems impossible to believe that people put up with it for twenty-seven years.

With a final backward glance we may spot Arthur Benjamin (of the *Jamaican Rumba*) playing Rachmaninoff's Third Piano Concerto (he gave his own *Concertino* in 1928); Clifford Curzon giving the première of a Second Concerto by Montague F. Phillips with its composer conducting – he also wrote 'Sing, Joyous Bird' and 'The Fishermen of England' for Chappell and Co.'s Ballad series; soprano Dora Labbette (her name later changed to Lisa Perli) and pianist Betty Humby performing at the same Prom – both were very close to Sir Thomas Beecham, Betty Humby eventually marrying him; Eric Blom, critic and lexicographer, joining Mrs Rosa Newmarch* as a programme annotator for the Proms; and Harriet Cohen choosing for her Proms debut the *Symphonic Variations* by her dear friend Arnold Bax.

In these immediate post-war years Alcock and Brown had flown across the Atlantic, Amundsen over the North Pole; James Joyce had written *Ulysses*, T. S. Eliot *The Waste Land* and Bernard Shaw *Saint Joan*, Walter Gropius had founded the Bauhaus at Dessau and Eisenstein had filmed *The Battleship Potemkin*; an Anti-Broadcast Lobby had declared that for Suzanne Lenglen to give her impressions of the day's play at Wimbledon over the air competed

---

* The indefatigable Mrs Newmarch succeeded Edgar Jacques in 1908, writing programme notes until 1940. Edwin Evans wrote them in 1941, and several annotators have shared every season since then.

unfairly with newspapers; and Britain had been through a short-lived General Strike. The Proms looked more secure than ever after the unprecedented success of the 1925 season.

'Fresh from his triumphs at the Hollywood Bowl', where Charles Chaplin had been among the huge audience under the stars, came Sir Henry Wood in 1926, Chevalier de l'Ordre de la Couronne (Belgium), of the Légion d'Honneur (France), Gold Medallist of the Royal Philharmonic Society, and Fellow of the Royal College of Music; Edward, Prince of Wales had attended the celebration dinner and roared at his own gaffe ('Stanford wrote the Hallelujah Chorus').

Decorations and celebrations were the order of the day. Sir Henry had received an illuminated address on the Last Night of the twenty-fifth season (and every member of the audience a souvenir brochure); there had been bouquets of white chrysanthemums and a chaplet of bay leaves for him since then. Now the Promenaders cheered every section leader coming on to the platform for the First Night of 1926, with a special cheer for Charles Woodhouse, Leader from 1920 until he retired in 1935 due to poor health. Then finally 'the king' with his red carnation: Sir Henry Wood, who (in the words of Victor Gollancz) understood, as by no means every conductor understands, that a concert should be an act of communion, with soloists, orchestra, every member of the audience and the conductor himself participating. 'We really did love everything and everybody on those Prom nights: the music, the performers, our neighbour and Henry Wood.'

Radiating confidence as he launched the thirty-second season, Wood had not the slightest premonition that less than three weeks after it ended he would have the red carpet ruthlessly and painfully pulled from beneath his feet. His dear friend and helper, the man who believed in him and made him, whose integrity was a rock to depend on in trouble, Robert Newman, who hardly had a day's illness in his life, suddenly fell grievously ill and was rushed into a nursing home. He died on 4 November; and Sir Henry was quite certain he would never look upon his like again.

Different Drummers

1927-1932

If a man does not keep pace with his companions, perhaps it is because he hears a different drummer. Let him step to the music which he hears, however measured or far away.

(Henry Thoreau, *Walden.*)

W hen your weekly wage as an insurance clerk is twenty shillings, you think very carefully before spending two of them on an evening out. Which is why seventeen-year-old Elvira Ketterer was standing in a queue for the Promenade, outside Queen's Hall on the first Wagner Night of the 1927 season. Her opera-loving father, having christened two daughters Elsa Margaretta and Leonora, turned to Mozart when naming a third and brought her up on Wagner.*

Leaving school the previous year, she joined the Old Girls' Dramatic Society and found several members eagerly looking forward to the Proms. Intrigued, she timidly asked to go along with them. Queen's Hall with its silk-shaded chandeliers was already familiar to her through complimentary tickets for symphony concerts; but not the friendlier look that the pool, fountain,

---

* There were three northern brothers, Elgar Hone, Haydn Hone and Handel Hone. Handel played the trumpet. Having a composer for a *middle* name allowed the Fawcett family to ignore it if they chose. They had two Handels, one Mendelssohn, Schubert, Elgar, Rossini and Weber, and two Verdis. Several played in Wood's orchestra. One of the Verdis became Beecham's first Royal Philharmonic orchestral manager. There was composer Haydn Wood; and there is conductor Elgar Howarth. Parents do take a chance though; suppose their children were unmusical?

palms and flowers gave to its usually more austere turquoise blue and gold interior on Promenade nights. Once inside the Arena she had no trouble insinuating her small frame up to the front, at the feet of the mighty as it felt to her. She did not realise it, but the oddly-shaped black box suspended high in mid-air above her head was something new. The first thing seasoned Promenaders noticed this year was the BBC microphone.

Elvira knew nothing of the struggle going on behind the scenes for some months before the season could begin. Not everyone in the audience would have known. Those who did were heartily relieved that the doors had opened at all. 'Things fall apart; the centre cannot hold,' wrote W. B. Yeats; and Robert Newman's death rapidly proved how truly he had been at the centre, holding a delicate balance. It really did seem soon afterwards that there might be no more Proms.

A strong lobby against broadcasting had Sir Thomas Beecham as a spokesman, and the support of Chappell and Co., as concert promoters and lessees of a hall for hire – Queen's Hall, which also provided a focal point for the lobby. The BBC had existed for nearly five years, but no microphone had ever been allowed inside. The premise was that if a public entertainment could be heard over the wireless at home nobody would buy tickets for the live show. This was a view sincerely held, and there was no alternative argument. No one could be certain, not even the BBC itself. Proof or disproof lay some time ahead.

The BBC had already anticipated some of the problems regarding the future of the Proms, and not only out of self-interest in wanting to broadcast from Queen's Hall. Director-General John Reith had some preliminary discussions with Sir Henry Wood as early as February 1926. He was inclined to take a share in the Proms, though not exclusively with Wood, whose grip on them Reith attributed to possessing his own music library! Landon Ronald and Hamilton Harty were among the other conductors considered. Percy Pitt, by this time Music Director at the BBC, thought the Proms would not be the same without Sir Henry. The BBC also had its own Wireless Orchestra, which might be cheaper to use than the one at Queen's Hall.

To Chappell and Co., the second part of every Prom had been a shop window to promote their Ballads. The first part lost them increasingly large sums of money. Broadcast entertainment was lessening the need for domestic music-making. Ballads were on the wane, and so was Chappell and Co.'s interest in the Proms. The hire of Queen's Hall was a different matter. A much higher rent was quoted to the BBC who found it unacceptable. Chappell and Co. said in that case there would be no Proms at all. Not so, Reith replied, the BBC would run their own season at Westminster Central Hall. Chappell and Co. countered with an alternative scheme for Proms conducted by Sir Thomas Beecham, whose name was sometimes invoked in connection with the most unlikely projects. The BBC turned down a request to call it the 'New Queen's Hall Orchestra by arrangement with Messrs

Chappell's Ltd' and opted for 'Sir Henry Wood and his Symphony Orchestra'.

All this jousting had only one purpose, to fix a price for the future hire of Queen's Hall by the BBC. Once having obtained quite favourable terms, Chappell and Co. withdrew from the arena altogether.

Sir Henry Wood was extremely worried about the BBC running his Proms. Their younger music men might not allow him the same artistic freedom he had enjoyed with Newman. Wood knew *he* could be trusted; but could he trust the BBC? He hinted at a substantial offer to conduct abroad. The BBC saw through that, but nevertheless offered him higher fees. Any initial tension between them is understandable, for they heard different drummers. Wood was desperately anxious to preserve intact his life's work; but, at fifty-eight, time was beginning to run out for him. The BBC was only five years old, and feeling its way carefully into the future; it had all the time in the world.

Private fears were not paraded publicly. 'With the whole-hearted support of the wonderful medium of broadcasting', said Sir Henry, promoting the 1927 season, 'I feel that I am at last on the threshold of realising my lifelong ambition of truly democratising the message of music and making its beneficent effect universal.' The BBC was quietly pleased: 'The Corporation has been anxious to do whatever was in its power consistent with its wider obligations. Negotiations have been in progress for several months. Ultimately agreement has been reached. A six weeks' series of Proms is to be given by the BBC, conducted by Sir Henry Wood. Moreover, the microphone is no longer banned from Queen's Hall for other occasions.'

The immediate effect was that everyone connected with the Proms put their prices up. The BBC was obliged to negotiate a new contract for the Queen's Hall Orchestra with the Musicians' Union. Other changes included the neater, fuller Prospectus we know today (instead of the previous newspaper sheet) with forty-eight postage-stamp-sized photographs of performers, composers, and Mrs Rosa Newmarch; programmes the same size with eight pages and notes; the reintroduction of a cheap Season Ticket to the Promenade; and the abolition of 'royalty Ballads' in part two of the concerts. Tickets were now obtainable from 'The BBC, Savoy Hill, Chappell and Co.'s Box Office, Queen's Hall, and Agents'.

There were unprecedented scenes on the First Night in 1927, when more people queued up beforehand than Queen's Hall could hold. Once Elgar's *Cockaigne* Overture started, there were audible sighs of relief from various parts of the hall – the Proms had come back to life! Another audience remained outside, listening at the doors and the open windows, clapping as loudly as if they had got in.

More than fifty years later, Elvira Ketterer would still have vivid memories of her first Prom. No one who goes to the Proms can forget the experience. For young Walter Loynes, who had never heard of them until he went to study at Regent Street Polytechnic, the sight of Queen's Hall opposite proved

4. At Appletree Farm, Chorley Wood, in 1924. Sir Henry Wood, Benno Moiseiwitsch, Daisy Kennedy, Lady Muriel Wood, Arthur Brooks of Columbia Graphophone Co, and daughter Avril. (*Courtesy Avril Wood*)

irresistible. From then on he divided his life between engineering and Beethoven, cheerfully walking the five miles home afterwards, his fare money gladly spent on a Promenade ticket.

Hundreds of soloists played at these concerts, yet even the most regular Promenaders always seem to remember the same names; artists who besides their artistry possess some other magic which an audience instantly feels and never forgets. Myra Hess playing Beethoven, Brahms, or Schumann, and sometimes 'an arrangement' (her own) of 'Jesu, Joy of Man's Desiring', despite the ban on encores. Solomon – after his Rachmaninoff Second Concerto in 1930 a critic could not understand why it had become so neglected. Moiseiwitsch, massive and impassive, thundering forth the *Emperor*. Cyril Smith, twenty-one, fresh from the Royal College of Music, in full command of the Brahms B flat Concerto. Eva Turner, whose 1928 *Turandot* at Covent Garden was so sensational, soaring over the full orchestra on Wagner Night. Albert Sammons, and Beatrice Harrison (who once played her cello to a nightingale) in the Elgar concertos. Arthur Catterall's refined tone and line – Leader of the Hallé and later the BBC Symphony, and always

5. Dame Myra Hess. Rehearsing with Jelly d'Aranyi at the BBC, Savoy
Hill, in 1928 (*BBC Copyright Photograph*)

a popular soloist. Clifford Curzon – Henry Wood thought no one played Schubert's *Wanderer Fantasia* more poetically. Harriet Cohen, dramatic and chic with black sleek hair and Paris gown, often disregarding convention by playing from her music. She raised funds to present a silver salver to Sir Henry, engraved with the signatures of a hundred of his soloists, and a pair of gold cuff-links, after nearly forty years of the Proms. Perhaps those were the cuff-links that sometimes rattled when he conducted.

So many other soloists are still remembered. Nor will anyone present on 24 August 1927 forget Daisy Kennedy, a pupil of Sevcik and later married to Moiseiwitsch, who lost her way in the Brahms Violin Concerto and told an astonished audience that it was because she had not had a rehearsal, ending, 'I hope my courage tonight will secure more rehearsals for other artists'. Then she burst into tears off-stage. It was not the last interruption at a Prom. Wood never moved, never complained, never made a scene; the score was produced, and the concerto finished. Reverberations went on for days. 'No work with which I am connected is ever performed in public unrehearsed,' Wood told the Press. (He had piano rehearsals with soloists in private.) 'Absurd,' said the BBC, 'all new or difficult works are rehearsed; there are four or five rehearsals every week. The Brahms Concerto has been performed by the Queen's Hall Orchestra 150 times; it hardly needs a rehearsal.' 'A lapse of memory . . . disaster only averted by the imperturbability of Sir Henry Wood . . . if soloist and orchestra are proficient, and the conductor knows his business, it should be all right,' wrote the Press. Critic Ernest Newman thought nothing a fiddler had done for a long time had given him so much pleasure. Under such conditions was music made; and a brave girl protested. Two nights later Isolde Menges lost her way in the Beethoven Concerto, which was held to confirm that soloists, not orchestras, are fallible.

A significant number of Proms performers and composers joined the BBC as music administrators – Percy Pitt, W. W. Thompson (Robert Newman's lieutenant; the organ obbligato of Teresa del Riego's 'Homing' in 1919 was his first Prom), Steuart Wilson, whose performance of Beethoven's 'An die ferne Geliebte' was a feature of several seasons; Arthur Bliss, Victor Hely-Hutchinson, composer and concerto pianist; and later Herbert Murrill, Maurice Johnstone, Anthony Lewis, William Glock – directors of music, concert organisers, planners, the future of these famous concerts, which by 1932 the Press was starting to call a festival, safely in their hands. Percy Pitt was at the BBC during the take-over. W. W. 'Tommy' Thompson ran the 1927 season from Chappell and Co. and joined the BBC in 1928, Percy Pitt's secretary Dorothy Wood (no relation) being seconded to him as an assistant. Her meticulous organising served successive planners for thirty-five years.

'Up under the roof of Station 2LO at Savoy Hill, a musician with years of broadcasting experience sits with a score, and a control for adjusting volume; he too is an artist, and his judgment is final.' By 1931 he had five microphones in Queen's Hall. *Amateur Wireless* carried a feature on them 'hung up on immensely strong but very slender RAF cable, almost impossible to see'. Critics began to listen at home, praising the sound, apart from a slight lack of bass resonance. Audiences sweltering in the hall envied those listening in the cool of their gardens. Wireless detection vans were out catching pirate listeners in 1931; 12,000 people suddenly took out licences! The first commentary on the scene at the Proms was broadcast between items in 1932, by which time an enormous hole in the ground on the other side of All Souls' Church from Queen's Hall had become Broadcasting House, headquarters of the BBC.

Resolving the problem of having two orchestras exercised Sir Henry and the BBC for some time. It was rumoured that Sir Thomas Beecham might create a new one absorbing the Queen's Hall players; but Beecham loved the limelight. Plans were also announced for his new opera house, for a new concert hall, for taking over the Proms during Sir Henry's alleged illness – Wood had to state publicly that he had never felt better. What actually happened was that the crack BBC Symphony Orchestra in white ties and waistcoats sprang to attention at Sir Henry Wood's entrance on the First Night of 1930. Adrian Boult had created it, with players from Queen's Hall and the Wireless Orchestras, and auditioned applicants from the Hallé and elsewhere. They were allowed to wear soft shirts after 1931, summer nights in Queen's Hall being unendurably hot.

Arthur Catterall was the Leader; but Wood's relationship with Charles Woodhouse was such that he asked for, and got him, to lead at the Promenade Concerts. He often worked into the night to copy Wood's bow markings into the string parts. Catterall had borrowed Woodhouse's violin the previous year, when his E string broke during a concerto. Woodhouse was such a good concerto player himself that he could take up the solo line immediately when someone like Daisy Kennedy had a lapse of memory. Colleagues found him rather superior, and always right. 'Do you know', said one in exasperation, 'that the players call you "God"?' 'Really?' Woodhouse replied. 'How did they know?' He also conducted orchestral works in the second half, allowing Sir Henry to catch the train from Baker Street to his home in Chorley Wood. Walter Loynes recalls the contrast between the two – Wood handsome, dark, and heavily built, using a long baton; Woodhouse tall and slim, slightly gingery, conducting with a short stick.

The BBC considered that Beethoven and Brahms were now beginning to overtake Wagner's previously unshakeable supremacy, and in 1930 they introduced British Composers' Concerts on Thursdays, which improbably succeeded (but were not much broadcast) to a point where evenings of Elgar, Vaughan Williams, or Delius could be given. In 1931 Elgar, who at seventy-four had taken to conducting seated, produced a *Nursery Suite* dedicated to the Duchess of York and her daughters Princess Elizabeth and Princess Margaret Rose. Next year he recorded his Violin Concerto with Yehudi Menuhin, then sixteen years old. Delius heard the premières of *A Song of Summer* and *A Song of*

6. The sparkling new BBC. To the right of All Souls' Church, Langham Place, is Queen's Hall with its canopies; and below it, the roof of the Langham Hotel (1932) (*Aerofilms*)

the High Hills on a wireless set the BBC had sent to him in France. Other single-composer nights were tried – Tchaikovsky, Schubert, Mendelssohn, Schumann – while a concert with Madrigals and folk songs in 1929, a Russian Saturday and a cornet solo in 1932, 'Una voce poco fà' from Rossini's *The Barber of Seville* played by the wizard of the age, Jack Mackintosh, harked back to earlier years. 'Whoever decides the programmes,' someone wrote to a newspaper, 'it is evident that they like their music thick.' However when the great Funeral March from *The Dusk of the Gods* was played in tribute to the composer's son, Siegfried Wagner, who died in 1930, not everyone in the audience stood up.

It is quite clear that Henry Wood liked his Bach thick also. Massive strings playing the third *Brandenburg Concerto*, a syrupy arrangement for cello, harp and organ of the Bach-Gounod 'Ave Maria' (once the only Bach in a season),

77

his orchestration of the *Toccata in F* ('magnificent, but it was not Bach'), all these things must be forgiven for the inescapable fact that single-handed, through the Promenade Concerts, Wood created a vast audience for Bach out of a darkness in which he was hardly ever performed. He was the first conductor to give the *Brandenburg Concertos* their rightful place beside the symphonies of Beethoven. It became a standing joke that Bach wrote the concertos for multiple keyboards for the benefit of the Royal Academy and the Royal College of Music, since representatives of each commonly performed them. By 1930 it was quite impossible to get a seat for Wood's Bach Nights, his gospel being handsomely reinforced by the wireless. And it was Bach who gave Wood a sweet revenge on his critics.

Whenever he acknowledged a Bach transcription as his own, Wood was at once accused of ruining it with Wagnerian scoring. On the Last Night in 1929 he conducted the organ *Toccata and Fugue in D minor*, a programme note (not by Mrs Newmarch, who may have been in the secret) stating it to have been transcribed by 'Paul Klenovsky, a pupil of Glazunov, whose early death lost Russian music a master of orchestration'. It was scored for colossal forces, full strings, sixteen woodwind, fifteen brass, masses of percussion, and organ. 'Of all versions, this is the most exciting,' wrote the critics; 'it overrides any objections a purist might bring, and leaves the polyphony clearer to the ear than the organ can. It is superlatively well done.' They could not praise it too highly. Year after year it had tremendous success at the Proms. Some time later, as had happened with the *Sea-Songs*, Wood disclosed his authorship. He was 'Paul Klenovsky'. When the full score was published there was a Strube cartoon in the *Daily Express* and a fourth leader in *The Times* about the leg-pull. It gave Sir Henry enormous satisfaction. The joke was on the critics, who retreated in disarray like Beckmesser. One of them thought Leopold Stokowski had recorded it, but that was his own version. Stokowski used to go to the Proms night after night when he was the young organist of St James's, Piccadilly. He returned to them in triumph as a conductor in 1963.

Wood was not simply a pioneer of modern works. Besides his advocacy of Bach, a keyboard concerto by Thomas Arne was given in 1929 and listed under 'New Works', hitherto called Novelties. Arne specialist Julian Herbage had renovated it. Eric Blom thought it time Herbage 'came out into the open with more of his music'. Kodaly's visit to conduct *Hary Janos* in 1928 was a tremendously successful Proms 'first', with a specially warm welcome for the Hungaria Restaurant's cimbalom player. Giving the Proms première of *Tapiola* on a Saturday was deemed a mistake; to follow Sibelius's last masterpiece with *Zampa* an even worse one. His Sixth Symphony was also presented on a Saturday, no longer exclusively a popular night. Some blamed the BBC. Composer Paul Hindemith played the solo part of Walton's Viola Concerto in 1929. Quentin MacLean, by courtesy of the directors of the Royal Cinema, Marble Arch, played Hindemith's Organ Concerto (written specially for the broadcasting medium) the following year. It was roundly booed.

Elvira, Walter, and their Prom companions were coming to grips with Mahler's First and Third Symphonies at this time; Wood had the eight horns stand to play, which impressed everyone. They were also exposed to an early dose of Krenek and Webern, the pills beneath the sugar. 'A little Janacek is worth a lot of Mahler,' wrote one critic; another found Webern 'struggling hard, but so far in vain'. Promenaders came without prejudices, to make up their own minds. In time their opinions might decide who would survive. Their starting-point was nearly always Bach or Mozart, Wagner or Beethoven, by 1930 sold out on almost every Friday. Geoffrey Last used to go with his brother-in-law, who had a neat solution to that problem. His friend Ernest Gillegin, the BBC's timpanist, kept a small bench near him on the platform for extra percussion instruments. None being required for Beethoven, he would kindly remove the 'Reserved' notice and let them sit alongside him. It gave them a player's view of the conductor (if an earful of the horns). Geoffrey Last recalls Henry Wood's wide sweeps with the baton, making him ideal to follow, and his intentions absolutely clear. One wonders what he made of the two extra drummers!

Beethoven's *Choral Symphony* was given in full from 1929, thanks to BBC sponsorship. People had forgotten the 1902 performance, and, after twenty-seven years deprived of its choral finale, they formed queues all round Queen's Hall by eleven o'clock in the morning. Police had to be called, and every available steward, to deal with the crowds. By evening the hall was under siege. Soon after the doors opened, the Promenade had to be closed. Hundreds were turned away disappointed. Those in the know went to 'a place of refreshment' nearby, whose enterprising owner had an excellent wireless set upstairs. No waiter ever asked for orders until the interval, and some people even took scores along with them. A note in the programme warned people not to applaud after the third movement, which like Pavlov's dogs they were conditioned to do. The new BBC National Chorus had been trained by Stanford Robinson. Sir Henry started the great tune in the finale at a whisper, as though preparing to spotlight the voices; and if he took their music fractionally slower, what matter? Standing there, filled to the brim with music until she could bear no more, Irene Loynes remembers that first impact of the baritone voice, followed by a full quartet of soloists and finally the huge chorus, so quietly seated she had been unaware of them until the 'Ode to Joy'. She stood amazed at the privilege, at such a feast for two shillings. And when in 1932 Isobel Baillie soared effortlessly up to the highest note in the final quartet, Elvira Ketterer stood silent at the end, the tears streaming down her cheeks. Sir Henry caught for an instant her brimming, adoring eyes, and smiled, she swears, especially for her.

Such scenes helped to lay for ever the spectre of broadcasting as the death of live performance. 'It has stimulated concert-going,' said Sir Hamilton Harty, 'revived the Hallé's fortunes, and benefited the British National Opera Company.' (He tried to get his Hallé Orchestra included in the Proms when the BBC took over.) Concerts had begun to sell out two weeks in advance, where once there were always seats at eight o'clock. 'It gives me the greatest gratification', Sir Henry Wood told the Press, 'that the broadcasts have enormously increased our audiences. They have been heard as far away as Leipzig; I have received many letters, especially from Holland. BBC officials have worked all hours to ensure success; they are delightful. The future of music in England is most hopeful.'

These increased audiences formed a wide cross-section, from the beginners to the intensely musical, from poor students to successful businessmen, to 'Eton-cropped shopgirls and typists puffing cheap cigarettes'. A different crowd came for different concerts: some came in flannels and sporting dress, or shorts on the hottest nights. Occasional shirtsleeves were seen even in the Grand Circle. One steward was observed slipping out to change his stifling dinner-jacket for a cooler lounge suit. Girls ate ice-cream on the steps of All Souls' Church at the interval.

They listened to Marian Anderson singing Debussy, Quilter, and 'Sometimes I feel like a motherless child', twenty-five years before she became the first coloured singer in opera at the New York Met. They saw the exotic xucalhos and Reco-Reco, Brazilian percussion played in *Choros 8* by Villa-Lobos; the one-armed Paul Wittgenstein playing Strauss's *Parergon* and Ravel's Left-hand Concerto, both written for him. When Dame Ethel Smyth described some novel features of her Violin and Horn Concerto they called out 'We came to hear music, not speeches!' The exuberant Francis Poulenc played his witty *Aubade* to them; Lionel Tertis his own arrangement for viola of Elgar's Cello Concerto. Philip Heseltine, alias Peter Warlock, conducted his *Capriol Suite*: and someone complained that programme notes 'are not read by musicians, and not understood by amateurs'.

One major event was the debut of John Ireland's Piano Concerto, a Proms favourite for nearly thirty years. Written for his young friend and composition pupil Helen Perkin, who gave the première, it quoted from a string quartet of hers and used muted trumpets, which Ireland first heard in Jack Payne's Dance Orchestra.

Wagner was cancelled on Monday 21 September 1931, Queen's Hall being needed for a Faraday Centenary Convention, to which Sir Henry Wood was invited. Just over a fortnight later, in far-away Leeds, Dr Malcolm Sargent shook the oratorio world with the shattering première of Walton's *Belshazzar's Feast*.

Promenaders quite properly felt that a festival like theirs deserved an appropriate end-of-term send-off. They had stood wall to wall for a whole season (nobody ever sat on the floor) and they regarded the other audience above them merely as onlookers. These were *their* concerts. Their rituals began with rhythmic foot-tapping during Wood's *Sea-Songs*, in an effort to do the Hornpipe faster than the BBC Symphony Orchestra. On the Queen's Hall carpet this sounded like muffled drums emphasising each *tum-tum-tum*.

They never clapped, or tried to drown the players. Sir Henry conducted them with relish, and then the whole audience, rising to their feet to sing 'Rule, Britannia', 'Land of Hope', and the National Anthem; but that was not the end. Time after time they called him back, cheered him, waved programmes and handkerchiefs, threw hats and umbrellas into the air. Twenty times the debonair beard and red carnation bobbed back on to the rostrum, beaming with pleasure as they sang 'For He's a Jolly Good Fellow'.

Finally he appeared wearing an overcoat, despite the heat, flung wide his arms, signalled the orchestra to leave, pleaded for the house lights to be extinguished, and then went outside, to be forced through the waiting crowds with Lady Wood to their car, amid more cheering and shouts of 'See you next year!' The last Promenaders left Queen's Hall more than three-quarters of an hour after the concert ended. Even then small groups still lingered round the all-night coffee-stall at Oxford Circus.

Diary of a Young Man
Proms 1933–1934
Portraits of the thirties

S it with us in the Grand Circle of Queen's Hall on the First Night of the thirty-ninth season of Promenade Concerts, the twelfth day of August 1933. My companion is a gifted young man, whose musical perception is already extraordinary. Perhaps sensing that the times are exceptional, he has been keeping a diary of his concert-going. We shall benefit from his acquaintance, for the extent of his knowledge and the ever-widening circle of his friendships among both performers and composers. We can also sneak a look at his scores.

Grinding out his days at some underpaid office job, his spirit awakens fully only when work is done. True, there are the lunch-time discoveries in a quick dash to the music section of Foyle's bookshop: the score of Bantock's *Omar Khayyam* (Part II) for two shillings, perhaps; Debussy's *L'Enfant Prodigue* for only half-a-crown. In the evenings, after coffee and *petits fours* at the Pâtisserie Bruxelloise in Oxford Street, his musical awareness is at full stretch like steel piano wires, receptive, sensitive, and missing nothing.

He seems to have been everywhere, dashing from the first half of one recital to the second part of a concert in another hall; then on to a supper party with an assortment of musicians. Among such company his eyes come alive with recollection and the still-vivid sounds of music. His chatter bubbles enthusiastically. These extracts from his diary are experiences he might have recounted during the interval of any Promenade Concert. Were there ever such times?

'I met Zoltan Kodaly at the Robert Mayers', and afterwards saw him conduct at the BBC; he's a very forceful personality, with a disconcerting habit of looking you straight in the eyes. And a businessman too, as well as a

7. Sir Henry Wood inherited a craftsman's skill as well as precocious musical gifts (*Radio Times*)

composer; I hear that if one of his scores is to be published at 19/- he wants 18/11d in royalties!

'Sergei Rachmaninov played his *Corelli Variations* here for the first time a few weeks ago; he must be the world's greatest pianist. I saw Paul Hindemith there when Henry Wood conducted his *Unaufhörliche* wonderfully well; and then Hindemith conducted his own *Mathis der Maler* and *Conzertmusik* – he's definitely someone to reckon with in modern music. Vladimir Horowitz gave a phenomenal performance of the First Tchaikovsky Concerto at Queen's Hall. It is a reflection on London's music public that Fritz Kreisler, whose tea-shop programmes get steadily worse, is presented at the Royal Albert Hall, while Josef Szigeti, whose recitals are pure joy, plays only at the Wigmore Hall.

'Not long ago Arnold Schoenberg gave his own *Variations for Orchestra* here. He was staying at the Strand Palace, where I got his autograph. Anton Webern conducted Berg's *Lyric Suite* at Broadcasting House, with Ernst Krenek in the audience. I found Schoenberg's *Gurrelieder* gorgeous, music in which you can just wallow effortlessly – wonderful chords! – and the BBC Symphony Orchestra strings absolutely ravishing in *Transfigured Night*. They played the Sibelius Seventh Symphony under Serge Koussevitsky, and never played it better. There was evidence of very thorough rehearsal, quite unlike Beecham's well-known technique of keeping the players guessing about his intentions until the actual concert, thus forcing each one to watch his every movement. Koussevitsky's interpretations were mellow, with wonderful discipline; he made Beethoven's *Eroica* live in every bar, while his Sibelius Second was on a par with Beecham's definitive performance earlier this year with the BBC. (*This is now available on records*.) After Koussevitsky conducted the *Tallis Fantasia* Vaughan Williams lumbered on to the platform in his countryman's tweeds! Tchaikovsky's *Pathétique* and Stravinsky's *Rite of Spring* were both unforgettable experiences under Koussevitsky.

'Incidentally I saw Stravinsky play the solo piano part in his *Capriccio*, and he played it very badly, being inclined to splash around the keyboard throughout, and at one point he forgot completely. I met him not long ago when he was giving a recital with Alexander Dushkin at the BBC. He's a funny little fellow, immaculate in evening dress, but his mouth seemed to be all teeth, north and south. He signed my score of *Sacre* rather impatiently.

'I found the BBC Orchestra rather cool towards Hamilton Harty when they played under him, they seemed too tired to clap him; but Alan Rawsthorne told me they had applauded him terrifically at rehearsal. Sibelius 5 caught Harty in a sympathetic mood and the performance was fine and clear, with a great deal of attention paid to detail. His *Corsair* overture was almost Beechamesque. Wilhelm Backhaus played the Schumann Piano Concerto impeccably. There was a miserable audience for the BBC's first British Concert in Queen's Hall, despite the fact that Eric Fenby came over from the Delius home in Grez specially for *A Song of the High Hills*, or that

Solomon was playing the solo part in Lambert's *Rio Grande*.

'The BBC have just installed an organ in the Concert Hall of Broadcasting House. I went to the official opening – with tea and a biscuit in their canteen afterwards! It may sound all right over the air, but it sounds awful in the hall. I really hate that thing! They have just rebuilt the organ in the Royal Albert Hall; Alcock, Thalben-Ball, Cunningham and Grier gave the opening recital, invitation only, and the damned thing sprang a fifteen-minute cipher! I heard Elgar's *Organ Sonata* the other day; not a successful performance. I must say I much prefer those BBC studio concerts *without* an audience, they are so delightfully informal. There's no immaculate announcer in evening dress to wave his hand for silence. Someone just shouts "shut up" before the light comes on, and you're off!

'I bumped into Francis Poulenc in Chester's music shop recently, and quickly bought one of their picture postcards of him, to get it autographed. Poulenc took it out of my hand, looked at the face on the front, and said "Who is this monster? How ugly he is!" You know, nearly everyone is here at one time or another. I saw Serge Prokofiev coming out of Queen's Hall after Bruno Walter conducted Brahms 4, really one of the best performances I have ever heard. Walter also played and conducted a Mozart piano concerto from the keyboard. Ernest Ansermet has been back again, conducting Elgar with his usual Gallic persuasiveness. I met Elgar only once, back in 1931 when he conducted the Second Symphony at a Prom. It proves that you can size up a man pretty well even while you're asking him for his autograph. He was all people said he was, noble and gentle, a truly great man.

'Alfred Cortot's performance of Chopin's Second Piano Concerto is surely a standard to judge all the others by; I heard him at one of the Courtauld-Sargent concerts. You should hear John Ireland play the piano! Great heavings, and whistlings through his nose – but sensitive playing, for all that. For someone so keen on modern music (he clapped the suite from *The Nose* by Shostakovich like a two-year-old, and sat through all the repeat performances at a BBC Contemporary Music Concert) surprisingly little of it shows in his own work. His *Soldier's Return* is dedicated to Edward Clark, the chap behind all that modern music put out by the BBC. He drinks an awful lot of whisky, and runs to flights of fancy when talking to you about plans, but he does get the stuff performed.

'Ernest Bloch has been over from America; he's shaved off his beard. He conducted his *Helvetia* at Victoria Hall and Lady Cunard talked through it to a gigolo-like companion the whole time. I saw Bloch rehearsing at Queen's Hall; it seemed to me Paul Beard was impatient with him; but he's a remarkably sincere and humble man, with lustrous shining eyes, and he just didn't seem to notice. Maurice Eisenberg, a handsome chap, was doing *Schelomo*. He rehearsed from memory, and with great fervour, as only the son of a rabbi could, he said. Mrs Bloch guards her husband's dressing-room like Cerberus, but everyone seems to get past her.

'Havelock Ellis was at the actual concert; I spotted his magnificent white mane from afar off, and even had a short conversation with that man of God. Bloch got an ovation; it could have been even greater if there had not been so many blasé celebrities in the audience. Henry Wood came into the Green Room afterwards and introduced himself with "Je vous embrasse, vous avez fait un grand triomphe". Arnold Bax and Tania were there too; and Gustav Ferrari. Bloch met Szigeti the next day, then dined in a Piccadilly restaurant where he found Moritz Rosenthal eating a simply colossal meal, and went over to greet him. The Boyd Neel Orchestra gave a magnificent performance of Bloch's *Concerto Grosso* that evening; I'm sure we shall hear more of these players.

'Tania? That's what everyone calls Harriet Cohen. She's always with Arnold Bax; they're inseparable. She's so beautiful, with a complexion like alabaster, and marvellous green eyes. And she plays all the moderns, Ireland, Walton, Bax himself; a splendid person. She played Bax's Fourth Piano Sonata at the Wigmore, and Frank Merrick introduced me to Bax afterwards. Cassadò gave the première of his Cello Concerto (it's dedicated to him) but even under Harty, and with symphonies by Brahms and Mendelssohn, it was badly attended. The London Symphony Orchestra has a style very much its own; quite a pleasant change after . . . well, never mind which. I heard the new Bax Quintet for Strings too, full of nature, Celtic twilight and the rest of it. The man is so damned prolific he seems to be churning it out lately. But he can't churn out Second Violin Sonatas, or *Tintagels*, or *November Woodses*, for all that.

'They gave Walton's *Belshazzar's Feast* again in January; after hearing every London performance of the work so far I still marvel at it. I see a wonderfully strong and sure hand; and it still thrills. Walton's a genius, and *Belshazzar* is his *Messiah*. Benjamin Britten's Oboe Quartet was played at the College of Nursing – he's a masterful lad. It is possible to get to grips with many of the new works at the Robert Mayer Study Circles, after supper at his flat. I met a woman there who had been a pupil of Clara Schumann, played piano accompaniments for Joseph Joachim, and had met Brahms, Liszt, and Cosima Wagner! A lot of our younger men go along, like Walter Leigh, Benjamin Frankel, and Alan Bush, as well as performers like Sophie Wyss.

'Then there's also the Proms Circle, a strange gathering! The Chairman, who also founded the Kipling Society, complained to me that there was never enough Chopin in the programmes. I pointed out that one of the piano concertos in a season represented exactly fifty per cent of Chopin's entire orchestral output. "Oh, indeed?" was his reply, with a sniff and a huffy lift of an eyebrow; absolutely typical of the enthusiastic but abysmally uninformed amateur.

'It cost me only two shillings to go to a Beecham concert a little while ago, including some Berlioz and Bax, and never was money better spent. Prince George was in the audience. A couple of weeks later Beecham gave a whole concert of Delius at Queen's Hall, including *Appalachia*. I managed to get into the Green Room afterwards and met him for the first time; it made me resolve to get to know him better, if possible. He left in that thick grey overcoat of his, with the lapels folded back to his chin, and a Trilby hat set at an angle. He looked just like Edward VII when getting into his Daimler. There was a lot of cheering, and he raised an arm in acknowledgment. Do you know that he took on a Philharmonic concert with the Sibelius First Symphony, which he'd never conducted and didn't know at all? He borrowed the records from a student at the Royal College, studied them for a week, and then did it from memory! I saw something of his magic during *Tapiola*; most of the way through it he just stood there half-asleep, then suddenly lashed himself and the whole orchestra with him into an absolute fury for a shattering climax near the end. You should see those electrifying eyes of his!

'They say that when he was at Oxford his rooms were open house for parties, but that *he* was always in another room studying at a piano. They used to try to get him to join in the fun; he'd just wave one hand graciously saying "That's all right, old fellow; *enjoy* yourselves" and carry on playing. Some of the things he says are quite deliberately outrageous. For instance in a speech to the Royal Manchester College of Music he said there was no college in the country capable of producing a really good singer! In January I heard him give a superb performance of *The Prison*, which Ethel Smyth thinks her best work; but do you know, Reginald Goodall told me Beecham hated the piece! Ethel had been badgering him to do it ever since she finished it, and he finally gave in. She made a speech saying it was worth waiting to be seventy-five to have Beecham conduct your music. Goodall himself seems to be going from one conducting triumph to another; I'm absolutely convinced he's a genius. Ethel Smyth made a really weird speech at another of those all-women concerts at Queen's Hall; she's an extraordinary sight in her Trilby hat and trousers!

'Bronislaw Hubermann played Tchaikovsky's Violin Concerto on Sunday afternoon at Queen's Hall with Beecham, an absolutely marvellous performance, and there was Delius's *Paris* as well. A few days later Beecham had a huge success with the première of Bax's *Tale the Pine-Trees Knew*. I heard him do Elgar's *Enigma* on the wireless – I was too broke to go to the concert – but I found it rather superficial compared to a performance I remember with Landon Ronald, who looked like a saint illumined when he conducted it.'

Diary of the 1933 Season

Our well-informed companion was among those enthusiasts cheering individual members of the BBC Symphony Orchestra into Queen's Hall from seven o'clock onwards. The players in their turn nodded to recognised 'regulars', himself included. Sidonie Goossens seemed to him just as lovely as ever; but he missed Marie Wilson, whose customary place at the front desk with the Leader Charles Woodhouse would be occupied this season by Laurance Turner.

12 August The First Night. There was tremendous applause at Sir Henry Wood's entry on to the platform; then he launched the orchestra headlong into Ravel's *Daphnis and Chloë*. Following from a score, I judged it an even more polished performance than Wood gave at the Symphony Concerts. Dora Labbette sang Mimi's song well – she's a lovely woman! Marcel Dupré played a Handel organ concerto in a style quite properly disliked by *The Times*; and chose thoughtless and clumsy registration for his encores, a quiet Bach *Chorale Prelude* and his own *Carillon*. How could one have known what he was enduring? Not until October did I discover that his mother died a day or two before this concert, and he had completely cracked up. The Bach *Prelude* had been her especial favourite.

15 August Benno Moiseiwitsch played the Tchaikovsky Concerto in splendid style; he's a very great pianist. Chief attraction was the première of *Kaleidoscope* by Eugene Goossens, selected numbers from his Piano Suite of the same name, as anticipated. Critics thought the slight originals could not stand orchestration, but I found the scoring perfectly delicious.

17 August The day may yet come when Ravel's Piano Concerto is as popular as Mendelssohn. Such elegance, such polish! Sir Edward Elgar conducted his Second Symphony, which enthrals me whenever I hear it. How glorious that bit where high cellos imitate leaping violins in the first movement. The performance may have been a little ragged, but the spirit was there, and Sir Edward had a huge ovation. [*Elgar was seventy-six and had only six months to live.*]

19 August *Cockaigne*! – what a ripping work! It was good to hear three movements from Holst's *Planets* again; and Ravel's *Bolero* sent the audience into a frenzy of delight.

22 August Harriet Cohen played the Vaughan Williams Piano Concerto – how ever did I think it diffuse and muddy? It now seems clear-cut; which just goes to show. Ravel's *La Valse*; the man in the street ought to be able to whistle it by now.

24 August Endured a Mozart and Haydn first half for the sake of Hindemith's *Philharmonic Concerto* after the interval, which I enjoyed more than ever.

26 August The divine Harriet played *Nights in the Gardens of Spain* divinely, and a solo Bach transcription with great feeling. Enesco's first *Roumanian*

Rhapsody got a run-of-the-mill performance with isolated passages of distinguished playing.

31 August Katharine Goodson – we remarked for the first time how exactly like Jelka Delius she looks – tripped up in the Grieg Concerto; she was distinctly below her best form. Vaughan Williams obtained a fine reading of his *Pastoral Symphony*, so all that flapping of his wings when he conducts gets results! It is perhaps the most English music I know. A not very good performance of the *Walk to the Paradise Garden* under Wood.

2 September Another Saturday Prom. Roger Quilter conducted two of his songs sung by Heddle Nash. Pouishnoff splashed about in the Rachmaninoff Second Concerto, but a musicianly performance. At the interval I cajoled Mr York at Door 15 to take a photograph down to the Green Room for Quilter to autograph for me. Nothing of importance played in the second half!

5 September The worst attended Prom in living memory. The mentality of the Proms audience is unfathomable. Always before a season in which he has included Elgar's *Falstaff*, Sir Henry Wood makes a special point of mentioning it to reporters who interview him. The Press then makes known his fondness for the work, and how many extra rehearsals are to be devoted to it. Behold, the day of the performance arrives, and where has all the audience gone? Where are even those insatiable imbeciles who stand there with a crazed look in their eyes muttering knowledgeably "horns!" whenever they hear trumpets in a Beethoven symphony? One would think that if only out of loyalty to Sir Henry, they might at least turn up to hear *Falstaff*. [*Sir Henry Wood once went down into the Promenade during an interval to enquire why people stayed away from* Falstaff. *He was the only conductor ever to do such a thing. The work had to be cancelled at a 1926 Prom and 'Tod und Verklärung' by Strauss substituted.*]

6 September Josef Szigeti played the Brahms Violin Concerto wonderfully! I heard he was suffering from a terrible cold; but you would never have guessed he was not physically up to scratch. I met Alan Frank [*of Oxford University Press*] in the interval, with the beautifully-produced full score of Lambert's *Music for Orchestra* which he conducted himself tonight. I was struck by the fine quality of the scoring; Lambert's a good contrapuntist.

7 September A Liszt concert of great interest. Felix Mottl's orchestration of *St Francis Preaching to the Birds*; the First Concerto, a bravura performance by Pouishnoff; and the interminable *Faust Symphony* which I enjoyed immensely. It makes you realise the colossal influence Liszt has had on our present music. So much grandeur was the wrong preparation for Butterworth's pastoral Rhapsody *A Shropshire Lad* after the interval.

9 September   I sat through an awful lot of tripe in order to hear Alexander Dushkin play the Stravinsky Violin Concerto. I like the work. Some people don't.

14 September   The great annual event of Arnold Bax coming on to the platform to acknowledge applause after his Third Symphony. Invariably a lump rises in my throat. What a work that is! Miniature scores are a boon. They show that a performance once thought exemplary has in fact a few ragged edges. Myra Hess played the Schumann; and dear Dame Ethel Smyth bowed from the Grand Circle after the Prelude to Act III of her *Wreckers*.

15 September   Stuck out an enormous dose of Ludwig van Beethoven just to hear Arthur Bliss conduct his excellently-scored *Introduction and Allegro* which I nearly missed through jawing at the interval to Tommy Thompson, the BBC external concert manager.

16 September   For a Saturday, the English première of Honegger's *Third Symphonic Movement* seemed a bit dry. The best thing by far was Percy Grainger's *Handel in the Strand* conducted by Charles Woodhouse. (Yes, really! He was encored in fact.) Grainger's stuff is contagious. Even the ultrasophisticated Edward Clark was bubbling over with enthusiasm in Ridinghouse Street afterwards. [*The first of Honegger's Symphonic Movements is the famous* Pacific 231, *the second,* Rugby. *Charles Woodhouse, Leader of the orchestra, was now and then allocated a piece to conduct, by Sir Henry.*]

19 September   I stood in the Promenade through a saccharine performance of the Mendelssohn Violin Concerto, and the 'heavenly length' of Schubert's Ninth Symphony, my patience being amply rewarded with Bartok's provocative Suite from *The Amazing Mandarin*. It turned some people white and speechless with hatred.

23 September   What a jolly Saturday programme! Hindemith's *News of the Day* overture, Mahler's *Adagietto* (Fifth Symphony), the catchy Poulenc Concerto for Two Pianos, and the inevitable Dukas [*The Sorcerer's Apprentice*].

25 September   A Wagner Prom with the Love Duet from *Siegfried* as its highlight.

26 September   Sibelius Night, attended by Ralph Vaughan Williams, Arnold Bax, Tania, and many others.

---

8. Harriet Cohen (*left*) and Eileen Joyce (*Erich Auerbach*)

28 September Haydn-Mozart Proms tend to drag when one is waiting for the first two Debussy *Nocturnes* in part two. I followed them from score; accurately played, but unimaginative.

30 September The most enjoyable feature, *Façade*, conducted by its long and lanky composer (Walton) in his usual slick and square manner.

2 October Old favourites from *Tristan* and *Götterdämmerung* with Norman Allin and Florence Austral; Liszt's interesting *Orpheus*: and an exceptionally fine performance of *The Swan of Tuonela*.

3 October The audience was startled tonight by sudden loud roars after the première of a new *Idyll* by Delius. What they could not know was that a few of us had promised Jelka and Frederick Delius to cheer, knowing they would hear it over the wireless in Grez-sur-Loing. I dashed off to the College of Nursing to hear Ethel Bartlett and Rae Robertson play new British music for two pianos. Alan Frank introduced me to a charming young lady, Phyllis Tate, whose *London Waits* they performed amid great merriment. [*Alan Frank and Phyllis Tate later married*]. Then I hurried back to Queen's Hall in time to hear Benno Moiseiwitsch play some encores. Afterwards in Ridinghouse Street I caught sight of the delightful Delius niece Peggy, in London to trace Sir Thomas Beecham and ask him to visit Frederick in Grez.

5 October Sophie Wyss sang Roberto Gerhard's *Catalan Songs* admirably – so much better with orchestra; the piano version is a makeshift. Albert Sammons gave his splendid account of the Elgar Violin Concerto.

7 October The Last Night.
> [*The record of Albert Sammons playing Elgar's Concerto with the Queen's Hall Orchestra under Sir Henry Wood has been reissued. 'A magnificent reminder of one bygone era's stylistic freedom and a true display of heartfelt Elgarian rubatos – closer, perhaps, to Elgar's ideals than any other. The scorching intensity sustained between soloist and conductor is little short of miraculous. Possibly the greatest of all its distinguished recordings.' – Classical Music magazine.*]

A week before that 1933 season began, our young diarist went on the pilgrimage of a lifetime, to visit Frederick Delius at his home in Grez-sur-Loing. You could hardly stop him talking about that! He had gone first by boat-train to Paris for a little sightseeing. In St Sulpice a small altar organ was tactfully accompanying some antiphonal singing. Suddenly the great west end organ joined in, to thrilling effect; the church filled with a glorious blaze of reed tone, an excellent introduction to French organs. He asked a woman selling candles who might be playing the west end organ – it was

Charles Marie Widor himself! Using a card of introduction to Vierne (whose name fortunately was not on it) our bold friend eventually inveigled himself into the organ-loft to sit beside Widor – 'his old hands gnarled and knotted, his feet difficult to manipulate accurately, but still, what playing!' – and prevailed upon him to autograph a copy of the Fifth Symphony [*the one with the famous Toccata finale*].

He then went by train from the Gare de Lyon to Grez-sur-Loing. There in the courtyard of the white house stood the wheelchair of Frederick Delius. Behind it, the riot of colour which is *In a Summer Garden*, a paradise for butterflies in the shade of a twelfth-century Norman church; and a view beyond which was perhaps *The Paradise Garden*. In the spacious living-room the sad, pathetic spectacle of the blind seated Delius, immaculate in white shirt and cravat, creased cricket trousers and white tennis shoes, the legs like sticks of wood, and the lean aesthete's face exactly as in the James Gunn portrait. [*Anyone who saw Ken Russell's unforgettable film on Delius for BBC television would find his way easily around these memoirs, so precisely do they coincide in detail.*]

Fresh garden plums were offered; but the perfect host intervened: 'My dear, surely the gentlemen are not going to eat plums before wine?' – then he insisted that Mrs Jelka Delius change the fine white glasses for even more exquisite green ones.

The talk was of Sibelius, and weird stories of him Arnold Bax and Cecil Gray had brought with them to Grez; of the visit of Elgar, who had been very pleasant indeed, and quite different from how they had imagined him. As to the possibility of Delius visiting England again, absolutely not by plane ('I should not like to be burnt up'), perhaps by sea, which held no terrors for him; and definitely if they did his *Village Romeo and Juliet*. He longed to 'see' his beloved Yorkshire Moors once more.

Delius enquired after Malcolm Sargent, debarred from conducting for at least a year because of tuberculosis. Jelka said no wonder he cracked up on such a punishing schedule, travelling all night and conducting all day.

It was confirmed that Alexandre Barjansky, and not Beatrice Harrison as stated in Philip Heseltine's book on Delius, gave the Cello Concerto's première. After Delius went blind, Barjansky discussed with him the idea of dictating his music to an amanuensis. They had to dismiss all the possible names as having too intrusive a personal style. Then Eric Fenby's letter arrived, followed, despite all attempts to put him off, by Fenby himself. Barjansky and he spent the day rehearsing and then playing to Delius his Cello Sonata and Concerto. Delius, overjoyed by Fenby's sensitive playing, dictated everything to him for the rest of his life.

Jelka had just received a printed copy of the *Idyll*; she and Frederick were greatly amused by the idea that a special 'bravo' should be broadcast from the première, and promised to listen in. Delius was also hoping that Beecham would record his *Paris* – 'He plays my music *beautifully*!' (Those records were delayed by French customs, being eventually delivered to Grez two days after Delius died. He had asked continually for them until the time of his death.)

Delius became restive and exhausted, so the visitors thanked him for his courtesy and departed quickly. Crossing the courtyard they heard Delius through the closing door behind them ask his German male nurse, '*Sind wir allein?*'

When the Master of the King's Music, Sir Edward Elgar OM, died on 23 February 1934, it struck our young diarist friend as strange to think of the blind and paralysed old Delius outliving so many of his friends and contemporaries – Elgar, Peter Warlock and later Gustav Holst. Listening to the wireless on 10 June the same year, he learned of the death of Delius.

Diary of the 1934 Season

11 August   The First Night. Henry Wood came on looking very fit indeed, and opened the season with the Prelude to Elgar's *The Kingdom*, hardly appropriate; *Cockaigne* would have done much better. A Bach organ *Prelude* transcribed for strings was effective, but similar treatment of the E major Violin Partita produced a mad scramble. Maggie Teyte sang Mimi's song exquisitely; her lovely bell-like voice and clear enunciation are always a joy. She also made the best of Liszt's "Kennst du das Land" – not very good Liszt. [*Not very good planning, either; Mimi's song also began the 1933 season.*] Franck's *Symphonic Variations* are invariably entrusted to a woman at the Proms; neatly played by Irene Kohler, a product of the Royal College of Music. Splendid performances of "Mercury", "Saturn", and "Jupiter"; and I followed *Till Eulenspiegel* and *Capriccio Espagnol* with the scores.

14 August   There is a satisfying sonority about Tchaikovsky! Lionel Tertis played Bax's Phantasy for Viola – oh what happy moments of ecstatic light-heartedness I owe to Arnold Bax. May Blyth sang Berg's three *Wozzeck* fragments; unhesitatingly I say "a masterpiece". Henry Wood showed that he knows the score of *La Mer* very well.

15 August   Terrific crush tonight. Honegger's *Chant de Joie* well worth the effort. A Brahms audience found it all very bewildering and knew not whether to clap or no. Another pearl cast! They were in raptures for Solomon's Chopin Ballade in F and two encores, and rightly so. Charles Woodhouse conducted Weber's *Turandot* Overture, a novelty if ever there was one; I wonder who knew of its existence?

16 August   Arthur Cranmer's "With Joy th'impatient Husbandman" and Joan Cross singing "Dove Sono" both excellent; also the Robertsons playing Mozart's two-piano concerto. Haydn's *Drum-Roll Symphony* I always enjoy.

Goossens's fine *Sinfonietta* is a masterly piece of scoring, and made a much clearer impression than at a performance earlier this year.

18 August   Met a woman who used to go to the Diaghilev *Ballets Russes* three or four times a week during their first wonderful London season. She had also heard Scriabin play the piano in London, quite unperturbed by all the people hissing his music from various parts of the hall.

20 August   Ernst Toch's Second Symphony deserved a better audience for its first performance; Toch played with all his usual finesse and clarity. There are moments of real lyrical beauty, but for the most part it tintinnabulates on in pleasant tinkles. Mary Jarred sang Harty's *Sea-Wrack* (a doubtful work?). Turina's *Procession del Rocio* is very superficial, though the sound is intoxicating.

23 August   Delius Memorial Prom. A patch in the slow section of the *Double Concerto* (around page 25 of the score) is Delius at his highest level of inspiration. The lovely *Idyll* was sung by Roy Henderson with great feeling, and artlessly by the delightful Dora Labbette (I noted some cuts). Clifford Curzon played the Piano Concerto magnificently, stressing the best points of a not altogether successful work. Henry Wood gets the chunky result he asks for in *Brigg Fair*, but it is disappointing compared to Beecham, except for Aubrey Brain's exquisite horn playing. At the interval I met Charles Lynch who called *1812* a beautiful work; is this carrying musical enthusiasm a bit too far? Dora Labbette sang two songs in what she imagined to be French. Woodhouse conducted a monstrous transcription of Bach's *Toccata in F*.

25 August   Benno Moiseiwitsch played the Third Rachmaninoff Concerto with his customary finesse and some cuts. Charles Lynch once reminded him that in 1921 he had played four concertos with orchestra right off. "Ach," he replied, "in those days I was young and foolish. Now I never play more than three."

After Frank Titterton sang his celebrated "Sound an Alarm" there came an unprecedented interruption. A man in the Promenade, seemingly sober, shouted out: "I PROTEST AGAINST THE CUTTING OUT OF THE ORCHESTRAL CRESCENDO!" There was an awesome stillness for a second or two. Wood took absolutely no notice. The orchestra were intrigued. The voice continued: "FIRST YOU MUTILATE WAGNER, NOW YOU HACK HANDEL!" Booing and hissing began, and he was effectively silenced. Wood waited a moment and then started on de Falla's three dances from *Tricorne* – irresistibly attractive music, this! Frank Titterton sang "Love Went A-Riding" as an encore in the second half, and Wood did Grainger's *Shepherd's Hey* to end.

27 August Bought the score of Foulds's *World Requiem* for 1/6d at the antiquity shop in Great Portland Street. [*This was the Great War's equivalent of Britten's* War Requiem, *and was once performed almost as frequently.*] Foulds lapses into trivialities; and he believed in spirits. Not wishing to hear the interminable *Tannhäuser* Act III introduction at the Prom (it might just as well be the entire Act) retired to the Buffet and discussed Arnold Bax. Apparently *The Happy Forest* was so badly performed at a Prom in 1925 that Bax simply went out and wept. He was far too nice ever to complain about either the playing or the conducting. After the interval Elgar's masterpiece *Falstaff* was excellently played.

28 August Elsie Suddaby's lovely soft high pianissimos in "With Verdure Clad". A shocking performance of the Haydn Piano Concerto; Mozart's K543 in E flat later was altogether better. A different soloist in part two; Tania played John Ireland's *Legend* wonderfully. After the concert I met Freda Swain in the foyer and asked her what she thought of the Ireland. "I *still* think it's a good work", she replied. I am a bit slow on the uptake, and said I believed nobody thought otherwise. "I *still* think it's a good work," she repeated, for my benefit; adding archly "*despite* the rendering." – Bowl of cream for Miss Swain!

30 August Prokofiev's Violin Concerto is an astonishing work for that *enfant terrible* of former days. Nothing blatant about it, beautifully spaced, and such lovely writing. Antonio Brosa played it magnificently. After the interval Marcel Dupré and Henry Wood between them mishandled Handel's Organ Concerto in B flat. I'm ashamed to think that not so many years ago I too roared approval of such concave distortions as did the feeble-minded organists present this evening. I am now getting sick of this sort of performance.*

1 September Strauss Concert. Enjoyed *Don Juan*, hated the *Burleske*, clumsily played by Lamond, thrilled to Oda Slobodskaya singing the *Salome* Closing Scene. *Don Quixote* I liked more than ever.

4 September Deserted the Proms and went to Gloucester with Eric Thiman to hear Elgar's *The Kingdom*, Kodaly's *Psalmus Hungaricus* and the Vaughan Williams *Pastoral Symphony*. Saw George Bernard Shaw in finely-pressed trousers, lanky and lithe, with a wonderful complexion. Heard a nice Three Choirs story about Walton. Gloucester asked him for a festival work, so he sent them *Belshazzar's Feast*. They returned it with the comment that it was

---

*This Prom began with three winners of *The Daily Telegraph* competition: Cyril Scott's *Festival Overture* (first prize) Frank Tapp's *Metropolis* (second) and Arnold Cooke's *Concert Overture No. 1* (third).

hardly suitable for performance in a consecrated building. Whereupon Walton sent them a copy of the Old Testament.

6 September   A glorious performance of Elgar's First Symphony, followed by the Arthur Benjamin Violin Concerto – Sammons indisposed and replaced by Louis Godow. E. J. Moeran looked suspiciously tight when he came on to acknowledge applause for that jolly hotchpotch *Farrago* Suite of his.

7 September   Sweltering hot! Heard Tania play Walton's *Sinfonia Concertante*.

8 September   Had my first swimming lesson this morning. *Hary Janos* at the Prom; and the pretentious *Californian Sketches* by Frederick Converse.

14 September   To the second half for Schoenberg's *Five Orchestral Pieces*, which thrilled me a second time! Harsh in places? Yes! But undeniably music.

20 September   Met a German music critic yesterday who heard Jeritza sing at Covent Garden some years back in the flimsiest of undies, with a powerful arc light behind her revealing her no doubt exquisite contours. Reviewing in a Berlin newspaper he had written that the representation of Sieglinde as a French harlot was a new one on him! The prima donna's solicitors threatened court proceedings; whereupon he offered to withdraw the word "French".

   Stood in the Promenade with Boyd Neel who had a miniature score of Liszt's *Faust Symphony*. Even with cuts it is a lengthy work. Leslie Woodgate shared my score of the Liszt E flat Piano Concerto in the second half. He seemed a charming fellow.

22 September   Sweltering hot again; the biggest Saturday night crush I can remember. Heddle Nash's top C and all that led up to it in "Your Tiny Hand is Frozen" should have stirred even the most frigid highbrow! *La Valse* is irresistible, now that repeated hearings have reconciled me to the percussive climax. Kodaly's new *Dances of Galanta* made a well-strung and gracious set. I stayed to hear Henry Gibson's *Gaelic Pipe March* but I can't remember a thing about it.

25 September   The Bax Third Symphony is now a solemn rite at the Proms. Having spent many hours in railway carriages with reams of manuscript paper, arranging it for two pianos from the miniature score, I can claim to know a little about it. This performance was competent, rather than overwhelming. How dated Lambert's *Rio Grande* sounds already!

26 September   A packed house to hear Myra Hess play the Brahms B flat Concerto. John Ireland conducted his *Mai-Dun* splendidly with a good, firm downbeat, obtaining a performance as lucid as it was rugged and noble.

Holst's *Somerset Rhapsody* we followed from its clear score. Debussy's *Fêtes* made a badly-played finale.

27 September Vaughan Williams Night. How thrilling the subdivision of strings in the *Tallis Fantasia*! Another fantasia, *Greensleeves*, and a quodlibet of dance tunes, *The Running Set* were both first performances, and exhilarating. Marie Wilson played *The Lark Ascending* faultlessly, and Keith Falkner's *Songs of Travel* were a joy. Vaughan Williams, who had conducted the "Novelties", also flapped his way through the *London Symphony*, a work for which one's affection increases as time goes on. I endured Handel's D minor Organ Concerto, for which H. J. Wood has done his worst. G. D. Cunningham was the soloist. I'm glad I stayed for Herbert Howells's *Procession* though – a topping little work.

28 September On learning that my miserable salary was to be reduced for one month, as punishment for having made a mistake at work (swapping two contracts in the usual rush to catch the late-fee post at Fenchurch Street) I handed in my resignation this evening. With a lighter heart than for many years, no matter what the future holds, I arrived late at Queen's Hall to hear Bax's *Tale the Pine-Trees Knew*.

29 September The former managing director of the firm offered me another job this evening, as his personal assistant. (He was Norman T. C. Sargant, Chairman of the London Metal Exchange, a pillar of the Methodist Church, father of Dr William Sargant the world-famous psychiatrist, Tom Sargant of Amnesty International, and the Bishop of Bangalore.) I heard the Prom on the wireless, at his home – Ireland's Piano Concerto and the Respighi orchestration of Bach's *Prelude and Fugue in D major*. Afterwards I walked for hours all over the West End.

1 October Heard a little *Parsifal* just before the interval, and met Leslie Woodgate again just after it. We both searched through a score unsuccessfully for three Bartok *Dance Suite* movements, which must have been from another suite, and sounded quite innocuous.

2 October All-Russian Concert, with the Glazunov Piano Concerto in F minor played by Stephen Wearing, and Trefor Jones completely out of his depth in his Welsh-French version of Rimsky-Korsakov's *Chant Indou*.

3 October Bach Night. *Brandenburgs*, Suite No. 3, Two-piano Concerto; but best of all, the Delius *Dance Rhapsody No. 1* in the second half. Then the first performance of Herbert Murrill's *Three Hornpipes*, deft and pungent.

4 October Followed Hindemith's *News of the Day* Overture with a score. Myra

Hess played the Grieg Concerto; and I greatly enjoyed Strauss's *Ein Heldenleben*. The *Circus Suite* by Deems Taylor was a humorous novelty as expected, crude, but good fun in its way.

6 October   The Last Night. The beautiful Eileen Joyce played Busoni's *Indian Fantasy*; and I followed *Scheherazade* from score. Afterwards I joined the other stalwarts to push Sir Henry's car right across the road, as we always do. I was the most persistent of them all, and thanked him through the car window for another wonderful season. He thanked me with his usual courtesy; and so ended the fortieth season of a concert series which perhaps serves mainly as an ear-opener. When the thrill of going to one's first Prom has passed, real musical education can begin. Probably it would be a mistake to hear Beecham first; impossible to appreciate anybody else ever after!

Sir Thomas Beecham conducted an all-Delius concert at Queen's Hall on 10 March the following year; for our young friend, a day in a million. Paul Beard and Carl Pini played the Double Concerto; ' . . . it moves me with its sheer beauty each time I hear it, and I hope it may be a long time before ever I tire of it.' *Eventyr*, the *Fair Scene* and *Walk to the Paradise Garden* from *A Village Romeo and Juliet*; *Over the Hills and Far Away*, and the Piano Concerto played by Katharine Goodson at the top of her form. 'Good heavens! If I had heard the work played like that before, I should have had a very different opinion of it. Even bad Delius has its wonderful moments, and Beecham can do his amazing best for even the weakest passages. It was a great and exalted musical experience.'

The next time he saw Beecham conduct Delius was in May at Limpsfield church in Surrey, where the composer's coffin was brought from France for reinterment in England according to his wishes. Lionel Tertis, Albert Sammons, and Ralph Vaughan Williams were among those who came to pay homage. The one person conspicuously absent was Delius's widow, Jelka. She caught pneumonia on the boat coming over, and within five days was herself buried beside her husband in Limpsfield churchyard.

Those extracts were selected and edited from an unpublished diary of Felix Aprahamian, who was just nineteen years old in 1933. He became Assistant Secretary and Concert Director of the London Philharmonic Orchestra in 1940; and since 1948 he has been deputy music critic of *The Sunday Times*.

They are interesting enough to be read at more than one level: as readable gossip, conjuring up the period atmosphere of London's music-making between the wars; or as informed comment on performing standards, and a guide to the way taste has altered in the forty years since then. It is a very great privilege to have been allowed unrestricted access to such treasure.

Sir Henry Wood's Jubilee
Proms 1935–1940

Sir Henry Wood once broke three batons in the first hour, he was in such a bad temper. That was most unusual; but things do not always go according to plan, and not only at concerts.

The breakdown of a marriage is a melancholy affair, painful for the principals, their relatives and close friends, often embarrassing to bystanders. There is nothing to be gained searching for cause and effect; the fact is that by 1934 Sir Henry and Lady Muriel Wood had drifted apart. Sometimes literally so. Dame Eva Turner once chanced upon Sir Henry, dishevelled and despairing in his suite at the Langham Hotel opposite Queen's Hall. His wife was holidaying in Japan. Sir Henry's feelings can be gauged only from his customary silence, the silence of total omission of any reference to his second wife or their family throughout his entire autobiography *My Life of Music*, published in 1938. 'Whatever has happened to old Timber?' asked players used to firmer direction from him. None could have guessed that, with applause still ringing in his ears, 'old Timber' dreaded going home.

When Major John Linton MC died in 1932, his widow began to consider resuming a singing career interrupted by marriage and a family. After twenty years' absence there would be lost ground to make up. She knew the very man, perhaps the best coach in the country, if he were not too busy conducting. She wrote to him, in her professional name of Jessie Goldsack, and received an enthusiastic offer of Proms and festival dates as well as the tuition. Such a splendid and tactful woman would never have commented on his unkempt dress or occasional lapses of concentration when accompanying her lessons; but one evening in 1935 Sir Henry unexpectedly rang her with an unmistakable cry for help.

It is a great relief to unburden oneself to a trusted friend. The crux was, would she agree to look after him? Womanhood overtook artistic ambitions. Jessie Goldsack made his well-being her sole concern. Earlier that year Sir Henry had received a warning in the form of a mild stroke after conducting in Rome. The first task was to build up his strength with a peaceful holiday in France and Belgium before the Proms began. It was the old, familiar, 'Timber', who faced his players on the First Night, spruce, vigorous, thoroughly in command, a buoyant and genial young man of sixty-six.

There was one further problem. In 1935 it would have been easier for a camel to pass through the eye of a needle than for a divorced person to enter the Royal Enclosure at Ascot. Divorce was out of the question for a national figure like Sir Henry Wood. The dilemma was resolved with kindly legal advice. Jessie adopted by deed-poll the prior christian name 'Lady' and the surname 'Wood'. Lady Jessie Wood was wholeheartedly welcomed wherever they went together.

The players facing Sir Henry on that opening night also had a new lease of life. In May the BBC organised the first London Music Festival, in which the BBC Symphony Orchestra was conducted by Arturo Toscanini, undoubtedly the greatest conductor in the world (if it was not Wilhelm Furtwängler). Some listeners felt the unforgettable experience of working with him could still be detected when they heard those same Brahms and Beethoven symphonies at the Proms under Wood. Toscanini conducted the orchestra again in 1937, 1938 and 1939. It was rumoured at the time that he had been offered a dozen concerts in 1936, later altered to eleven, with a proportionate reduction in fee. No more was heard from the Italian maestro that year.

Attendances at the increasingly successful Proms proved that the best artists produce the best results. The 1935 season saw the debut of Elisabeth Schumann, Elena Gerhardt, Piatigorsky, Adolf and Hermann Busch in the Brahms Double Concerto, Arthur Rubinstein in 1936 playing the Ireland Piano Concerto and Beethoven's Third; Szigeti once more in the Brahms and Beethoven Violin Concertos; cellist Emmanuel Feuermann in 1938, and Richard Tauber's Proms debut in 1939. The young Elisabeth Schumann delighted everyone; her grave charm, in Schubert *Lieder*, alternating with a merry twinkle of eyes and voice, stayed long in hearts and minds. Elvira Ketterer once saw her turn away from the packed Queen's Hall auditorium to sing, as the last of many encores, Brahms's *Lullaby* specially to those sitting behind the orchestra – 'and how we cheered her after that!'

The period parallels pre-1914, where welcome visitors like Backhaus and Egon Petri also added lustre to the seasons; though in 1937 critics were lukewarm about Soulima Stravinsky, and the next year about Elena Glazunov, composers' children playing their fathers' works with something less than distinction.

In 1934 Marie Wilson was deputising for an ailing Charles Woodhouse, who nevertheless went on conducting works in the second half for some time. She became Leader of the BBC Symphony Orchestra herself for the next two seasons, a remarkable player who could bring out the best in all her colleagues just by her presence, a rare gift she was herself unaware of. Paul Beard paid generous tribute to it, and none understood better than he. Standing before her as soloist in Hamilton Harty's new violin concerto in 1935, he sat beside her as the new Leader in 1937, rapidly becoming a great favourite with everyone. Within five years critics were declaring his performances of such difficult, exposed works as *Ein Heldenleben* 'superior to nearly all the concerto soloists appearing in the season'.

The centenary of Camille Saint-Saëns's birth on 9 October was marked a month beforehand by the first and so far the last concert of his works at the Proms. Marcel Dupré played in the Third Symphony, Pouishnoff the Fourth Piano Concerto, Thelma Reiss the A minor Cello Concerto, and there was also *Phaëton*. Important anniversaries by 1935 received such an accolade, as did the birth centenaries of Dvorak in 1941, and of Grieg two years later.

There were complaints of less broadcasting from the Proms in 1936; only sixty per cent as much, according to some; nothing but snippets, according to others. Constant Lambert joined the attack in his alternative role of newspaper critic. The teenage BBC, still groping towards a policy, put out a specious argument: '. . . despite the fact that many people can listen to good music every night of their lives, a block of music occurring at the same time for forty-nine successive evenings is not in the interests of listeners as a whole'. More and more radio stations abroad had begun broadcasting the Proms, for no more than the cost of circuits from London. Artists were simply told, 'It may interest you to know that your performance will be relayed in Switzerland, Germany, Spain, Belgium, Italy, Holland', etc. Orchestral players were already querying this by 1934! A courteous but sad reply from Spain to the BBC in 1936 tells its own story: 'Owing to the prevailing conditions in our Country it is impossible for us to make any transmission of these concerts. Nevertheless we are extremely obliged to you for your kind offer'.

Queen's Hall was redecorated before the 1937 season, recarpeted, equipped with new heating, lighting and ventilation. Some works new at the Proms had been written for the Coronation of King George VI in May that year, including Walton's *Crown Imperial* which got its composer many recalls, as did Bax's *London Pageant*, dedicated to the BBC Symphony Orchestra and played on the Last Night. A harp concerto by Germaine Tailleferre, the woman member of *Les Six* in Paris, was played on the First Night by Sidonie Goossens. She was still the orchestra's Principal Harp forty-three years later at the age of eighty, the only founder member still with them in 1981. 'Mother' to generations of new players, she was never known to speak ill of anyone, and was universally adored. Tailleferre's Concerto for two pianos, mixed chorus, saxophones and orchestra had been played for the first time

9. Sir Henry Wood in 1938 (*BBC Hulton Picture Library*)

here at the 1935 Proms, the season Sigurd Rascher first appeared, as soloist in the Saxophone Concerto Lars-Erik Larsson dedicated to him.

All seven Sibelius symphonies were played in 1937 for the first time in a single season, and the first Sibelius Night was tried. The great Finnish composer cabled his thanks to Sir Henry, next year sending his daughter to visit him during the Jubilee. All nine Beethoven symphonies used to be played once every season also, and all four Brahms, as if the same audience came every night. When the Proms were young they knew better, repeating the *New World Symphony* or Schubert's *Unfinished* four times in eight weeks. Beethoven's *Choral Symphony* could easily be given twice today, except for the law of the quart and the pint pot – something else would have to come out.

Sir Colin Davis began his career as a clarinet player and once said 'You know you're a conductor when people start paying you to do it'. They first paid Henry Wood in 1888, so the 1938 season was declared his personal Jubilee. The Prospectus proudly listed forty-nine of the works introduced by him to this country at the Proms, including *Casse-Noisette* and many other Tchaikovsky scores, much Delius, even more Sibelius, *The Firebird*, Franck's *Symphonic Variations*, *Scheherazade*, music by Ravel, Debussy, Bach, and *Le Carnaval des Animaux*. During the First Night interval Sir Henry broadcast an appeal for his Jubilee Fund, to endow beds in London hospitals for musicians. This was heard inside Queen's Hall by means of loud speakers, as they were then called. There were some notable British works in the Jubilee; Lambert conducted his *Horoscope* ballet music; a very young Benjamin Britten played solo in the first performance of his Piano Concerto ('the Playboy of Music: musical wisecracking' wrote the critics) and also conducted his *Variations on a Theme of Frank Bridge*. There was the première of Walton's Second Suite from *Façade*, and an *Overture for Unaccompanied Chorus* (wordless) by Anthony Lewis, 'a member of the BBC staff' who went on to lay foundations of music in the Third Programme and to become Principal of Wood's old Academy; Arthur Bliss conducted *A Colour Symphony* and Ralph Vaughan Williams his *Pastoral*; and a bronze bust of the Founder was installed in Queen's Hall from the opening night of the season.

One day early in 1938 Eva Turner met Sir Henry and Lady Jessie Wood on Paddington Station, as today one runs across people at the world's great air terminals. There was talk of a special Jubilee Concert, of special music, of many colleagues being asked to take part; not enough time for every singer to do an aria of course; but would she consent to sing just a few notes? 'I'd be happy to do just a cough and a spit!' was the Oldham-born diva's characteristic reply. Which is how, just after the Proms ended, she came to be singing in the exquisite *Serenade to Music* at Queen's Hall with fifteen fellow singers (all the sopranos were still alive in 1980, as she likes to point out!) and with Vaughan Williams ambling down into the Stalls to hear Wood rehearsing his Jubilee offering. Wednesday 5 October was chosen for the Jubilee Concert to suit Sergei Rachmaninoff, who came over specially at his own expense, to play his Second Concerto in tribute to Wood's services to Russian composers, but would not lift his absolute ban on being broadcast even for this occasion. (How strange, when he made so many records long before editing was possible.) It nearly upset negotiations with the BBC, though they did not broadcast a record of the concerto whilst he was playing it, as Rachmaninoff expected they would. His generous gesture did solve the problem of which pianist to engage for the Jubilee; Moiseiwitsch had suggested twenty-four of them playing the concerto simultaneously on twenty-four grands in the Arena of the Royal Albert Hall.

As well as everything else he did, Wood also kept scrupulous notes on every Proms performance; his Jubilee may be a good moment to recall some of those pungent observations: 'A stringy voice, but what a fine musician! Should only be given difficult modern works no one else will sing.' 'Do let us give the César Franck Symphony a rest.' 'It is not possible to rehearse two concertos and two other works in a morning.' 'Always comes in a bar too soon, and swallows silent rests.' 'A bad performance of Tchaikovsky; should only play Beethoven in future.' 'By all means let us repeat Rachmaninoff's Third Symphony.' 'Let us drop the *Choral Fantasia*, it is poor and dull; and we do not want a piano on the platform during the *Choral Symphony*.' 'A mistake. The last piece should always be for full orchestra, the public do not like to see only a dozen players on the platform, they feel they are not getting their money's worth.'

Life had achieved a certain stability by 1939, of which unchanged admission prices to Promenade Concerts for the past nineteen years was one small symbol. The season began on 12 August with tested favourites, Moiseiwitsch playing Rachmaninoff's *Paganini Variations*, Joan Hammond singing Verdi, Kodaly's *Hary Janos*; and the front desks of first and second fiddles playing Vivaldi's B minor Concerto for Four Violins. Four nights later there was Bach's version of it for four keyboards, a juxtaposition such as festivals delight in; yet this obvious link was not mentioned in either programme note. Royal Academy student Denis Matthews was one of the four pianists on 16 August, just a fortnight before war was declared; he next played the night it ended, VJ Day, 15 August 1945.*

Later in the season came Solomon and the Bliss Piano Concerto, direct from the New York World's Fair which commissioned it. Britten's three Rimbaud Songs (later *Les Illuminations*) marked 'a spiritual change which may prove decisive'. Thelma Reiss bravely played Tchaikovsky's *Rococo Variations* with a plaster on her forehead; Sir Henry carried her cello on to the platform, as she had been knocked out by its case falling on her in a taxi accident en route for the concert. Léon Goossens in Rutland Boughton's Oboe Concerto was declared 'the best performance of the week . . . he sets a phrase in a clear light and gives it a glowing beauty'.

---

* The final Victory in Japan Day; Victory in Europe was on 8 May 1945.

On 1 September a critic went to Queen's Hall on purpose to see how many people turned up in the black-out. It was not crowded, but Sir Henry, smiling as always, got an enthusiastic welcome. Some uniforms were seen amongst the audience, and people had to grope their way home afterwards in the dark. Sir Henry broke forty-five years' silence from the platform: 'Owing to the special arrangements for broadcasting which are now in force, the BBC very much regrets that the Symphony Orchestra will no longer be available for these concerts in London. I am therefore very sorry to say that from tonight Promenade Concerts will close down until further notice. I must thank you, my dear friends, for your loyal support and I hope we shall soon meet again.'

Only thirteen years after those acrimonious exchanges prior to the BBC taking over the Proms in 1927, it all started up again over who should run them during the Second World War. When the Lord Privy Seal stopped public entertainment in London from 2 September 1939, the BBC Symphony Orchestra was evacuated to Bristol; out of the frying-pan and into the fire as it turned out, the Luftwaffe bombing Bristol before London. Theatres soon opened again, and police permission was given for concerts at Queen's Hall. It was felt that the BBC ought to carry on with the Proms. Wartime concerts were turning money away. There was a mounting thirst for good music, the packed National Gallery Concerts run by Myra Hess being a prime example. Preliminary discussions were set up between representatives of Chappell and Co. and the BBC, but the negotiators were soon far apart. The BBC could not predict what might happen to forward planning during hostilities; they wanted a War Clause (which protected concert promoters forced to cancel performances), and anyway their orchestra was no longer in London. Chappell and Co. did not want the War Clause, and hinted that Queen's Hall might be turned into a cinema unless the BBC made up its mind. Henry Wood said he and Chappell and Co. were being approached by 'other interests' willing to run his Proms. Copious correspondence flew about; there were telegrams, letters to the Press, misunderstandings on all sides, legal quibbles and threats, with no one in possession of all the facts at any one time. The BBC Director-General's letter to *The Times* fairly sums it up:

'In spite of having only a single Home programme in wartime, the BBC hoped to continue the Proms, but the war's hazards not being fully known, caution and delay resulted. Queen's Hall's owners told the BBC two other interests wanted to run the Proms. The BBC offered to co-operate with either, only to learn that both had fallen through. When the BBC then decided to run a shorter season themselves, they were told that the Hall was fully booked. All this time they could make no firm offer to Sir Henry Wood, who suggests in letters to the Press that this casts doubts on his integrity. Nothing could be further from the BBC's intention.'

And so on and so forth.

The sudden appearance of Mr Keith Douglas with Mr Owen Mase to run a 1940 season of Promenade Concerts under the auspices of the Royal

Philharmonic Society may have seemed a *deus ex machina* to the BBC, but it can hardly have been unexpected by Chappell and Co., since all dates were safely booked at Queen's Hall, and Sir Henry Wood had already agreed to conduct. Not surprisingly, none of the concerts was broadcast that year.

Keith Douglas was a wealthy amateur of music, whose father had been Chairman of the Bradford Dyers' Association. He played piano and horn at Rugby and Oxford, wrote criticism, conducted, managed and endowed for ever the Bradford Philharmonic; and was the arranger 'with advice from Sir Thomas Beecham' of a Waltz and Intermezzo from *A Village Romeo and Juliet* by Delius, which Wood had conducted on the First Night of the 1939 Proms. (Beecham was certainly one of the 'other interests' mentioned by Chappell and Co., but he immediately went off to the United States.)

'Sir Henry Wood's Forty-sixth and Farewell Season' – a stunt devised by Keith Douglas to coax people into Queen's Hall in spite of black-outs and bombs – showed signs of hurried planning. In the absence of the BBC's resources, programmes were kept very safe to make ends meet. With the London Symphony Orchestra, and Gerald Moore as official accompanist, things went quite well. Five nights into the season, Basil Cameron joined Sir Henry as Associate Conductor for the first time. The closing scene from *Götterdämmerung* on Wagner Night was sung with 'splendid dramatic power' by Eva Turner, 'technically flawless'. Margaretta Scott was released from a play at the Apollo Theatre to recite Grieg's *Bergliot* 'and did it very well indeed' – the Scandinavian Evening was not full, but on the whole things were starting to pick up. One of the most striking new works was Lennox Berkeley's *Introduction and Allegro* for two pianos and orchestra, played by the composer and William Glock, who next year became music critic of *The Observer*. American Ambassador Joseph Kennedy, father of John F., Robert and Edward, joined the audience during this noisy season, which was once more cut short, four weeks earlier than intended, because of air raids.

Henry Wood conducted the BBC Symphony Orchestra in Bristol later in the year, then went on to Manchester for concerts with the Hallé from October to January. The Hallé committee offered him the conductorship, but he declined, the position later being filled by John Barbirolli, recently returned from the New York Philharmonic. In this time of clothes rationing Lady Jessie appealed to the Board of Trade for extra clothing coupons to help Sir Henry through the rigours of many winter journeys. Their refusal indicated that 'all dance-band leaders are allowed the same number of coupons'.

Beyond the Call of Duty

Arthur Reckless made his Proms debut on Monday 26 August 1940, singing Wagner with Eva Turner. It was the night of the first air raid on London. The music ended abruptly whilst an official advised the audience to remain, as all transport had ceased. (Later, in the Royal Albert Hall, red or green lights flashed during performances, signalling an air raid or the all clear.) Then the concert continued. Afterwards the buffets reopened until sandwiches and coffee gave out. Standing Promenaders were invited to occupy vacant Circle seats. Some phoned parents to say they were staying, then everyone settled down to enjoy impromptu entertainment during the night, to the distant sounds of bombs and gunfire.

First of all books of words were handed out, Sir Henry leading the audience in 'Charlie is My Darling', 'Loch Lomond' and other community songs, with the official accompanists Gerald Moore and Berkeley Mason. Gradually most of the orchestra came back on to the platform, some in shirt-sleeves or smoking pipes, like a Haydn *Farewell Symphony* in reverse. Both Eva Turner and Arthur Reckless sang extra items, orchestra and conductor showing real musicianship by playing without any music. (In 1944 Dame Eva's Kensington home was destroyed by a flying bomb; only her typewriter was saved, by its wooden case, and her Blüthner grand when a blast wrapped the curtains round it.) Whenever there was an air raid, soloists might stay on to do an extra turn. Benno Moiseiwitsch even played cello with an orchestral group all using different instruments from their usual ones. Another night he turned the pages for an amateur pianist from the audience. Arthur Catterall played second violin to his daughter in Bach's *Double Concerto*. London Symphony Orchestra Leader George Stratton played the Mendelssohn, with Basil Cameron conducting from memory. Antonia Butler played a Handel Cello Sonata, and one memorable night joined Gerald Moore, Arthur Catterall and his daughter, and an LSO viola player, in an historic performance of

108

Schumann's Piano Quintet. The audience were swept along as the five of them made music together, unrehearsed and unforgettable, as if their lives depended on it.

There was no shortage of light relief. Basil Cameron would play excerpts at the piano, in a contest to guess the composer and the work – prizes, free seats for a future Prom. Cameron and Sir Adrian Boult once came in around midnight, collecting for the Spitfire Fund in two wastepaper baskets labelled respectively 'Brahms' and 'Beethoven'. Coins were tossed in as they toured the hall, Beethoven winning by several pounds.

One night it was announced that Sir Thomas Beecham had flown in specially from Australia. The orchestra tuned up properly, the curtains were flung wide, and in walked Beecham to the life, his walk, his superior air, the quick glance to see what kind of audience he had, the imperious gestures, foot-stamping and hisses to the band as he conducted Mozart's *Figaro* Overture. Then followed a typical Beecham speech, accusing his orchestra (which had occasionally been sponsored by Jack Hilton) of 'gallivanting with a dance-band leader'. After that he conducted 'some contemptible modern music thrown off by a young friend of mine'. The whole of Queen's Hall was in fits of laughter, not least Sir Henry Wood, watching in shirt-sleeves from the wings. The brilliant performance had a cutting edge to it, for the real Beecham was believed to have evacuated himself to safety in the United States. There was an undercurrent of 'the orchestra is here, but where is Sir Thomas?' Ralph Nicholson, whose impersonation amounted to genius, is now Director of Guildford County Music School. As Nicholson left the platform Sir Henry said, 'I didn't know you were a conductor?' Still in Beecham's voice Nicholson replied, 'I hear you do some conducting too!' Then he joined the picnickers on the floor of Queen's Hall, where Geoffrey Last learned that the 'contemptible modern music' had been unscored, unrehearsed, and busked by the entire orchestra.

At about 2 a.m. Sir Henry appeared in his cloak to announce that he was going to bed, and it was now up to the audience to entertain the orchestra. There were some amazing results, including expert yodelling from the Balcony, an excellent Chopin recital by a young Promenader, and a Music-Hall comic who fell a bit flat, the style having passed right out of favour. There was also a young woman who apologised that she could sing only in German; did anyone mind? The house burst into spontaneous applause and, while German aircraft dropped German bombs on London, she sang German *Lieder* most beautifully. Perhaps it could only have happened in England.

Geoffrey Last once left while the impromptu concert and an air raid were both in full swing. He counted nine enemy bombers in the searchlights, and saw big fires blazing to the north; 'but inside Queen's Hall nobody gave a damn'. A section of the orchestra found strength to play Viennese waltzes, and couples danced in and out of Promenaders sleeping on the floor. Being young and fearless, they had no thoughts of danger. It was a magical

10. Sir William Walton hears his music in wartime (*Erich Auerbach*)

experience for twenty-year-olds, still vividly remembered. They bubbled over with excitement at the unexpected bonus of these extempore concerts. Afterwards came the thrill of leaving Queen's Hall in the early light of dawn, as London returned to life like the Sleeping Beauty. Buses, taxis, and tube trains all started up again at the all clear, and Promenaders made their way to the suburbs and breakfast, or to their day's work in City offices.

The bombs that destroyed Queen's Hall mercifully fell when none of this was taking place inside. James Lawrie was at the last concert there, *The Dream of Gerontius* conducted by Sargent on Saturday 10 May 1941. He gave short shrift to his companion, who had a feeling there might be an air raid and thought it something they ought to experience. At seven o'clock the next morning he was summoned back from Haslemere to help search for the body of his younger brother, one of thousands killed in London that night.

May Rudgley had seen bodies being dug out of demolished houses opposite her bed-sitter in Bayswater, and was looking forward to the afternoon concert to restore a sense of normality. She walked with a friend through Marylebone to Queen's Hall; their hearts sank when they saw the tangled mass of hosepipes, the smoke and the piles of rubble which were all that remained. Amid the debris sat a man at a trestle table, redirecting ticket-holders to the

Royal Academy of Music, where the concert was to take place in the Duke's Hall half-an-hour later than advertised. People were standing at the back and sitting on the floor. One woman complained that they should have arranged something better than this. May thought it marvellous that the concert was given at all, when players had spent all morning chasing around borrowing instruments people had fished out of their attics.*

One cellist had second thoughts in the act of leaving his instrument at Queen's Hall the previous evening, picked up the case, and carried it on his head in the black-out all the way to Hampstead, a thing he had never done before. His was not the only one to survive. Double-bass player Charles Stewart saw the ruins next morning, thought that was the end of that, and went home. An hour later he answered the doorbell to a colleague asking to borrow his instrument. He told him it had gone with Queen's Hall. 'No it hasn't, you lazy so-and-so,' came the reply. 'You didn't put it away properly in its box; you left it standing against the wall, and it's still there!'

The contrabassoonist was not so lucky. Such instruments are mostly made by Heckel in Germany, so replacement was impossible. Christopher Wykes, on service with the Army, read an appeal in *Musical Opinion* and, having an old but playable contra lying idle at home, asked his father to take it up to London, where it did yeoman service for the rest of the war. It was afterwards played by Gilbert Harding's uncle Cuthbert, until German contrabassoons were once more available. Christopher still plays it in the Leicester Symphony Orchestra, where it is affectionately known as the 'shower-bath'.

---

* One of them turned out to be a Sanctus Seraphim violin made in Cremona in the eighteenth century, worth £20,000. The London Philharmonic Orchestra's string section still take turns playing it.

Jubilee of the Proms
Seasons 1941–1944

When Sir Henry Wood first saw the ruins of Queen's Hall, he wept. Next time he was still numb with shock. But on the third visit he spotted his bronze bust standing intact above the debris – *'So I'm still here!'* Chappell and Co. were completely removed from all future negotiations, having no hall to let; and when Wood and the London Symphony Orchestra transferred to the Royal Albert Hall of the Arts and Sciences for the 1941 Proms season, the audience miraculously doubled to fill it.

The Royal Albert Hall had a notorious echo; a single drum-tap could be heard twice in certain parts of it. Various remedies were tried – baffles in the roof, curtains sprayed with gypsum behind the orchestra, a canopy above it, and so on. There was also the strange sight of empty seats in a supposedly sold-out hall, a legacy from subscribers to the original building costs having received seats in perpetuity which their heirs did not always occupy. People soon settled down to this being home to the Proms for the foreseeable future, though it was understood that Queen's Hall would one day be rebuilt. They could take shelter if need be in the Kensington Gardens and Hyde Park trenches, or in the subway down Exhibition Road. Free seats were given to the Forces where available, but a third of the season sold out. As the traditional solos after the interval would have been lost in the vastness of this new place, Promenaders might find Louis Kentner playing one Chopin concerto in the first half, and the other in the second.

Any pretence of a 'Farewell Season' was dropped. Keith Douglas planned six weeks; Sir Henry, feeling disorganised, obtained W. W. Thompson as his personal manager from the BBC, which broadcast from about twenty of the concerts this year. Popular soloists took part, including 'that gifted girl pianist Moura Lympany' and 'the Polish girl Ida Haendel, making Tchaikovsky's very ordinary Violin Concerto sound like a masterpiece'. Wood's suggestion that Cyril Smith and Phyllis Sellick play *Le Carnaval des Animaux* on the First Night was the start of a famous two-piano partnership. Compared with earlier and later seasons the Proms of 1940 and 1941 may seem uneventful, evenings of standard works with hardly any Novelties. Henry Wood said composers were busy on war work; certainly they and the poets were not being squandered as they had been in the Great War, though in Europe they were uprooted. Louis Aragon distilled the refugees' anguish in verse which became 'C', one of Francis Poulenc's finest songs, published clandestinely in Paris during the German occupation.

The Proms were held in conditions of extreme difficulty, but they *were* held. There may have been no real danger that they would cease, though other organisations did tend to regard the BBC as a goose with unlimited golden eggs. In fact they proceeded with caution and responsibility. Even though the two-year break in their management was the result of someone having pulled a fast one, they magnanimously took the Proms back under their wing. Henry Wood was delighted. Two seasons' absence made the BBC seem a safe harbour indeed; he was very glad to be back.

Two symphonies written whilst their composers were on duty as air-raid wardens were performed here in public for the first time at the Proms, Lennox Berkeley's Symphony in 1943, and the *Leningrad Symphony* by Shostakovich in 1942. The Russian began his in July 1941, shortly before the siege of Leningrad; most of it was written on the roof of the Conservatoire. In March 1942 it was played at the Bolshoi Theatre in Moscow. The dedication is to heroic Soviet citizens. Forty years later the posthumous memoirs of Shostakovich revealed that it had been conceived well before the siege, and that it mourns a Leningrad Stalin had destroyed long before Hitler attacked it. The longest symphony until then performed at the Proms, it was listened to with profound attention by an immense audience. Sir Henry had broadcast it in June 1942, after the last-minute arrival of the score, and correction of a mass of copying errors.

Alan Bush also conducted his Symphony in C during the 1942 Proms, an event seen by the Press as 'making amends for a ban on his works since he signed the People's Convention Manifesto last year'. A critic felt both composers had 'fallen victim to the notion that music must have a political or propagandist significance'. Not so Britten's *Sinfonia da Requiem*, 'the most mature work of his we have yet heard, a virtuoso of the orchestra'; nor Rubbra's Fourth, dedicated to Sir Henry, which Rubbra conducted in his khaki battledress uniform: 'it should be heard widely, and often'. Rubbra played solo piano in his *Sinfonia Concertante* in 1943, which he had refurbished during war service as an artilleryman.

The BBC's resources allowed more Novelties from 1942, and also provided two orchestras for the first time, with three conductors. The plan was simple. Wood conducted the First Night. He and Cameron shared the first four weeks' work with the London Philharmonic Orchestra; he and Sir Adrian Boult the last four, with the BBC Symphony. All three conducted something on the Last Night. The BBC accepted Lady Jessie Wood as fully representing Sir Henry in all matters, which freed him for the real work of preparing new scores. She was soon suggesting a season of ten weeks, with the London Philharmonic playing the second half, which was politely resisted.

Once a fortnight during 1943 there was a Prom in tribute to one of our Allies; the Berlioz *Te Deum* on Bastille Day; a Russian Night; U.S. Technical Sergeant Hugo Weisgall conducting his *American Comedy 1943* and Lieutenant Burgess Meredith declaiming Copland's *Lincoln Portrait*; but most sensational of all, both the Czech and Polish Army Choirs on stage on 12 August, the Czechs singing their marching songs, the Poles performing part of an opera, *The Haunted Castle* by their countryman Moniuszko, a kind of Polish Smetana. Works by Dominions composers were also being featured; Wood said the BBC's list of 'firsts' was very impressive, but in all honesty he had never heard of some of them.

Sir Henry had suffered another mild stroke in 1941 after a concert at Bradford. Only three nights into the 1943 season he had a bad one in full view of everyone at the Albert Hall. Towards the end of the Brahms Second Symphony he suddenly bent sideways; he could not lift his baton any higher than the music desk. He came off perplexed and cross – and was promptly confined to bed by Dr Skeggs and Lord Horder. He had to miss the visit by H.M. The Queen, taking H.R.H. Princess Elizabeth to her first Prom, a Bach-Handel Night on 23 June. He missed the Memorial Prom to his friend Rachmaninoff on 25 June. He was allowed to sit in the audience at the first Sunday Prom on the afternoon of 11 July, transferred from the previous Wednesday when the Government requisitioned the Albert Hall for a meeting to honour China on the sixth anniversary of the Sino-Japanese War.

Basil Cameron bore the brunt of extra conducting, coming to the fore with premières such as the First Symphony of Eugene Goossens. The BBC lent its own orchestra to Vaughan Williams for a run-through of the season's outstanding new work, his Fifth Symphony, dedicated without permission to Jan Sibelius. The London Philharmonic gave the actual première, directed by the composer. Sir Henry conducted the first and final items on the Last Night, for which both orchestras combined, though no appropriately large works were included.

Wagner Nights were gradually losing ground, being shared with Liszt or Tchaikovsky, reduced to only three in a season, and moved from Mondays, though for twenty years up to 1953 there was so much Wagner that the Prospectus divided his works alone into separate 'Orchestral' and 'Vocal' lists in the index. Bach Nights continued to gain ground, and were worth watching, with Fanny Waterman playing in 1942 and Antony Hopkins in 1943. The ever-present threat of air raids for once gave Beethoven's *Choral Symphony* its rightful place in a concert, when the early starting-time of 6 p.m.

11. Solomon *(left)* plays cards with Benno Moiseiwitsch. A stroke deprived Solomon of the use of his right hand, and the world of a great and beloved pianist *(Erich Auerbach)*

late in 1942 allowed it to be put last, and still end before the Nine O'Clock News. If ever there was a final work! – yet at first it used to be played incomplete; and later it was always placed before the interval (which was dictated by the BBC's main News) for lack of sufficient time after it. By 1943 the BBC's Director of Music was Arthur Bliss, ever on the lookout for brilliant young soloists. 'A boy called David Willcocks is very promising,' George Thalben-Ball told him, 'but he's in the Forces.'

The Proms were now fifty years old and Sir Henry Wood seventy-five; plans had long been laid for proper Jubilee celebrations in 1944. The BBC engaged a third orchestra, the London Symphony, the conductors remaining Wood, Cameron and Boult. British and foreign composers were asked for first performances (in England, at least). Shostakovich sent his Eighth Symphony, Stravinsky *Four Norwegian Moods*, and Hindemith the ballet *Cupid and Psyche*. *The Daily Telegraph* undertook to defray extra costs involved, including a special Birthday Concert in March. Their sponsorship helped to raise money for a Jubilee Fund to rebuild Queen's Hall as a lasting memorial to Henry Wood. Lord Horder was its chairman and the public was able to subscribe by paying 'a shilling a brick'.

In the months leading up to the Jubilee Proms every society wished to pay tribute to the great man. There were lunches given by the Performing Rights Society, the Savage Club (Wood had been made a life member), the Musicians' Benevolent Fund, and there was the Birthday Concert itself on 25 March. Vaughan Williams presented an album signed by fellow musicians from all over the world, and thousands of pounds were given to the Fund. After a lunch in June at Sir Henry's alma mater the Royal Academy of Music, Clifford Curzon and the Griller Quartet played for him. The Proms Circle became 'the Henry Wood Proms Circle' by his permission; John Masefield, the Poet Laureate, penned verse in his praise and sent a personal note which touched him deeply. Sir Henry wrote in *Radio Times* of what Proms broadcasts meant to the Forces far from home, of how it made them known to millions abroad, and of the loyal support his faithful audiences always gave to him even when faced with difficult new works.

At a Claridges lunch on 5 June he received a thousand guineas for the Fund from the BBC and by prior agreement offered his life's work to them – 'I hope with all my heart they will carry on my Proms as a permanent institution for all time'. Sir Adrian Boult accepted the 'Henry Wood Promenade Concerts' on the BBC's behalf. Three days later, just forty-eight hours before the season opened, King George VI invested Sir Henry with the Order of the Companion of Honour and asked after the new concert hall Fund. If 'old Timber' had not fully realised it before, he knew it now; he was loved, respected, honoured.

Queues began to form outside the Albert Hall from 10 p.m. on Friday evening; advance booking was such as had never been known. One Prommer would never forget the First Night of 1944. At about 4 p.m. on a sunny Saturday afternoon Elvira Ketterer joined a friend in the queue who was working in a government department and had brought her boss along, 'a gentle man with a quiet wit named Donald Selsby'. Whilst waiting for the doors to open he and Elvira had a lively argument about the merits of Elgar compared with those of Wagner; but perhaps their hearts were really elsewhere, for many concerts and several years later they were married and truly did live happily ever after. For how many such liaisons, one wonders, have the Proms been responsible?

A huge roar of welcome greeted Sir Henry on the First Night as an audience of 7,000 rose to its feet to cheer his entrance. Most of them had not been born when he started the Proms; but to the oldest and the youngest he was the

Grand Old Man, the most famous musician in Britain. The Jubilee Season had been brought forward to 10 June because daylight hours were comparatively safe from air attacks. The BBC's *Fifty Years of the Proms* was on sale; *Queen's Hall* by Robert Elkin had just been published; proceeds from both went to the building Fund. Some of the works in the printed programmes bore the date when Wood had first introduced them, Tchaikovsky's *Cossack Dance* (1899) and *Swan Lake* (1901), the Delius Piano Concerto (1907), the Bach-Wood *Sixth Suite* (1916). 'Never in the history of the Proms' Wood had said of the 1944 season, 'has the novelty net been more widely cast' – including violin concertos by Samuel Barber and Arnold Bax, both played by Eda Kersey, who, sadly, died soon afterwards. The BBC was broadcasting to Africa, the Pacific, North and South America, the General Forces programme,* and Europe. The Press warned of the danger that microphones might pick up an air raid siren alert above the music, confirming to the Germans that their flying bombs were on target above the capital. Neither the sirens nor the 'doodle-bugs', Hitler's secret weapon for winning the war, could distract the audience in the Albert Hall; but there was increasing official concern about such a vulnerable concentration of people. On Thursday 29 June, more than a month before the actual Jubilee, the Government and the BBC once more suspended the Proms; but without a public announcement, not to let the enemy know how effective their pilotless bombs and rockets had become.

There was a very disappointed man in Harley Street. Dr George Cathcart, one of only five surviving from the original planners and players in 1895 (W. A. Peterkin was another), had been looking forward to a night of triumph on 10 August. He was too old for wartime travel to Bedford, where Sir Henry was obliged to join the evacuated BBC Symphony Orchestra, to carry on with a modified season from 3 July, turning up in a camouflaged car to play for a studio audience of only 200 in the Great Hall of Bedford School or the Corn Exchange. What bitter irony that the Proms, which once resisted broadcasting, should become broadcasts and nothing else! What anticlimax that Sir Henry should have to approach the Jubilee of his concerts so far from the tumult of the audiences he felt it such a privilege to serve!

In shirt-sleeves and summer dresses the BBC Symphony Orchestra played only those parts of the original concerts which would have been broadcast from the Albert Hall, usually the solos or a symphony, Myra Hess, Moiseiwitsch, Lionel Tertis and many others staunchly going out to wartime Bedford for their one item, Sir Henry conducting only occasionally in the first four weeks, husbanding his strength for the Jubilee in August.

Sir Adrian Boult conducted the Shostakovich Eighth Symphony. Julian Herbage, the BBC's Assistant Director of Music, wrote in *Radio Times*: 'The Union of Soviet Composers' accusation that he was "formalistic and insin-

---

*Norman Collins, Director of the Forces Programme, later became one of the founding fathers of Independent Television.

cere" caused Shostakovich to purge himself of much that was superficial and caustic in his style and to develop the more profound and introspective side of his genius'. Some officers and farmers in the small audience 'looked a little dazed; and even members of the orchestra seemed surprised at the noise they were creating'.

Through July *Radio Times* stopped referring to these broadcasts as the Proms, though works such as Khachaturyan's *Ode to Stalin* and his Piano Concerto played by Moura Lympany were heard as planned. (From 1 August to 10 August *Radio Times* called them 'Sir Henry Wood Jubilee Concerts'.) Joan Hammond sang 'Ah, perfido' on Beethoven Night, Friday 28 July, and Maurice Cole played Mozart's popular A major Piano Concerto K488. Lady Jessie Wood has written of the unusual, fretful morning rehearsal at which Beethoven's Seventh Symphony was left almost untouched. In the evening Sir Henry leapt upon it like an exploding supernova, exhausting his players with an incandescent performance. 'Those of us privileged to be there', Sir Adrian Boult later recalled, 'were thrilled at our old friend's perennial energy and youth.'

That giant star, that great heart and iron will, had finally burned itself out. He never raised a baton again, but lay feverish, alternately worse and better, until he knew the nation had heard the 10 August Jubilee Concert on the Home Service. Sir Adrian Boult conducted it and George Thalben-Ball played the Handel Organ Concerto which Sir Henry Wood had recently orchestrated. On his behalf Lord Horder made the appeal for donations to the building Fund. BBC announcer Stuart Hibberd read Wood's final message: 'Give my love to all my dear musicians and my dear friends of music. I am disappointed I cannot be with them today, but tell them I shall soon be with them again and then we'll finish the Jubilee Season with a Victory Season'. The Forces Programme followed with a feature on 'Fifty Years of the Proms' and part of a Prom originally broadcast to the BBC's Pacific Service on 1 July, which both Sir Henry and Sir Adrian had conducted.

Wood was moved to Hitchin hospital on 14 August at the request of his physician Dr Basil Skeggs, whose son Peter Sir Henry nicknamed 'Gerontius' because of his great love for the work. He had promised the young man Elgar's own marked score, and on his death-bed kept asking when 'Gerontius' could come to see him. 'I know why he's agitating,' Peter Skeggs told his father, 'it's about that score.' Lord Horder visited the hospital on 18 August. The same night Lady Jessie Wood and Dr Skeggs were called urgently; Sir Henry had asked the nurses to send for his beloved Jessie. She stayed beside him until he died the next day.

There was a funeral service in St Mary's Church, Hitchin, with the BBC Symphony Orchestra and Singers. Sir Adrian Boult and Basil Cameron conducted and George Thalben-Ball played the organ. Then the orchestra was off to give concerts at Forces' camps in conjunction with Walter Legge of ENSA. Sir Adrian conducted those, as he did Wood's old student orchestra in a special Royal Academy concert for the man in whose memory *The Musicians' Diary* was later published. The ashes were buried in the Church of the Holy Sepulchre without Newgate, where Sir Henry's musical life had begun sixty-five years before. A stained-glass window has been followed by others to Walter Carroll, Dame Nellie Melba, John Ireland, and memorials to Coleridge-Taylor, Kathleen Ferrier, Malcolm Sargent and many others, establishing it as 'the musicians' church'. After every Last Night the Promenaders take the wreath of laurel from Sir Henry's bust in the Albert Hall and lay it on his tomb in the church, where it remains until it withers.

When a conductor has ceased to conduct, it is no longer possible to touch the magic; it lives only in the memory of those who experienced it.

IDA HAENDEL: 'As a child I hadn't that much contact with him, but I was aware of his kindness. He was a grandfather to me and I loved playing with him.'

PAUL BEARD: 'He appointed me Leader of the Birmingham Symphony Orchestra in the twenties. I don't think any young player has ever had more reason to be grateful.'

DAME MAGGIE TEYTE: 'One never refused him; after all, he was Sir Henry Wood, and had all the concerts and halls at his disposal.'

CYRIL SMITH AND PHYLLIS SELLICK: 'We owe our careers to Sir Henry.'

SIR ADRIAN BOULT: 'Even his worst performances were jolly good by any standards. He gave you the printed page, in the best sense of that expression.'

DAME ISOBEL BAILLIE: 'His accompaniments were always sympathetic, he knew when you were going to take a breath; it is so rare.'

PAUL BEARD: 'He was always ready with a word of praise and encouragement. There were no inquests; he said we were all entitled to make a mistake, but never the same one twice.'

DAME EVA TURNER: 'He knew his stuff utterly, never wasted time, his scores were already marked, revised, I don't know how he did it all; he was one of those conductors who simply made the rehearsal and the concert a joy for the performers.'

PROMENADER: 'His were good sound performances by which to judge others in our later years; and yes, it is true, we loved him.'

The King is Dead
1945–1949

The death of the Founder caught those concerned with running the Proms on the left foot. It precipitated a crisis which made the earlier financial crises, and even the destruction of Queen's Hall, seem no more than flecks in the path of progress. It was five years before Wood's true successor emerged, and then it was neither the succession envisaged by Sir Henry nor the solution anticipated by the BBC.

In these years Lady Jessie Wood became the custodian of Sir Henry's ideals and ambitions for the Proms. The role she assumed acted as a useful curb against possible excesses, by ensuring that the riderless horse did not gallop away out of control.

The stunning numbness which emanates slowly outwards following the death of a great and active celebrity like Sir Henry Wood was felt first and keenly at the BBC, finding itself owner of a familiar ship which suddenly had no captain to give the orders. Their backing had been financial and administrative; the motive power, inspiration, and main design of the concerts always flowed from Sir Henry himself. Running the Proms with him at the helm was one thing; to be faced with running them without him offered quite a different prospect. How do you replace a man like that in the public consciousness? It had never been seriously considered.

Not that there was any shortage of conductors. A whole new generation of men like John Hollingsworth, Trevor Harvey, and Norman Del Mar were lining up behind the senior established names such as Beecham and Boult. Interestingly enough for a nation which only thirty years before was still insisting that musicians had to be foreign to be any good, there was now not one foreigner in sight. Giovanni Battista Barbirolli, for all the steaming saucepans of spaghetti with which he was apt to sustain guests around midnight after a successful concert, was a Cockney, and quite properly proud of it. His Manchester orchestra, however, was founded in 1857 by Sir Charles Hallé from Hagen, Westphalia, which exactly illustrates the point.

So does Basil Cameron, Wood's chosen associate from 1940. Cameron was not his real name. He was born Basil Hindenberg, of a German father and a Scots mother. As Hindenberg he founded and conducted the Torquay Municipal Orchestra before the Great War, profiting from that British penchant for musicians with foreign names. It became too uncomfortable-sounding a surname to live with in Britain after 1914, when Field Marshal von Hindenburg's armies were killing our soldiers in Flanders, so from then on he adopted his mother's maiden name and became plain Basil Cameron.

There may be those who appoint associates precisely because they show potential for doing the job even better in the future; such selflessness and altruism may be less rare than one suspects. Sir Henry Wood no doubt did express the wish that Basil Cameron might succeed him; but he cannot seriously have regarded him as a rival in his lifetime. His death left Cameron with more in his hand than just a baton; he also held the ace of trumps. He had the longest association with the Proms of any conductor now that Sir Henry was laid to rest. He had been his associate for the past four seasons, and established a *rapport* with the audience. He was in a very strong position indeed – the natural choice to preserve continuity, to ease the Proms through an awkward hiatus. The BBC quickly retained his services.

For the past two seasons Sir Adrian Boult, founder and conductor of the BBC Symphony Orchestra and the first BBC Director of Music, had enjoyed conducting works like Ravel's *Daphnis and Chloë* and Elgar's Second Symphony for Sir Henry, but the Proms were never in his bloodstream as they had been in the Founder's. Boult was always a magisterial interpreter, one of very few conductors whose grasp of Schubert's 'Great' C major Symphony may be compared with Wilhelm Furtwängler's. Whether or not it was fully realised in 1945, Sir Henry's second Proms associate was a man whose musicianship outshone by many candle-power a worthy conductor like Cameron, or even Wood himself. Sir Adrian has always been an obliging man who would never let the side down. There is no question that in 1945 he had no need of the Proms, nor has he really needed them since. They have needed him, and Promenaders have always recognised what they were being offered whenever he appeared before them. He now obliged by helping these concerts at a most difficult moment in their history, regarding his participation more as first aid than as any final cure.

The 1945 Prospectus reinforced optimism in the future with a slogan, 'Promenade Concerts – Possession of the Whole Nation', and an article, 'The Proms Go On' in which C. B. Rees wrote that 'the season begins in the happy consciousness of victory achieved in Europe'. He recalled 1942, when two outside orchestras had been used, drawing a parallel with the engagement of both the BBC Symphony and London Symphony Orchestras this season.

Basil Cameron and Sir Adrian Boult were shown as joint conductors, not alphabetically, doubtless at Boult's insistence. Whereas in the past Wood brought them both in as associates, they now in turn brought in Constant Lambert.

This was an imaginative choice. Lambert, then just forty, was something of an *enfant terrible*; he had been discovered by Diaghilev, and was the first English composer he commissioned to write a ballet. He was the other reciter with Dame Edith Sitwell in the 1923 première of Walton's *Façade*; and he had invoked jazz when composing *The Rio Grande*. His book *Music, Ho!* was required reading on modern composers.

People were pleased to see that the 1945 Prospectus once more showed who was conducting what, information tacitly withheld the previous year because in 1943 Sir Henry Wood had been ill for so long that almost everywhere his name appeared someone else had substituted for him on the actual night. Decisions such as whether to print conductors' names against the works allotted to them were not taken lightly at the BBC. It was in its nature to think carefully and to plan far ahead. The quality of those it consulted about the Proms was a further guarantee. There were the conductors involved. There was Lady Jessie Wood. There was also a succession of BBC Music Directors of impeccable lineage, Victor Hely-Hutchinson and Herbert Murrill, composers whose music had been performed at the Proms, followed by Sir Steuart Wilson, who had actually sung at them under Wood. Additionally there was the steadying hand of Julian Herbage planning the programmes. A musicologist of conservative tastes, he was probably best known to music-lovers as co-editor of BBC Radio's *Music Magazine* with his wife Anna Instone, who had built up the BBC's gigantic record collection.

A three minutes' silence was observed on the First Night of 1945 in tribute to Sir Henry Wood. 'It was a nice idea', said one Promenader, 'to put his bronze bust salvaged from Queen's Hall on a pedestal below the rostrum.' There were equally visible signs of a determined effort to return his concerts to their pre-war glory. Elisabeth Schumann (now an American citizen) was invited back immediately the German surrender made it possible. During the war years she had become a little elderly woman with white hair, and was quite obviously apprehensive about her reception here. There was a queue a mile long for her concert; some of the hundreds who failed to get in surrounded a car with a wireless set outside and heard her on that. Those inside stood to cheer her: within living memory there had not been a greater show of enthusiasm for any artist. Tears of joy and gratitude streamed down her face, and down the faces of many in the audience too.

There were other reminders of the past six years, Martinu's deeply-felt threnody *Memorial to Lidice*; William Schuman's setting of Walt Whitman's

---

12. Basil Cameron *(Godfrey MacDomnic)*

verses about America at war, 'Free Song'; movements from a wartime film score, *The Story of a Flemish Farm*, by Vaughan Williams; and Army Sergeant-Major Alan Rawsthorne acknowledging the applause after his overtures *Cortèges* in 1945 and *Street Corner* the next season.

A crop of international soloists appeared for the first time at the Proms, a bumper crop it seems now – singers Kathleen Ferrier, Owen Brannigan and Peter Pears; the Polish pianist Witold Malcuzynski; violinists Ginette Neveu in 1945, Yehudi Menuhin in 1946 (the Promenaders stamped and applauded right through the interval after he played the Elgar Concerto) and Arthur Grumiaux; the welcome return of Josef Szigeti, spellbinding in Prokofiev, Max Rostal brilliant in Bartok; and William Primrose (who also settled in America) playing Walton's Viola Concerto.

For two seasons Proms Novelties showed signs of the old flair. 'By far the most interesting event', according to William Glock in *The Observer*, was the debut of Schoenberg's Piano Concerto in 1945 with Kyla Greenbaum and Cameron; 'given its traditional climaxes, pregnant rhythms, and more normal curves of melody as against his middle period works, most listeners will have found some stimulation in it'. They also heard for the first time Shostakovich's Fifth Symphony conducted by Lambert, Cameron giving the première of the jollier Ninth at the First Night of 1946, and of Prokofiev's Fifth the same year (the composer had conducted it when Moscow was celebrating victory in the Ukraine); Bloch's *Suite Symphonique*, two marches by Darius Milhaud, Hindemith's *Cupid and Psyche* at last (scheduled for the Jubilee season, but not played) and his *Symphonic Metamorphosis of Themes by Weber*. Out of admiration for Léon Goossens, Richard Strauss lifted his ban on further performances of the Oboe Concerto he wrote in 1945 aged eighty-three. 'Goossens played it with the mastery and delicacy of a Kreisler,' wrote a critic, 'but there's not a note of music in it later than 1912.' Boult conducted the Sea Interludes from Britten's *Peter Grimes* only a few months after the opera's première at Sadler's Wells; Peter Pears sang *Les Illuminations* with Britten, and Michael Tippett was cheered for a performance of his *Concerto for Double String Orchestra*.

When Vaughan Williams directed his *London Symphony* again in 1946 Sir Adrian stood in the Promenade to listen, 'occasionally peeping over the shoulder of a girl in front to look at her pocket score'. The audience saw Vaughan Williams bend down to whisper something in his Leader's ear during the applause for his fifth recall. A word of praise for the performance, perhaps? What that rough-hewn, splendid composer really said to George Stratton was 'Why do they keep on calling me back? Are my fly-buttons undone, or something?'

'Where Does the Uttered Music Go?', Walton's setting of the Poet Laureate's verse, came to the Proms from Sir Henry Wood's memorial service and was sung by the BBC Chorus and Choral Society under Leslie Woodgate. Handel's *Alexander's Feast* (Part 2) was another Proms first; Sir Adrian conducted it and Ireland's popular 'These Things Shall Be' the same evening.

Four Wagner Nights were each devoted to a single *Ring* opera in 1946, as they had been in the early twenties, but this did not revive their former popularity. Sibelius joined Brahms, Beethoven and Vaughan Williams by having *all* his symphonies played – 'for the first time in a Promenade season', Julian Herbage wrote in the 1946 Prospectus, an uncharacteristic slip : Wood did them all in 1937. Each of the solo vocal quartet lines in Beethoven's *Choral Symphony* was allotted to *two* of the BBC Singers, 'a daring experiment amply justified'.

Frustratingly for an ear, nose and throat specialist who was also a music lover, Dr George Cathcart had become too deaf to hear music except on the radio. Two players from the pioneering days of 1895 were also about in 1946. At seventy-eight, Second Clarinet George Anderson was the only member of Wood's first orchestra still playing; trumpeter John Solomon was ninety that August. He was the real subject of a legendary story about an off-stage trumpeter in Beethoven's *Leonora* Overture, which has since been variously ascribed. A policeman in Queen's Hall did once try to stop him playing in the corridor, but 'I didn't take any notice of him'.

The 1945 and 1946 seasons were a brave beginning after wartime austerity; but the momentum was not maintained. The reasons had roots in what went on behind the scenes immediately afterwards. Everyone respected Sir Adrian Boult's wish not to continue beyond 1946; he had not taken a proper holiday since before the war. Even so he had to wait another year. Would Basil Cameron therefore become Wood's successor *faute de mieux*? It was not unremarked that he disliked sharing a concert with someone like Constant Lambert, nor that he would have preferred the London Philharmonic Orchestra as in the past. He was always complaining to the management about something; for a while his chances looked a bit shaky.

There were other considerations. People were being turned away night after night. Could the season be extended to nine or even ten weeks? Would another short season of Winter Proms be successful?* Ought the concerts to begin half an hour later at 7.30 p.m? Was this the moment to resume the pre-war level of broadcasting, or should it wait until the Third Programme came on the air? Would a third orchestra be an advantage, and if so, which? Should there be *three* principal conductors and one associate? What about Dr Sargent?

Lady Jessie Wood, determined to preserve what she conceived as her late consort's ideals, thought outside orchestras should not be used at all. Sir

---

* Several experiments with similar concerts in January have had no real influence on the development of the Proms. They took place in an atmosphere of gumboots, overcoats and draughts, and consisted mainly of the standard repertory, though the BBC did commission three works in 1949 to celebrate the birth of H.R.H. Prince Charles (*Festal March*, Gordon Jacob; *Dances*, Herbert Howells; *Birthday Suite*, Michael Tippett). Spike Hughes wrote in the *Daily Mail*: 'Winter Proms have been a complete flop'. They do not form part of this book.

Henry had engaged the London Symphony and London Philharmonic orchestras in 1942–3 only as an expedient, she said; he really preferred one orchestra under one conductor, playing better and better as the season progressed.*

The London Philharmonic had dropped out after 1944 over a question of fees. Now they were reluctant to come back because of the BBC's wish that any Proms conductor should work with any of the orchestras engaged. The LPO was always quite happy to play for Cameron; but it was an open secret that they were less than keen to work with Dr Malcolm Sargent, by that time reliably rumoured to be in the 1947 season.

Sir Adrian Boult thought concerts might with advantage be shortened, but Lady Jessie Wood was against that. What she called Sir Henry's 'Mission' (a concept popularised by Carlyle) would be defeated by shorter programmes. That 'Mission', as she never ceased to point out, had been to give the public what it wanted to hear, to slip in new works Sir Henry believed they might come to enjoy, and to present new, promising young performers.

The London Passenger Transport Board's consent to a 7.30 p.m. start was finally obtained; after all it was they who had to provide buses for the crowds. When the 1947 Prospectus appeared it showed three main conductors, Basil Cameron, Sir Adrian Boult, Dr Malcolm Sargent, and three orchestras, the BBC Symphony, London Symphony, and London Philharmonic. Constant Lambert had left to compose, and to conduct the Sadler's Wells Ballet; the new associate was Stanford Robinson of the BBC.

'It is at least tempting to describe this season as a Festival,' wrote Julian Herbage in a foreword. The Third Programme made it possible to hear every concert on the radio; nevertheless 10,000 people applied for a pair of seats each, so a Ballot was instituted for the First and Last Nights. Dr Sargent opened with Smetana's *Bartered Bride* overture, later conducting Tchaikovsky Nights, a Delius Prom, the Plague Choruses from Handel's *Israel in Egypt*, and Britten's *Young Person's Guide*, which he had originally done for an educational film, then taken all over the world with enormous success.

Among the novelties was Stravinsky's *Rite of Spring*, negotiated by Basil Cameron 'successfully, if with something less than complete abandon'. Susi Jeans played a Haydn organ concerto reconstructed from parts she found in her native Vienna (she married astronomer Sir James Jeans in 1935). There were new works by Elisabeth Lutyens, Rubbra, Rawsthorne; but not even Sargent's advocacy could redeem Starakadomsky's *Concerto for Orchestra*, 'pretentious futility' from one of Miaskovsky's students, highly regarded among the younger Russians. Sargent introduced his own arrangement of the *Nocturne* from Borodin's Second String Quartet (little more than doublings and an added double-bass); the following season he orchestrated the *Four*

---

*The reverse was the case, which is why Sir William Glock later brought in as many as twenty orchestras in a season. They came fresh and better rehearsed.

Serious Songs of Brahms for Kathleen Ferrier. Did he already see himself in Wood's shoes?

Promenaders started to queue twenty hours before the Last Night, at which a strict pecking order was observed. Sir Adrian opened it; Stanford Robinson came into the first half, Sargent into the second; Basil Cameron conducted the final works. BBC television cameras were present; for the first time those with sets saw most of the first half in their homes. When the 1947 season came to be evaluated, one thing was abundantly clear; Sir Malcolm Sargent was the man of the hour. (He had been knighted in the King's Birthday Honours List.) Sir Adrian Boult saw in him a real Proms man, able to switch from one artistic world to another, night after night, a man of ideal characteristics for these concerts. He was all in favour of retaining him for half the 1948 season. This was typical of Boult, generous and unselfish, a big man in every sense. There was perhaps just a whisker of personal relief in it also. His opinions were widely shared.

Naturally Sir Malcolm realised that he had been a success; and as naturally he wanted to know how things stood for 1948. His increasing fame, not to mention his knighthood, was bringing invitations from abroad. He had offers of engagements from Australia and America; he wished to know how to reply. Nothing is ever quite that simple. There were more problems to be solved before a definite answer could be given. Sargent was wanted for the Proms, that was quite clear. Sir John Barbirolli was also being approached. So was Sir Thomas Beecham, though with little hope that such a consummation would ever be achieved. A love-hate relationship existed between him and the BBC, with little of the love shown on his side, possibly because his prediction that broadcasting would kill public concerts had been proved wrong, or that being himself a British institution he did not care to admit the existence of another. A strong lobby favoured having only two principal conductors rather than three. If Barbirolli or Beecham accepted, what would happen to Basil Cameron? Neither did in fact accept, so the Proms settled down for the next sixteen years with Sir Malcolm Sargent and Basil Cameron in charge.

Through 1948 the Promenaders looked with increasing rapture towards the new man on the rostrum, and he looked back at them with irresistible confidence. Nothing that year – not the acoustic experiments with a new aluminium canopy or rearranged orchestra seating to combat the Albert Hall echo, not the novelties by Kabalevsky, Auric, Martinu and others, nor even the return of white-haired Zoltan Kodaly to conduct *Hary Janos* – could compare with the dazzling impact of Sir Malcolm Sargent. He had easy authority. There was a clash with the orchestra over a correct speed for *On Hearing the First Cuckoo*. Sargent won that battle of wills. Beethoven's *Choral Symphony* was halted part-way into the slow movement when a flash-bulb went off behind the violins. Sargent sent the photographer packing: 'I can't concentrate with you fiddling about like that; will you please go'. He made a speech on the Last Night, thanking everyone, and announcing Winter Proms in January. It was not what he said, but his sheer personality that unleashed an almost hysterical outburst from the packed crowd.

Not everyone approved of the way things were going. Lady Jessie Wood thought the atmosphere of the place contributed to an audience coming more for a good time than for self-improvement. It is always tempting to think of the bull-ring and the circus in the Royal Albert Hall. She also had in mind the more sober hall she hoped would be built in Sir Henry's memory. Some of the audience, who had not just come for a good time, disliked the others making themselves heard between items. 'Hooliganism was rather too evident' reported *The Times*; 'high-spirited gratitude must not be confused with sheer bad manners.'

There was an inquest. Basil Cameron thought it might help to omit the repeat of the Hornpipe. Stanford Robinson would have been happy to let the *Sea-Songs* be thrown overboard altogether. Those guiding the Proms forward were in a dilemma. There was some feeling that the Hornpipe and all that were human touches worth preserving; but there was no doubt at all that audience behaviour had been getting out of hand, especially on the Last Night. They decided to ask Sir Adrian Boult to conduct it next year.

He returned in 1949 well refreshed, even after a punishing schedule of concerts abroad; and there was a tremendous welcome for Sir Malcolm Sargent. Vaughan Williams wrote in the Prospectus: 'It takes 1,000 bad composers to make one good one; Prommers have to endure 1,000 failures to be sure not to miss the 1,001st, the man who has the heart of the matter in him'. The season's Novelties did rather better than that; Bloch conducted his *Concerto Symphonique* for Piano and Orchestra, there were the Strauss *Duet Concertino* for Clarinet and Bassoon, Honegger's *Liturgical Symphony*, and the Shostakovich Concerto for Piano and Trumpet played by Noel Mewton-Wood and Eric Bravington, plus a number of British works. Max Rostal played the Alan Bush Violin Concerto, in which the programme annotator detected a struggle between the individual (violin) and world society (orchestra). Lennox Berkeley wrote *Colonus' Praise*, a setting of Sophocles's eulogy of his birthplace, for the twenty-first anniversary of the BBC Choral Society. H.R.H. The Duchess of Kent was in the Royal Box on 18 August, and in Sargent's box Margaretta Scott and Guilhermina Suggia who had come to hear Pierre Fournier play Elgar's Cello Concerto. Sir Adrian conducted a concert for John Ireland's seventieth birthday in which Eileen Joyce played the Piano Concerto, and Ireland took a bow from the platform, as he had done many times before at these concerts.

Sir Malcolm Sargent made his last appearance this year a fortnight before the season ended; but through him the Promenaders had already found their identity. Not all Sir Adrian Boult's soldierly bearing and dignity could prevent them indulging in their new-found freedom. The noise which assaulted him from the vast well of the Albert Hall he did not enjoy. He endured ordeal by fire trying to maintain some order on the Last Night; but it was no more than an ineffective rearguard action, a parting shot aimed at the unruly Promenaders. They had discovered this could be their own show. Much as they liked Boult, Sargent was the man to lead their dance. From 1950 onwards they would have their own way on the Last Night, especially in front of the television cameras. In Sir Malcolm Sargent both the Promenaders and the planners knew in their hearts exactly the right conductor had been found to take the Proms confidently forward into the future. He was a man who walked with kings.

Sargent:
The Golden Years
1950–1959

Promenade Concerts entered the second half of this century with quite the nastiest Prospectus ever designed for the series. A single folded sheet the size of a desk top, it had to be fully opened out before any programme could be read.* There was no index of works, it was universally disliked, and the experiment was not repeated. Other changes in 1950 were to last much longer.

After a second conductor had been introduced in 1940 the opening concert of each new season was always shared. The 1948 and 1949 First Nights were jointly conducted by Cameron and Sargent. Sir Malcolm approached the 1950 season as Chief Conductor of the BBC Symphony Orchestra (Boult left at sixty, the BBC retirement age) and under contract for the Proms. For the next seventeen years he alone conducted First Nights, only illness preventing an unbroken run of eighteen years. Basil Cameron never appeared at them again. Sargent also opened every Last Night and conducted the whole of the second half; Cameron was given a couple of works before the interval. From 1965 Sargent conducted the First and the Last Nights himself. All this provided a splendid send-off and climax, both for Sir Malcolm and for the audience, welcoming him back with great enthusiasm each season. His hope to see them all again next year was addressed to scenes of wild carnival revelry on the Last Night; people had immensely enjoyed themselves during the Proms. Members of that audience overlapped each other. Some for whom no place would ever be quite like Queen's Hall rubbed shoulders with others

---

* A format originally devised in a smaller size for Winter Proms.

who identified Promenade Concerts with the Royal Albert Hall. For one part of the audience there could never be another Henry Wood; to another part Sir Malcolm Sargent was the embodiment of all the excitement and uplift they derived from these concerts.

Two dialogues continued throughout the next decade on subjects of increasing concern. One was between critics and Proms planners over lack of enterprise in the repertoire. The other was about audience behaviour, particularly on the Last Night. Press and public alike deplored falling standards. Sir Malcolm defended 'my beloved Promenaders'. ('Why *his?*' queried Eric Blom.) The first malaise would in time respond to treatment. The second appears to be incurable.

Critics fired the first broadside after the 1950 season. 'There has been an undercurrent of dissatisfaction and boredom with the programmes this year. An unenterprising series, with no new works. The BBC must take the blame for falling short of the standards Sir Henry Wood established. A feeble, hackneyed and flatulent eight weeks of music. Out of 240 works the only novelty was the Viola Concerto by Elisabeth Lutyens.' (She called it a disgraceful state of affairs herself.) Herbert Murrill of the BBC replied in 1951 that 'bearing in mind last season, there is an average of one new work per concert' (meaning 'new to the Proms', not premières); and he wrote in the 1952 Prospectus: 'In Henry Wood's day the Proms gave premières where few others did. Now many do, including the BBC, whose Proms' aim is still to bring as much fine music as possible to as large an audience as can be reached. We have considered as "Novelties" any works not previously performed at the Proms.' The critics regarded this as a very weak evasion of the real issue.

R. J. F. Howgill succeeded Murrill as the BBC's Controller, Music, in 1953: 'There are few actual firsts; second and third performances are the most important to a composer. The three premières this season are British, as befits Coronation year. We are consolidating the Proms into what Sir Henry Wood intended.' Sir Malcolm Sargent felt that 'good new works' ought to be kept for BBC Symphony Concerts in the Royal Festival Hall, the 'doubtful ones' for studio broadcasts. 'Many new works are not likely to survive in the repertoire, therefore new music is hardly worth playing at all.' Ralph Vaughan Williams and Peter Racine Fricker tartly replied, 'He must have a very low opinion of the Promenaders. The pity is that Sargent conducts new music very well; it needs only a lead from someone of his calibre.'

Critics returned to the fray in 1955: 'There were hopes that the last two years might have seen the BBC lifting the Proms out of the Slough of Despond into which they have fallen since the war.' To which Julian Herbage, who scrupulously planned the Proms for over thirty seasons, always keeping faith with music-lovers who knew what they liked, made answer in 1956: 'There is no doubt that this vast audience is attracted mainly by the standard fare. There are works this year which show what is going on abroad.'

This will repay closer scrutiny. 'What is going on abroad' was represented by Roussel (who died in 1937) Kodaly (then seventy-four, by his *Peacock Variations*), Frank Martin (sixty-six, Swiss), Prokofiev (sixty-five), Milhaud (sixty-four), Harald Saeverud (fifty-nine, Norwegian), Aaron Copland (fifty-six), Shostakovich (fifty), and Samuel Barber (forty-six). In 1956 Olivier Messiaen was forty-eight; not a note of his music had ever been played at the Proms. Pierre Boulez was thirty-one, Hans Werner Henze thirty, and Karlheinz Stockhausen twenty-eight. Promenade audiences knew nothing of their work.

C. B. Rees of the BBC wrote in the 1957 Prospectus: 'With no Diamond Jubilee [which was in 1954], programmes naturally follow a more traditional pattern' – though there was a creditable performance of Henze's *Ode to the West Wind* by cellist Christopher Bunting, conducted by John Hollingsworth, 'Webern made easy' as one critic commented. Someone shouted 'Rubbish!' which caused *The Times* to ask 'What if it had been a piece by Boulez or Stockhausen?' This did not pacify the critics. 'Does the BBC really think Arnell or Martinu likely to arouse interest in modern music in an audience come to hear Brahms or Tchaikovsky?' Again in 1958: 'Unfortunately the selection of twentieth-century music remains for the most part as limp and lopsided as ever, compared to Liverpool's *Musica Viva* concerts ' – a concept borrowed from the Munich series of that name directed by Karl Hartmann, who at fifty-three was also still unheard of in the Proms.

Maurice Johnstone (BBC Head of Music Programmes) regretted 'an inescapable necessity to leave things out; there is far too much, just as there are too many plays and actors for one Shakespeare season at Stratford-upon-Avon'. Even in 1959 when the Proms ran four 'Masters of the Twentieth Century' concerts the critics still complained that 'they do not represent the finest of today's music'.

Sir Malcolm Sargent had the final word: 'Tell those critics who say the Proms are becoming a bore, that they are suffering from musical indigestion. Our bookings are bigger this season than last. Music they call "hackneyed" is good music; it has stood the test of time.' In one Last Night speech he even had this to say to contemporary composers: 'If music be the Food of Love, play on – if not, shut up!'

The other dialogue concerned the deteriorating behaviour of Promenaders. There is always a temptation to hold Sir Malcolm responsible but he was hardly to blame for having been born with star quality. 'These things just did not happen in Queen's Hall', as someone observed; but who would mind a very pretty girl waving a scarlet umbrella being hoisted on to a young man's shoulder in the Arena, the better to be seen? That was in 1947, when the real culprit first appeared at the Royal Albert Hall. Those in the Arena had instantly realised that television cameras would swing towards such a pretty sight; that it was part of their function to show what went on in the hall, especially between items.

Season after season the range of paraphernalia held aloft for the television cameras steadily increased. There were coloured streamers, paper darts, balloons, Union Jacks, comic hats, umbrellas, the skull and crossbones; even items for sound as well as vision – bells, whistles, rattles, alarm clocks, toy trumpets, and motor horns. In 1952 a firework smuggled in to add pyrotechnic effects to Tchaikovsky's Overture *1812* unfortunately exploded prematurely while the imperturbable Amy Shuard was singing Tatiana's Letter Song. Three years later there were also streamers on the First Night, which was televised from 1954; Sargent and Moiseiwitsch both pulled some out of the piano. Bangs were not funny on the Last Night of 1955, when detectives were mingling with the audience because of anonymous threats to the life of Gina Bachauer. Sargent had to reassure viewers and listeners that the loud reports they could hear were only fireworks.

Sargent was criticised by the Press, as the 'real pal of this audience', for condoning their behaviour; but it was R. J. F. Howgill who thought the BBC ought not to begrudge young people their end-of-term relaxation; and *The Times* which pointed out that 'this is the same audience which stood for an hour and a half in absolute silence listening to *Gerontius*'. Sargent may secretly have enjoyed his reception being compared to Frank Sinatra's at the London Palladium, and the Last Night to a football match – 'If people can get as enthusiastic about music as about football – good!' – but he drew the line at pennies being thrown and toilet rolls unfurled. Twice he walked on to the platform half-an-hour before the Last Night started; in 1952 to point out the danger to orchestral players of throwing coins at them; and in 1955 to ask Promenaders not to hurl 'streamers of excessive width'.* He may have felt like the Sorcerer's Apprentice vainly trying to stem the rising flood, or he may have had his tongue in his cheek; but, as he quite accurately claimed, whenever he raised his baton you could hear a pin drop.

Those planning the Proms made Sir Henry Wood's *Fantasia on British Sea-Songs* the scapegoat for the Last Night turning into a jamboree, and reasons were soon conjured up for abandoning it. By now, Sir Henry would probably have thought up something else. There was no place for 'selections' in these programmes. What had been fine for the centenary of Trafalgar was no longer appropriate. Sir Malcolm was ready with an alternative, the vocal arrangement of Arne's 'Rule, Britannia' he had made to inaugurate the Royal Festival Hall in 1951; and, to avoid ending with this, Parry's splendid 'Jerusalem' as the final item. A press conference to announce these changes was considered: 'Sargent could bring it off without any disturbance if he chose to identify himself with his employers for once'. No one could be quite certain that he would, so the idea was scrapped. The 1953 Prospectus was published, omitting the *Sea-Songs*.

---

* Some years later he warned them again, mutely supported by a police sergeant he took on with him; two for the price of one, as someone remarked.

13. Sir Malcolm Sargent, as Promenaders remember him (*Erich Auerbach*)

That did it. As soon as the season started 'Three Arena Members' distributed the following message:

All regular attenders of the Henry Wood Promenade Concerts are asked to be present at a meeting on the steps of the 'Little Albert' behind the Royal Albert Hall at 5.30 p.m. on Saturday, 22nd August, to discuss the removal of the Sea-Songs from the last night Prom, and determine how we may best bring our dissatisfaction at this move to the notice of the BBC's Programme Planners, the Press, Musicians and people of influence, in particular with the BBC.

Under mounting pressure the planners decided on a compromise. The *Sea-Songs* would be played on the Last Night as an encore, but not broadcast or televised. The same stratagem was resorted to in 1969 when Sir William Glock and Colin Davis tried to remove 'Land of Hope and Glory', though for a more artistic reason, and were met with equally effective protest. After the Last Night in 1953 Sir Malcolm Sargent was thanked by the BBC 'for keeping the audience in a good temper, and for sending them away happy, despite his great worry throughout the season over the omission of the *Sea-Songs*'.

There is more to a decade of Promenade Concerts than such little local difficulties; the fifties were particularly rich in celebrations and anniversaries. There were complaints that the Bach Bicentenary Prom in 1950 was not broadcast. Relays from the Edinburgh Festival and other Third Programme commitments deprived listeners of some other important Proms events, Elgar's Second Symphony, Schubert's Ninth, and so on; but the audience did see Victoria de los Angeles sing Strauss, Mozart, Gounod and de Falla at her debut, and the blind Greek pianist George Théméli play Schumann's Concerto, which he learned from Braille, one hand at a time. (His favourite relaxation was cycling, one hand steering, the other on the shoulder of his brother, pedalling alongside.) Sir Malcolm Sargent, with a white carnation and a black eye (from a car accident), joined Ernest Lush and sixteen BBC Singers in the Brahms *Liebeslieder Waltzes*, playing the four-hand duet on *two* grand pianos. 'Much more comfortable,' said Sargent, sensibly. Another casualty was Harriet Cohen, who had injured her right hand and played the Left-hand Concerto Sir Arnold Bax wrote for her. Marjorie Avis of the BBC Singers deputised for Ena Mitchell in Beethoven's *Choral Symphony* at only four hours' notice.

The 1951 Festival of Britain, with the new Royal Festival Hall, brought the anticipated drop in attendances at the Proms, and also lessened the need for giving any Winter Proms. Sir Malcolm Sargent was taken ill and did not return until 30 August, when he sat to conduct Beethoven. Lord Horder examined him during the interval, just to be on the safe side. John Hollingsworth, who had to sit up all night studying scores, took over most of Sargent's concerts, with Trevor Harvey. Sir Adrian Boult obliged by rehearsing a choral concert, fully knowing that Sir Malcolm might be back to conduct the performance. The one-armed Paul Wittgenstein, brother of philosopher Ludwig, played the Ravel and Britten left-hand concertos, both dedicated to him. Moura Lympany married an American radio executive at 10.15 a.m. on the anniversary of the first Prom, rehearsed Beethoven's Fourth Piano Concerto at noon, performed it at the evening concert, and then went on to her wedding reception. A high spot of the season was Zino Francescatti playing a Paganini violin concerto 'accompanied by an awed and attentive orchestra'.

The truth about rebuilding Queen's Hall was now out. Chappell and Co. had sold their lease to the London County Council, who bought it precisely to ensure that there would be no rival to their Royal Festival Hall. The Jubilee Fund of some £80,000 had lost its original objective. As far as possible, money was returned to contributors; but many could no longer be traced. The Trustees applied to the courts for directions as to the substantial sum still left, to prevent it remaining for ever in Chancery. Many people wonder what became of their 'shilling a brick' and other donations. The Henry Wood Memorial Trust has given grants to the Henry Wood Hostel for Music Students, a Henry Wood Rehearsal Hall for London Orchestras at Southwark (one of his dearest wishes come true), one in Glasgow for the Scottish National, and another in Newcastle for the Northern Sinfonia. The balance has provided a Graduate Conductors' Scholarship at the Royal Academy, and a Royal Society of Musicians' fund for orchestral players, whose well-being was always a priority with Sir Henry.

The St George's Hotel and Henry Wood House (BBC offices) now stand on the original site of Queen's Hall. The hotel's manager, Peter Mereweather (an ex-Promenader), has had the five small and previously anonymous conference rooms named after the conducting knights chiefly associated with the Proms, Sir Henry, Sir Malcolm, and Sir Adrian; one of the most celebrated soloists still living in 1981, Dame Eva Turner; and a man who had his finger in everything musical, the Pied Piper of Mannheim, centenarian Sir Robert Mayer. In 1954 the BBC took over the old Langham Hotel opposite, where Sir Henry Wood had a suite, and used to entertain the whole BBC Symphony Orchestra to dinner during the Proms season.

Before the 1952 season it was decided to hold auditions, which achieved the distinction of turning down the young Australian soprano Joan Sutherland. Quite properly they were abolished in 1954, the year of her triumphant Proms debut in Lisa's Aria from Tchaikovsky's *Queen of Spades*. The 1952 Prospectus listed artists making a debut – Helena Braun, Set Svanholm and Jess Walters, magnificent in Wagner, pianists Gina Bachauer, Edith Vogel and Peter Katin, violinist Manoug Parikian and cellist André Navarra; and the sensational Larry Adler playing the *Romance* Vaughan Williams wrote for him. The composer was present when it was played through at Sir Malcolm's flat near the Albert Hall, and took a bow after the première. The second performance took place immediately; it was the first piece in Proms history to

14. Larry Adler, always generous with gifts of harmonicas, puts Sir Malcolm through his paces (*BBC Copyright Photograph*)

be repeated on the spot by public demand. Larry Adler's artistry was compared to Segovia's; he played at other seasons, giving the premières of Arthur Benjamin's Harmonica Concerto in 1953 and Malcolm Arnold's in 1954, the composer conducting; both were dedicated to him.

All the Vaughan Williams symphonies were given in 1952, his eightieth year (he conducted the Fifth himself); but a projected Stravinsky Sixtieth Birthday Concert was faint-heartedly abandoned. Basil Cameron had done the *Symphony of Psalms* with the London Philharmonic Choir in March, which was brought into the Proms instead, a forerunner of the 'repeats' policy which so enriched these concerts from the 1960s onwards. With Bartok's *Concerto for*

Orchestra in the same concert, it just about emptied the Albert Hall. Jacques Ibert acknowledged the applause for a ballet suite, *Diane de Poitiers*, which he wrote for Ida Rubinstein, and Malcolm Arnold 'blew the cobwebs off the Proms' with his *English Dances*.

Sir Malcolm rotated the BBC string players to give all a chance to play in the front desks; his Mozart was criticised by *The Times*, and there was controversy over his large-scale Bach; BBC planners felt recent more authentic performances had converted the Bach-Handel audiences to smaller ensembles. The London Philharmonic Orchestra were discourteous to Basil Cameron at rehearsals. 'It would not be fair to attribute the trouble to Cameron's uninspiring personality,' was one BBC man's opinion, 'for he had none with the London Symphony Orchestra.' *Daily Express* critic Arthur Jacobs pulled a ton of bricks on top of himself by suggesting that standing in the Promenade was an obsolete, empty ritual. It may have been that newspaper's policy to provoke; Noël Goodwin was roundly attacked in 1955 for writing that 'the Proms today have no value – new music is ignored'.

Sir Malcolm conducted the first five concerts in 1953, including the special Coronation Concert on the second night. There were obvious works like 'The King Shall Rejoice' and 'Zadok the Priest', but also the *Te Deum* Walton wrote for the Coronation of Her Majesty Queen Elizabeth II; his Coronation March *Orb and Sceptre* ended the First Night. Sir Malcolm was in his element with the combined BBC Choral Society and Goldsmiths' Choral Union. Sargent having been invited with the BBC Symphony Orchestra to the Edinburgh Festival, Sir John Barbirolli and his Hallé Orchestra played for a week at the Albert Hall, a scoop expected to revitalise the Proms. They gave Vaughan Williams and Elgar-Brahms Nights, Friday's Beethoven Prom; Evelyn Rothwell (Lady Barbirolli) played Castelnuovo-Tedesco's Oboe Concerto, there was *Swan Lake* and *España* and a Viennese Night on the final Saturday. Sir John made a speech, effectively creating his own mini-Last Night in this and subsequent seasons.

The *Liebeslieder Waltzes* were done again, and Sargent played solo piano in Bach's Fifth *Brandenburg Concerto*, with Leader Paul Beard and Principal Flute Douglas Whittaker. Promenaders heard the perfection of Dennis Brain's concerto playing, and the horn solos in Britten's *Serenade* which Peter Pears sang for the first time at the Proms; and there was a huge ovation for the exquisite artistry of Elisabeth Schwarzkopf.

The three real 'firsts' were all concertos, and properly all British in Coronation year – Benjamin's for harmonica, Berkeley's for flute, and Gordon Jacob's for violin. Also new to the Proms were Bax's Sixth Symphony, *Sinfonia Antartica* by Vaughan Williams, Martinu's Second Piano Concerto, and the Rubbra Viola Concerto played by William Primrose. Walford Davies's *Solemn Melody* had to be abandoned when the organ sprang a cipher; the BBC's W. W. Thompson retired after twenty-six years' service to the Proms; and Frederick Thurston was unable to play Mozart's Clarinet Concerto because of a cold following a lung operation. The season showed record attendances overall.

Sir Thomas Beecham's two Proms in the Diamond Jubilee Year were described everywhere in the Press as his debut; yet he had conducted in 1915. Probably no one connected with the Proms in 1954 had been involved in them forty years previously, when 'Mr Thomas Beecham' had given a Saturday evening of Lollipops in wartime, which was not reviewed by the Press. Sir Henry Wood, who wrote his autobiography mainly from memory, had evidently forgotten it. Robert Newman would have engaged Beecham, who alone might have remembered, but perhaps not among his many thousands of important concert and opera engagements since then. In any case Beecham would have been aware of the greater value of a late debut compared to a return after forty years. His two Diamond Jubilee Proms included Sibelius's Fifth, Sixth and Seventh Symphonies, the Violin Concerto with Henry Holst, *En Saga*, Schubert's Fifth and Haydn's Ninety-ninth Symphonies, scenes from Act II of *Irmelin* by Delius, some Wagner, Berlioz and Bizet. He gave Massenet's *Last Sleep of the Virgin* as an exceptional Lollipop encore; and made a speech about how ladies used to swoon into the fountain, a sight foreigners came from all over the world to see, which enchanted the packed Albert Hall.

Sargent had a lot to put up with; Barbirolli also made a speech after the Hallé's Viennese Night, so Sir Malcolm gave a press conference the Sunday after the season ended, as a countermeasure. He conducted the actual Diamond Jubilee Prom on 10 August, which included works special to the Proms at various times in their history. Wagner's *Rienzi* Overture, the first work ever performed; the *Serenade to Music* that Vaughan Williams wrote for Sir Henry's Jubilee, with ten of the original sixteen singers. There could have been eleven, but Eva Turner, who was in the audience, had not known she would be back from America in time. There was Sargent's own *An Impression on a Windy Day* which had precipitated his conducting career; Kodaly's *Hary Janos*; Wood's orchestration of Handel's B flat Organ Concerto played by his friend Marcel Dupré; Mark Hambourg (now seventy-five) with Liszt's *Hungarian Fantasia*; and the 'Bach-Klenovsky' *Toccata and Fugue in D minor*. The concert was televised. Sir Malcolm placed a golden laurel wreath on the Founder's bust, and there were loud cheers for Lady Jessie Wood, who afterwards lit the sixtieth candle on a birthday cake in the Green Room backstage.

It was Sir Malcolm Sargent's own sixtieth birthday just before the 1955 season began. The previous year he had indulged himself and the Promenaders in *Hiawatha's Wedding Feast*, which harked back to pre-war years when the full trilogy used to be enacted by his 'costumed Red Indians of the Royal Choral Society' as a joyful annual event. It stayed in the Proms for several seasons, with Webster Booth a notable Hiawatha. For his own 'diamond jubilee' in 1955 Sargent brought in another great favourite, a first half of excerpts from several of the Savoy operettas of Gilbert and Sullivan. The introduction of choral works and opera forms a substantial part of the advances achieved in this decade. Bach's *Magnificat* and Britten's *Spring Symphony* were done in 1954, also Act II of Wagner's *Tristan und Isolde* in the Hallé's week. (Sir John Barbirolli was ill in 1956; his associate, George Weldon, and Vilem Tausky deputised. In 1957 the Hallé did not appear at all. They returned to the Proms in 1958.) Selections from *A Garland for the Queen* commissioned by the Arts Council from leading composers, a kind of modern 'Triumphs of Oriana', were also performed in 1954 by Cambridge University Madrigal Society under Boris Ord. Madrigals enjoyed a brief revival at the Proms in 1956 when the Harvard Glee Club sang at a poorly attended American Night.

As well as the Gilbert and Sullivan in 1955 Sir Malcolm gave Act II of Walton's *Troilus and Cressida*, whose première he had conducted at Covent Garden the previous year, with the original stars Richard Lewis and Magda Laszlo. There was the first Proms performance of Fauré's *Requiem* given in memory of Lord Horder, physician to His Majesty The King, Sir Henry, and Sir Malcolm; patron of music, and first Vice-President of the Henry Wood Concerts Society. Dvorak's *Te Deum* and Delius's *A Mass of Life* were also in the season, the Delius at considerable cost to the BBC in Performing Rights when six of their regional stations decided to broadcast it as well. Verdi's *Requiem* was first done in 1956, followed by Orff's *Carmina Burana*, another *Belshazzar's Feast* performance, Part I of Haydn's *The Seasons* in 1958, the

15. Ursula and Dr Ralph Vaughan Williams OM, with Sir Malcolm Sargent (*Erich Auerbach*)

whole of his *Creation* in 1959 as well as a complete choral Prom that year including Honegger's *King David*. Act III of Wagner's *Die Meistersinger* packed the Albert Hall in 1956, as did Act III of Puccini's *Tosca* in 1958.

Anniversaries also played their part. The 1956 season provided Mozart's last six symphonies for the bicentenary of his birth, and concertos played by Jack Brymer, André Gertler, Raymond Cohen and Frederick Riddle (the *Sinfonia Concertante*) and a bevy of pianists – Rosalyn Tureck, Myra Hess, Denis Matthews, Clifford Curzon – as well as arias sung by Erna Spoorenberg and Ilse Hollweg. The great Wagner soprano Kirsten Flagstad donned Norwegian national dress in 1957 to sing at the Grieg Fiftieth Anniversary Prom, even in retirement effortlessly dwarfing the Albert Hall with that still magnificent voice. The Third Programme reached its own decade the same year. Real premières were commissioned by the BBC from Henze, Holmboe, Petrassi, Blacher, Panufnik (who conducted his *Rhapsody*; he was the first of the many artists to fly or leap from the East to the West.) John Ireland took a bow after his *London Overture* on the First Night of 1959, but was not well enough to be at his eightieth birthday Prom three weeks later.

Three centenaries occurred in 1958. The First Night honoured Robert Newman (born 1858), who sang the name part at the first performance of Parry's oratorio *Job* in 1892. There were six of his favourite works, including some Wagner and 'Softly Awakes My Heart'; Moiseiwitsch played piano solos in the second half as was the custom when Newman began the Proms in 1895. An exact centenary replica of the first 'Mr Charles Hallé's Grand Orchestral Concert' was given by Barbirolli, who also daringly included the first London performance of Bruckner's Fourth Symphony in the Hallé's week. Puccini's centenary brought Act III of *Tosca*; and there was a memorial concert to Jan Sibelius (who had died the previous September) with his Violin Concerto, First Symphony, and *Luonnotar* sung in Finnish by Liisa Linko. The eighty-five-year-old Vaughan Williams was at that concert; another night he hobbled on to the platform with the aid of a stick to acknowledge applause for his Ninth Symphony, the one with saxophones and flügelhorn. Three weeks later he was dead. By chance the *Tallis Fantasia* was due to be played on the day of its composer's funeral; Sargent conducted it, and also declared the *Gerontius* performance to be in memory of Vaughan Williams, asking the audience to stand silent afterwards. It was voted the best yet heard, with Richard Lewis at the height of his powers.

Third Programme Tenth Anniversary commissions apart, there was some truth in criticism that Proms Novelties were falling short of the standards set by Sir Henry Wood. To have encountered at the Proms Prokofiev's Seventh, or Shostakovich's Tenth and Eleventh Symphonies, and piano concertos by both for the first time in Britain was certainly exciting; but they were not premières such as Wood untiringly gave season after season. Ludicrous subdivisions were devised to conceal this: First Performance in Britain; First Public Performance; First Public Performance in England; First Performance in London; First Performance at the Proms; and all the rest of it. Even so, 'for one work by Bartok or Berg there were a dozen by Alwyn, Coates, Ibert, Gordon Jacob, Benjamin, Finzi, or Searle'. And what was Franz Reizenstein's Hoffnungesque *Concerto Popolare* doing at a Prom in 1958? (Mis-spelt *Populare*, the kind of trap which led to *serioso* and *pensivo* being engraved on the windows of Liverpool's Philharmonic Hall; both spurious, as Vittorio Gui pointed out. The Italian musical terms are *serio* and *pensoso*.) Four 'Masters of the Twentieth Century' Proms in 1959 included some great works, Debussy's *La Mer*, Berg's Violin Concerto, Stravinsky's *Symphony of Psalms*; but other masters were less effectively represented. The scheme also lumped all the pills together without any jam, a certain recipe for very thin audiences.

From the public's point of view the chief glory of these years may well have been the splendid array of soloists. People could depend on hearing virtually all our leading artists at least once every season; any omission would have been noticed immediately. One new work in 1958 brought four very familiar Proms figures together at the same concert – Sir Eugene Goossens conducting his *Concert Piece*, with sisters Marie, Sidonie and brother Léon forming the *concertante* of two harps and oboe. Proms history personified; Eugene had been a violinist in Sir Henry's orchestra at the first performance of Schoenberg's *Five Orchestral Pieces* in 1912; the revised version was played in this same 1958 season under Basil Cameron, and cheered. It was for Marie, Sidonie and Léon that Sir Henry arranged 'Home, Sweet Home' in his *Sea-Songs*; and Sidonie gave many a harp concerto its première at the Proms, including William Alwyn's on the First Night in 1954.

The Promenade audience has always been generous to newcomers too, and there were plenty of these, in the best traditions of Sir Henry. More than a hundred eager youngsters at one go in the National Youth Orchestra of Great Britain, which first appeared in 1955, Sir Adrian wearing a white tuxedo and seeming to shed twenty years when he conducted them. Allan Schiller played with them in 1957 under Hugo Rignold, and Kathleen Jones in 1959 under Walter Susskind, when they were televised. Both were fourteen; both played Mozart. The same season young Jean Harvey played Bruch's First Violin Concerto before the interval and Litolff's famous *Scherzo* after it, the first soloist to play in concertos for violin and piano at the same Prom. Misfortune preventing two other soloists playing that year, a pair of young men stepped into unexpected debuts, John Ogdon with Liszt's First Concerto, Malcolm Williamson to play his own Piano Concerto without time for a rehearsal. Heather Harper first appeared in 1956, a splendid debut in Haydn; and Julian Bream in his early twenties was playing Rodrigo's *Concierto d'Aranjuez* year after year. For prestige and full audiences, international soloists were invited every season – Sena Jurinac, Kerstin Meyer, Kim Borg among many singers; cellists Edmund Kurtz and Janos Starker; harpist Nicanor Zabaleta; pianists Shura Cherkassky, Andor Foldes, Hans Richter-Haaser; and many others hugely appreciated by the Promenaders.

16. John Ogdon (*Clive Barda*)

It was one of these, American pianist Rosalyn Tureck, who heralded a change in Bach performance at the Proms with her measured, precise, and perhaps controversial interpretation of the D minor Concerto in 1954. Boris Ord also revealed the cleaner, springier textures obtainable from a small choir singing in the *Magnificat*. George Malcolm played Bach's D minor Concerto on a harpsichord in 1955, for the very first time at the Proms (the audience kept very quiet). Next year John Hollingsworth conducted a small ensemble in the Fourth *Brandenburg Concerto*, using two 'Flutes (à Bec)' – recorders played by Carl Dolmetsch and Richard Taylor. The 1957 Bach-Mahler Prom was a flop, raising the question 'Is Bach in the original justified?' The second part of a 1958 Bach Night was given without the orchestra: Leslie Woodgate conducted the unaccompanied Motet 'Jesu, priceless treasure' and George

Thalben-Ball ended with the original organ *Toccata and Fugue in D minor*. A similar second half was given the next year.

Sir Malcolm Sargent retired from the BBC Symphony Orchestra in 1957, being succeeded by Rudolf Schwarz, but retaining the title 'Chief Conductor of the Proms'. The players commissioned a gift of a crystal decanter and seven goblets, each handsomely engraved with one of Holst's *Planets* and an animal, on opposite sides, to represent music and Sargent's Fellowship of the Royal Zoological Society, where sometimes he used to entertain the orchestra.

These were indeed the golden years; and one overriding consideration does much to explain both the poverty of the programmes and the richness of the performances: profit. A conservative repertoire and superlative soloists were a good recipe for full houses. For the first and perhaps the last time in their history the Proms took in more than had to be paid out. The surplus could be as much as the proceeds of four or five packed concerts. Whenever the profit fell, there was consternation. Those involved felt that the Proms could hardly do better than their fifty per cent full houses a season and more than eighty per cent overall attendance; obviously audiences were getting what they wanted. 'Once the programmes become stereotyped into an annual repetition of accepted works their days are numbered,' *The Times* had written in 1924. There were others about in 1959 who felt that the old spirit of adventure had been traded for security.

Checkmate: Sir William Glock
1960–1967

A nother twelve minutes and Sir William Glock might never have had
anything to do with the Promenade Concerts. He was short-listed for
Principal of the Guildhall School of Music in 1958, and had been
thinking along educational lines for some months. His were the right
qualifications: a Cambridge degree, three years with Artur Schnabel in
Berlin, music critic of *The Observer*, founder of Dartington Summer School of
Music and editor of its associated magazine *The Score*. He had played Mozart
piano concertos in London before the war, and in the première of Lennox
Berkeley's two-piano *Introduction and Allegro* with the composer at a Prom in
1940 under Sir Henry Wood. He and his wife directed the superb International Music Association club in South Audley Street, London, the like of
which musicians may never see again.

Glock had also nailed his colours to the mast. When the editor of *The
Observer* demanded no further articles from him about that noisy composer
Bartok, Glock wrote another the following week and was promptly sacked. He
told the BBC Music Advisory Panel that only two minutes of Webern had
been broadcast in a year. When the Chairman thought that was too damned
much, Glock never turned up again. The IMA Club's governing body
included the BBC's Controller, Music, R. J. F. Howgill, a chance which had
enabled Glock to arrange a BBC performance of *Le Marteau Sans Maître* by
Boulez in 1957, with the composer conducting. It was to Howgill that Glock
turned for one of eight references needed by the Guildhall School.

Howgill, who was about to retire, had a better idea. Why not succeed him
as the BBC's music chief? Glock was lukewarm, but at the urging of Michael

Tippett allowed his name to go forward. The suggestion took a long time to work its way upwards for top BBC approval. The night before Glock's final interview at Guildhall the BBC's Chairman of Governors had still not been contacted. Confirmation came the next morning, just twelve minutes before Glock should have left for that interview.

William Glock had been broadcasting for the Third Programme and the BBC Overseas Service's Université des Ondes since 1940. His talks ranged from Tallis, Wilbye, Byrd and Purcell, through Mozart to the modern world of Bartok, Berg, Stravinsky, Dallapiccola and Schoenberg. He had played Mozart and Schubert duets on the radio with Peter Stadlen; and he proposed to the Third Programme a three-week tour of Europe during which he would look for talent, define standards of performance, and find out what composers

17. Sir William Glock at Dartington Hall, with Peter Maxwell Davies, who succeeded him at the Summer School of Music (*Camera Press*)

were up to. Later he visited Canada, electronic studios in Paris, Cologne and Baden-Baden, and the Venice Biennale. He broadcast further talks, on Bartok's *Mikrokosmos*, music criticism, and the piano trio; and played Frank Martin's *Petite Symphonie Concertante* with the Boyd Neel Orchestra conducted by Georges Enesco.

To his Summer School, first at Bryanston and later at Dartington Hall in South Devon, came the greatest teachers and performers, among them Nadia Boulanger, Hindemith, Blacher, the Amadeus Quartet, Copland, Enesco, Stravinsky, Britten, Maderna, Schnabel, Berio, and Peter Maxwell Davies, who now carries on the traditions as Glock's successor. At the IMA Club in London a glittering parade of musicians from this country and abroad was always to be found, enjoying excellent meals and the society of colleagues. Pierre Boulez used to compose in an upstairs room when in London with Jean-Louis Barrault's theatre company.

The Summer School was a new musical world in miniature; Glock ran it with quiet flair. He proved that old and new could be complementary; that a Romantic work might need to be followed by some Telemann or Bach to 'clear the air' before a piece of astringent Stravinsky. He prepared more thoughtful meals than the standard soup, meat and pudding of overture, concerto and symphony. He challenged listeners to refine their palates, placed Indian ragas before them, brought medieval music to life out of the text books and into the concert room. He balanced the famous names who came to Dartington by commissioning unknown composers, a vote of confidence in younger men writing in the wilderness which Peter Maxwell Davies acknowledged twenty years later by dedicating his Symphony to him. The Summer School was like a cell needing only the right conditions to multiply. With Glock in control of the BBC's Music Division, the right conditions existed.

Peter Heyworth, Glock's successor on *The Observer*, called the London music scene in 1959 'arrantly provincial'. Britain's musical establishment held frostily aloof from all that foreign rubbish. 'Stravinsky's *Agon* cannot be danced to,' declared *The Times*, 'and dancing is about all his *Symphony in Three Movements* is fit for.' If that was the official view of Stravinsky, what hope for Berg or Webern, to say nothing of a rising generation of composers like Stockhausen and Berio?

With his BBC Thursday Invitation Concerts Glock lit a beacon; revolutionary in concept then, they have had a lasting influence on programme building. The lion lay down with the lamb. *Le Marteau Sans Maître* of Boulez was framed by Mozart Quintets at the opening concert in a series where Beethoven's Septet might precede Schoenberg's *Serenade*, or *Pierrot Lunaire* be followed with Bach's *Goldberg Variations*. Such illumination revealed taste and judgment spanning centuries. Glock had heard the very old and the very new; the flair with which he deployed them brought refreshment to lively and open minds. It also infuriated reactionaries, who dubbed them the 'Thursday Irritation Concerts'.

Was the Festival Hall fully booked ahead? Glock put on Midnight Matinées after the symphony concert audience had gone home. When Stravinsky conducted his *Oedipus Rex* at one of these, with librettist Jean Cocteau as the Speaker, not only was the hall packed, but the work went immediately into the repertory of Sadler's Wells Opera, with spectacular success.

To be convinced of your mission is only a beginning. To carry through your plan takes courage and determination. To succeed takes time. There was a whole year between each of the stages by which William Glock proceeded to inch the Promenade Concerts forward into the real twentieth century and to widen their range by going back beyond Bach, though this did not lessen their impact, nor the reaction they caused. One important principle was to achieve the highest possible standards of performance; and a way to do this was to bring into the Proms works which had already been rehearsed and performed elsewhere, not only the symphonic repertoire but big choral works, perhaps even a complete opera.

John Pritchard was making strides with the Royal Liverpool Philharmonic Orchestra, especially through their *Musica Viva* concerts of contemporary works. Glock invited them to play for a week in his first Proms season of 1960, to include Stravinsky's *Symphony in Three Movements*, Webern's *Six Pieces*, and Schoenberg's *Variations* on separate evenings, amongst the more traditional concertos and symphonies, and to give the first Proms performance of the *Grande Messe des Morts* by Berlioz.

Instinctively realising that the BBC Symphony Orchestra would relish the chance to play under someone as distinguished as Italy's Nino Sanzogno, Glock put on a short festival conducted by him at the Royal Festival Hall in May 1960. The plan was also to bring some of those concerts into the Promenade season a couple of months later. Sir Malcolm Sargent offered to take them over, as the BBC Symphony Orchestra would already have all the works at their fingertips; he was doubtful about having Sanzogno at the Proms. Lady Jessie Wood conveniently remembered a verbal undertaking by the BBC that Henry Wood's Promenade Concerts should never be directed by a foreigner. (Eduard Colonne had conducted them for a week in 1908, but that would long have been forgotten.) Just to make sure, she wrote to the Principal of the Royal Academy of Music, who upheld her view, which in musical terms is like having the Archbishop of Canterbury on your side. On the other hand, Sir Arthur Bliss felt that Lady Jessie Wood had no standing in the matter, and was all in favour of letting Sanzogno conduct at the Proms. This was seen as a vested interest by the Master of the Queen's Musick in obtaining reciprocal invitations from abroad to British conductors. At all events the Promenade audience was denied Sanzogno in 1960; and the question of foreigners conducting at the Proms was shelved for three years.

At a first glance the 1960 Prospectus appeared to offer an almost unruffled season, William Glock's introduction promising to 'represent all that is most vital from the eighteenth century to the present day' and 'to re-interpret the Proms in the spirit of Sir Henry Wood'. In a season where Beethoven Night was still on Fridays (but also once on a Tuesday), where Tchaikovsky, Brahms, Bach and Russian Nights were still reassuringly to be found, and the concerts looked more or less the same as usual, Glock had marshalled his principles with considerable subtlety. *Variations on a Theme of Paganini* were staple First Night fare had they been by Rachmaninov; instead they were by Boris Blacher and Sargent conducted them. Novelties were going to be more up-to-date and not thought of as Novelties but new music. A Beethoven audience returned after the interval to give Roberto Gerhard's Violin Concerto an encouraging reception. Pamela Bowden sang Berg's *Altenberg Songs* on another evening with poise and authority. Charles Ives's *Three Places in New England* had never before been heard in Britain. Schoenberg's six-minute *De Profundis* was sung twice, so that the audience might grasp it better. Alfons and Aloys Kontarsky with Heinz König and Christoph Caskel brought their astounding performance of Bartok's *Sonata for Two Pianos and Percussion* to the Proms straight from the Thursday Invitation Concerts, all four playing from memory. Explanations from the platform prepared the audience for the startling first experience of electronic tape music, Berio's two-track *Perspectives* played through loudspeakers above their heads. They were uncertain how to react to such alien, disembodied sounds. (They should have heard Stockhausen's four-track *Song of Youth*, but there was no suitable machine available to play it.)

There were other works new to the Proms, Beethoven's *Missa Solemnis*, Debussy's *Jeux*, Mozart's Piano Concerto in C, K503, a Vivaldi Flute Concerto, the Berlioz *Requiem*, all pure gain. In future seasons first Proms performances of works from the past would greatly outnumber the new music. Britten and Stravinsky were championed, in step with public acceptance; Peter Pears singing Britten's *Nocturne* and Colin Davis conducting *Oedipus Rex* from Sadler's Wells Opera were tremendous occasions in 1960, when Colin Davis was one of several young conductors Sargent generously welcomed on equal terms. Soon the world's finest artists would regard a Prom appearance as an accolade; already in 1960 regular favourites such as Joan Sutherland, Ida Haendel and Myra Hess were being supported by Elisabeth Söderström, Ingrid Haebler, Henryk Szeryng and many others. For the first time Prom audiences also heard Janet Baker, and the Amadeus Quartet's Norbert Brainin and Peter Schidlof in Mozart's *Sinfonia Concertante*.

William Glock was as determined to change the tastes and habits of audiences as Newman and Wood had been in 1895. There was an initial drop in attendances of about nine per cent, which Glock had expected. There was also an outcry from those who did not see that a performance of electronic music in 1960 was given in the same spirit as Sir Henry Wood offering Schoenberg's *Five Orchestral Pieces* in 1912. Tampering with the successful Proms 'could empty the Royal Albert Hall in a couple of seasons'. Some of

Glock's own music producers held meetings at the hall and sent complaints to BBC Directors about the monstrous policies of this man they had nicknamed 'Hitler'. Even the Albert Hall's general manager wailed doom and wrung his hands, though it had little to do with him.

For William Glock only to have prescribed further doses of Schoenberg or Stockhausen might well have emptied the hall. He had a great deal more flair than that. It seems amazing that after sixty-six years of the Proms one man should suddenly have had so many brilliant inspirations, accumulating year by year like the gifts in a Christmas song, until people wondered what he could possibly think of next, and the concerts became transformed into the biggest music festival in the world.

A Partridge in a Pear Tree

For most Promenaders, going to one of Glyndebourne Festival Opera's exquisite productions in their Sussex house would have been out of the question. Opening the 1961 Proms Prospectus they found to their astonishment that the whole of Birnam Wood was to be transferred root and branch to their own castle in South Kensington. The entire cast of Mozart's *Don Giovanni* had been prevailed on to remain together one more day after the Sussex season ended, to perform at the Albert Hall. Glyndebourne Opera at the Proms – and for only three shillings in the Arena! People talked of little else; and the reality far exceeded their expectations. A platform was built out from the organ loft above the orchestra, to allow a bare minimum of stage action, specially produced for the occasion by General Manager Moran Caplat, who has always done it since. György Melis as Don Giovanni, Richard Lewis as Don Ottavio, and Michael Langdon as the Commendatore wore tails, to distinguish the nobility from the *hoi polloi*, Geraint Evans as Leporello and Leonardo Monreale as Masetto, who wore dinner-jackets. Gerda Scheyrer and Ilva Ligabue wore long gowns as the two ladies; Mirella Freni something more suitable for a peasant girl. Their performance held the audience spellbound. John Pritchard drew ravishing sounds from the Royal Philharmonic Orchestra, and the apt twang of a harpsichord accompanied recitatives. As many people heard *Don Giovanni* in one night at the Albert Hall as would have kept the Box Office busy down in Sussex for the best part of a week. Promenaders laughed in all the right places, too; proof of homework done on the Italian libretto. Now they knew for themselves the perfection of ensemble obtained through the Glyndebourne system of living and working together *en famille* in one of the loveliest places in England.

This season being freed after thirty-two years from the tyranny of the Nine O'Clock News, Beethoven's *Choral Symphony* could regularly be played after the interval, instead of before it; and both halves of all concerts planned with greater freedom. William Glock introduced forty works never before heard at the Proms, from Mendelssohn's *Reformation Symphony* back in time as far as the

18. Sir Clifford Curzon, oblivious of the hubbub all round him, practises during a rehearsal interval (*Godfrey MacDomnic*)

magnificent forty-part Motet 'Spem in alium' by Thomas Tallis, including four Haydn symphonies and the Mozart *Requiem*. Marina de Gabarain and Teresa Berganza both sang de Falla, *El Amor Brujo* and *Seven Popular Spanish Songs* respectively, at their Proms debut. Of seventeen truly modern works, four were new BBC commissions. Of the rest, Tibor Varga played Schoenberg's Violin Concerto to a full house (but not at a repeat in 1962), Colin Davis introduced Stravinsky's *Les Noces*; John Carewe and the New Music Ensemble performed Webern's *Five Orchestral Pieces* twice the same evening, and gave the audience a first taste of Boulez. Sir Arthur Bliss conducted his *Colour Symphony* for his seventieth birthday, and Sir Adrian Boult, absent for three seasons, gave his magisterial reading of Schubert's Ninth Symphony on his return. But the abiding memory of 1961 has to be Glyndebourne Opera, and *Don Giovanni*.

Two Turtle Doves
Glock was successfully restoring the Proms to their former role as pathfinder; he also took account of a sudden surge of interest in Bruckner and Mahler, whose symphonies had started to fill other halls for the first time. Rudolf Schwarz did not conduct a Prom during his five years with the BBC Symphony Orchestra following Sir Malcolm Sargent; under him they played Bruckner's Ninth Symphony at his first Prom appearance in 1962, the year he handed over to Antal Dorati. Three nights later he also gave the *Adagio* from Mahler's unfinished Tenth Symphony with the London Symphony Orchestra, who had earlier in the season played Mahler's Third Symphony under Norman Del Mar. All three works were Proms premières. Symphonies by one or both composers have featured in every season since, sometimes three by each, and fourteen of them new to the Proms.

Many major choral works were introduced, from *Israel in Egypt* to *The Damnation of Faust*. Tchaikovsky's *Manfred Symphony*, and two Weber concertos were new, also the inclusion of Purcell's *Abdelazer* Suite, to show where Britten found the theme of *A Young Person's Guide*, which Sir Malcolm so brilliantly conducted on many First or Last Nights. When Maxwell Davies conducted his *Fantasia on an In Nomine by John Taverner*, one of three BBC Proms commissions, it was preceded by the original played on a tiny chamber organ.

Messiaen's *Oiseaux Exotiques* came into the Proms from Glock's BBC Symphony Concerts at the Royal Festival Hall. Colin Davis conducted a Stravinsky eightieth birthday Prom, and more of his works new to the Proms on other nights. Some people noisily left during Roberto Gerhard's First Symphony, but many more stayed to hear it. Henryk Szeryng was applauded right through one interval for his Beethoven Violin Concerto, as once happened to Menuhin, who nobly deputised for his pupil Alberto Lysy in Mendelssohn's Concerto this season. Glyndebourne Opera returned with Mozart's *Così fan tutte*; and 1962 saw the debut of Stephen Bishop, Peter Glossop, Jacqueline du Pré, Geza Anda, Hermann Prey and Vlado Perlemuter. On the Last Night Paul Beard retired after twenty-six years as Leader of the BBC Symphony Orchestra.

Three French Hens

It was unlikely that the battle over foreign conductors could be fought a second time. Sargent accepted Silvio Varviso conducting Mozart's *The Marriage of Figaro* at the 1963 Proms because he had been doing so at Glyndebourne; but he had heard 'a mischievous rumour' about a work in his own repertoire. It was no rumour. Carlo Maria Giulini brought his exciting interpretation of the Verdi *Requiem* to the Proms for the 150th anniversary of Verdi's birth, with the Philharmonia Chorus and Orchestra. He gave an orchestral concert three nights later. Once Sir Malcolm saw that applause one evening for Giulini did not mean less applause another evening for himself, and that his standing at the Proms was not being undermined, the question of foreigners was finally dropped. Along came Leopold Stokowski with Mahler's *Resurrection Symphony*; then Sir Georg Solti and the full Covent Garden Opera Company in Act III of *Götterdämmerung* for Wagner's 150th anniversary. Part or all of seven operas were given, including *Trial by Jury* on Gilbert and Sullivan Night for the first time.

Benjamin Britten's *War Requiem*, first performed in Coventry Cathedral fourteen months previously, was conducted by Meredith Davies and the composer on 1 August; his *Cantata Misericordium* for the Red Cross centenary in Geneva formed part of his own fiftieth birthday concert, which Britten conducted on 12 September. The audience would not go home until all the lights were put out. The *War Requiem* was repeated next season for the fiftieth anniversary of the First World War, though John Foulds's similarly conceived *World Requiem* had been as often played in the 1920s as Britten's work in the mid-1960s. Luigi Nono conducted his very different anti-war *Songs of Life and Love* (subtitled 'On the Bridge at Hiroshima') in 1963, a visionary work which gripped the audience. Sir Malcolm Sargent procured epic performances of the Fourth and Twelfth Symphonies by Shostakovich, both new to the Proms.

Four Colley Birds

The Amadeus String Quartet in white tuxedos began a Haydn night in 1964 with his 'Emperor', the first string quartet performed at the Proms. There had been other occasional chamber music, like the Beethoven Septet considerably spread over two evenings in 1906. Octets by Mendelssohn and Stravinsky began two other Proms this season, though the sound was not ideal in all parts of the hall. Chamber-sized performances of *Alexander's Feast* and *The Creation* were not yet well attended. After 1961 'composer nights' were no

19. Sidonie Goossens OBE, founder member of the BBC Symphony Orchestra in 1930, still playing with them in 1981 *(Magnus)*

longer named, but Haydn, Sibelius, Walton-Tchaikovsky, Elgar-Holst and others could still be found, even if Beethoven sometimes became a vestigial Friday presence.

A major event was the world première of Deryck Cooke's performing version of Mahler's unfinished Tenth Symphony. His Eighth, 'Symphony of a Thousand' had a tremendous reception also, sung by ten choirs from north and south, eight soloists, and the combined Royal Liverpool and BBC Northern orchestras under Charles Groves. Verdi's *Otello* by Covent Garden celebrated the seventieth anniversary of the Proms on 10 August, and incidentally the Shakespeare quatercentenary. (Victor Gollancz stood with Promenaders in the Arena to hear it.) The Royal Opera did Acts I and III of Wagner's *Die Walküre* in this year of Solti's first full *Ring* cycle. Sargent, who had been conducting Proms in New York before the season began, gave *Belshazzar's Feast*, the *Serenade to Music*, Sibelius's Fifth Symphony, and the Bach-Wood (Klenovsky) *Toccata and Fugue* on the twentieth anniversary of the Founder's death, for which William Alwyn composed and conducted a *Concerto Grosso* in tribute to Sir Henry, commissioned by the BBC. Another evening John Carewe conducted Richard Rodney Bennett's *Aubade* in memory of John Hollingsworth, who had died in December 1963.

Glyndebourne Opera gave a ravishing *Idomeneo* and David Willcocks the first Proms performance of Purcell's *Dido and Aeneas*. Ingeborg Felderer sang Schoenberg's half-hour monodrama *Erwartung*; Rostropovich and Ashkenazy both made stunning debuts; Rudolf Kempe deputised for Pierre Monteux, who had died aged eighty-nine before he could conduct a Prom; Boult stood in for Giulini, who was indisposed. The Prommers sang 'Happy Birthday' to Basil Cameron before he conducted his eightieth birthday concert on 18 August; his grip on the Proms had been dwindling since 1961; this proved to be his last season. From now on Sargent also conducted the whole of the Last Night. More Proms were televised, and seen in Europe, contributing to a total audience William Glock estimated at around fifty million.

Five Gold Rings

Sir Malcolm Sargent conducted his choice of works for a seventieth birthday concert (the actual day was 29 April 1965). Walton was there to hear his *Coronation Te Deum* and Holst's *Hymn of Jesus* sung by four choirs. Elgar's Cello Concerto was played by Jacqueline du Pré; his Second Symphony ended the celebration. Promenaders presented a silver coffee pot and a bouquet to Sir Malcolm. Even with twenty-nine conductors in one season (the Prospectus gave them a separate index section for the first time) Sargent still conducted at twenty-three of the forty-nine concerts. There were four notable newcomers. Antal Dorati had taken the BBC Symphony Orchestra to America for the first time in May, with Pierre Boulez; each included works from that tour in their first Proms. Gennadi Rozhdestvensky of Moscow's Bolshoi Theatre conducted Shostakovich's Eighth Symphony with the London Symphony

20. Gillian Weir (*Erich Auerbach*)

Orchestra. James Loughran brought the BBC Scottish Orchestra and a Proms commission, Elizabeth Maconchy's *Variazioni Concertanti*, with four principal wind players of the BBC Symphony Orchestra as soloists. Sir John Barbirolli, back with the Hallé, received the American Mahler Medal from Deryck Cooke (a previous recipient) after conducting the Sixth Symphony. Sir John's own Proms connection went back fifty years; he was a cellist in Sir Henry Wood's orchestra during the 1915 season.

The Royal Albert Hall organ was specially featured at five concerts. Gillian

Weir played Poulenc's splendid Concerto with Sir Malcolm on the First
Night. Three Proms ended with Bach organ works, and one with part of
Messiaen's *La Nativité du Seigneur*.

'More or less by chance', as William Glock wrote, the season included an
opera from each century, from Purcell's *The Indian Queen* to Schoenberg's
Moses and Aaron, the latter not to a full house, perhaps because it lacked that
Dance round the Golden Calf which had caused such a sensation at Covent
Garden.

Six Geese A-Laying

'The development of the Proms from the complacent, tradition-bound
institution they had dwindled into in the late 1950s to the wonderfully
enterprising, flexible and comprehensive music festival we now delight in has
taken another progressive yet logical step,' as *The Financial Times* put it – four
Prom concerts in 1966 by the Moscow Radio Orchestra (en route for the
Edinburgh Festival) under Gennadi Rozhdestvensky, with four young
Russian soloists and Janet Baker singing *Kindertotenlieder*. The BBC gave a big
party for the first foreign orchestra at the Proms. These very welcome visitors
made a huge impact on the audience. Their final concert was on a Sunday,
the first to be planned into a season; the one in 1943 had been by *force majeure*.

Glock's challenges were being met; his revitalised Promenade Concerts
were quoted with pride; audiences were flocking to where everything vital was
happening. With four operas, the Proms première of Delius's *A Mass of Life*,
the Amsterdam Concertgebouw, and Jascha Horenstein's magnificent
Mahler Ninth, a festival indeed! It was where many would hear *Ecuatorial* and
Déserts by Varèse, and Elliott Carter's *Variations* for the first time; but also
Cavalli's *Messa concertata* and Magnificats by Schütz. They would see ninety-
year-old Havergal Brian looking slightly bewildered by the applause for his
Twelfth Symphony, and the eighty-four-year-old titan Leopold Stokowski
bringing Tchaikovsky's Fifth to its exciting conclusion. A *Guardian* critic
trotted out the old legend of Londoner 'Leonard Stokes' changing his name in
America, a lie never properly refuted. The birth certificate shows Leopold
Anthony born in Marylebone on 18 April 1882, son of Kopernik Joseph
Boleslaw Stokowski, a Polish emigré cabinet-maker and his wife, formerly
Annie Marion Moore.

Sir Malcolm Sargent discovered that the First Night was his 500th Prom,
making great play of this with the Press.* Poor Sir Malcolm; for over fifteen
years Beethoven's *Choral Symphony* brought fresh sniping from critics who
found his reading 'dim, pedestrian, impersonal, prosaic; the three orchestral
movements unmemorable. He seems to encounter far fewer obstacles than
Beethoven did when he wrote it.' Brilliant handling of massed choirs they

---

*It was his 473rd, but who would have checked? Perhaps Proms in New York and elsewhere
were included.

allowed him, but not profundity. 'Inside the gleaming international maestro there is an Edwardian organist trying to get out – with great effect when the full charm and technique are beamed on choirs. Where other conductors mature, he has preserved his dash.' (Players nicknamed him 'Flash Harry'.)

The full charm is still remembered by huge choirs, who always gave him more than their best. Sargent felt completely at ease with them; but not always with professionals. Over-compensating for this sometimes led to orchestral musicians and soloists finding him arrogant and patronising. Relations were also handicapped because players who had once contributed five shillings a week to support Sargent in a Swiss sanatorium deeply resented it when later he spiked the idea of an orchestral pensions scheme (though there was talk of cheques quietly sent to players in difficulties). Even Henry Wood was abrupt and disliked in his early days as an opera conductor, but he mellowed. Sargent would argue with Paul Beard about bowing the *Till Eulenspiegel* violin solos, or spend an interval between rehearsal and broadcast criticising Cyril Smith's piano technique – he fled from the Green Room to escape, but a younger soloist's nerve might have been shattered. There are ways of doing such things which give less offence, as Wood discovered. One of Sargent's famous Brains Trust contributions brought a sharp reply from band-leader Geraldo – 'If you listen, you must realise my players rehearse as long as yours'. Sir Malcolm could even be rude to his hosts, descending in a dressing-gown to quieten the Ball at an ambassador's residence overseas, or ostentatiously returning a decanter of port passed to the right by the man at whose table he was dining. It was as though the coal-merchant's son from Stamford could never resist showing off what he had learned. No one could have called Sargent modest, but he sometimes underestimated his own impact. A rebuke could seem like a thunderbolt, precisely because he *was* Sir Malcolm Sargent. The memory of it might sting for a lifetime. He was not to the manor born; and though he revelled in being received on equal terms by kings, earls, and ambassadors, he perhaps never fully understood the obligations that are placed upon a gentleman.

Naturally there was more to him than this. He could be magnificent in a crisis, and had a tactful way with irritatingly persistent press reporters. Dame Eva Turner once saw quite another side to him in Manchester's Midland Hotel after a rehearsal. 'His young daughter Pamela was with him there in a wheelchair, already dying of tuberculosis. Sargent absolutely adored her; he was very tender with her, and kept her amused. He never let her see that his heart was breaking.'

We may never know just how much her death affected him.

Seven Swans A-Swimming

Sargent's own health caused some anxiety before the 1967 season. He had sufficiently recovered from an operation the previous December to go on his ninth Australian tour, seventeen concerts during April and May; to take a

21. Leopold Stokowski, once a Promenader, conducting

holiday swimming with dolphins in Hawaii in June; and to conduct two
concerts at Chicago's Ravinia Park Festival in July. He returned with a
temperature and in pain, but began Proms rehearsals on Monday before the
First Night. After two days the temperature recurred and he bowed to his
doctors. William Glock and Colin Davis (at this time conductor-elect of the
BBC Symphony Orchestra) put their heads together and covered Sargent's
eighteen Proms appearances with seven other conductors, of whom all except

at the 1963 Proms *(Godfrey MacDomnic)*

George Hurst were already in the season, the fortieth run by the BBC and Glock's eighth; advance bookings were up £6,000 on the previous year. The public learned that Sargent could not do the First Night. Colin Davis gave the programme unaltered; it was Fou Ts'Ong's first Prom appearance, playing the Grieg Concerto. BBC engineers ran a television cable across the road to a set in Sargent's bedroom at Albert Hall Mansions because the concert was being recorded.

The Polish Radio Symphony Orchestra under its conductor Jan Krenz played on the Sunday. On Monday came the season's new departure, a fully costumed, staged, produced and acted performance of Britten's *The Burning Fiery Furnace*, just as moving in the vast Albert Hall as it had been in tiny Orford Church. Because the stage had to be set in advance, Schubert's Octet was played on a platform above the goldfish in the middle of the Arena. Then came the news that Lord Cohen had ordered Sir Malcolm into hospital for a further operation to remove some internal obstruction. The names of those replacing him were released by instalments, as he still hoped to conduct before the season ended.

Meanwhile Bernard Haitink's 'organic conception' of Mahler's *Resurrection Symphony* made a contrast with Messiaen's work on the same subject two nights later, 'a score of surpassing obviousness' in one critic's view. Benjamin Britten conducted Bach's *St John Passion*, in contrast to Krzysztof Penderecki's *St Luke Passion* a week later, conducted by Henryk Czyz who had given the Munich première. All the whispering, shouting and vocal glissandi finished soprano Stefania Woytowicz, who could not sing Britten's *Les Illuminations* the next night. John Pritchard conducted Walton's *Belshazzar's Feast* instead of Sargent, at the first concert to be televised in colour in this country. Marcus Dods took over Sargent's Gilbert and Sullivan Night.

There were two orchestras and two sub-conductors in the Arena, and another orchestra on the platform, when Pierre Boulez directed Stockhausen's intricate *Gruppen*; after that he was off to Edinburgh while Bernard Haitink brought the Amsterdam Concertgebouw to give four concerts, one conducted by Colin Davis. Claudio Abbado and Hans Schmidt-Isserstedt began the final week, by which time it was generally known that Sargent could not conduct this season; and even he had accepted it. Sir Adrian conducted Beethoven's *Choral* on the Friday, Colin Davis a slightly amended Last Night. He also made a speech, and told the audience that Sir Malcolm Sargent was present in the hall, and that he would fetch him.

Sargent had reached an extraordinary decision during the week. He knew that he was dying of cancer. If he was going to see his beloved Promenaders again, it had to be on the Last Night. He asked if his doctors could give him enough strength almost literally to raise him from the dead; enough to cross the street from his flat to the hall; to stand once more on the platform of his triumphs; to speak once again before millions. He could not be talked out of the idea; a dying man's request is not easily refused. He was given glucose and saline injections for over seven hours, the energy equivalent of two weeks' nourishment. Colin Davis brought him gently up on to the platform from backstage, where the BBC had a stretcher, doctors, nurses and attendants standing by. From the clear, ringing tones of his speech the truth could not have been guessed, though a BBC Symphony Orchestra player afterwards said there was something about his shoulders she had not liked the look of. Sargent gave the opening date of next year's Proms, as he always did, and

22. Benjamin Britten conducting Bach's *St John Passion* in 1967 (*Godfrey MacDomnic*)

hoped to meet everyone again then. He stood for the National Anthem, left the platform with cheers ringing in his head, and was taken home. The energy charge lasted through a press conference he gave next day at the flat. Seventeen days later he was dead.

There may always be those who regard this farewell appearance as an outrageous piece of exhibitionism by a man on the threshold of death. Others may see reflected there Sir Thomas Browne's 'the long habit of living indisposeth us for dying', or Dylan Thomas's 'Do not go gentle into that good night . . . Rage, rage against the dying of the light'.

There may yet be another explanation.

Only the very greatest conductors are remembered for their conducting alone. Except for his connections with the Promenade Concerts, books would not still be written about Sir Henry Wood. Sargent had probably understood this a long time. It would explain many things, including his anxiety to retain the Chief Conductorship of the Proms. He certainly knew in his heart and by his intellect that history would not place him amongst the greatest conductors of all time. He probably felt, quite correctly, that he had contributed something to the Proms as Sir Henry's successor. He could not know that no one would succeed him. Wood had been forced by fate to end with a whimper, far from the adoring audiences he had done so much to create. Where Sargent lay on his death-bed they were tantalisingly close at hand. His last wish granted, his swan-song over, he took leave of friends, and made his peace with God.

'This man will ruin the Proms'
1968–1973

To be sure of getting the conductors, soloists and orchestras that he wanted, William Glock was planning far ahead; the 1968 season was already well advanced when Sir Malcolm Sargent died. A popular First Night would have been inappropriate as a Memorial Concert; but Glock could still start with one if he began on Friday instead of Saturday. Every season since then has opened on a Friday with a gesture suitable to such a big music festival, Verdi's *Requiem*, Mahler's Eighth Symphony, Beethoven's *Missa Solemnis* and so on.

Any lingering ambiguity about Sargent was dispersed before the 1968 season began. The BBC was asked to display his bronze bust by William Timyn on the platform next to the one of Sir Henry Wood. There is only one Founder of the Proms and he spent fifty years maturing them. Whatever Sargent's contribution, he made it during only seventeen years. The BBC very properly declined the request. (After Sargent's bust, whose? Boult's? Colin Davis's? In time, a totem pole of conductors' heads reaching to the Albert Hall ceiling?) The bust has since been installed in the main foyer of the Albert Hall, where Sargent is less well served by a painting in which he looks like the toreador in a Spanish bullfight poster.

Promenaders protested at the BBC's decision; and also at the proceeds from the Memorial Concert not having been given by the BBC to the Sir Malcolm Sargent Memorial Cancer Fund for Children. (There would not have been any, as it happened. The BBC donated £500 to the Fund.) Who did the Promenaders now think they were? Which of them protested? – for by no means all of them worshipped Sargent.

They formed a small part of a social revolution. Popular musical entertain-

ment, once provided by older professionals, had become the province of very young people with minimum talent and maximum amplification, whose stars became millionaires at twenty. (Wood had been right about the microphone but fortunately not in his own field.) Youth had money to spend; on clothes, the more outrageous the better; on social drinking, almost replacing older drinkers in pubs which brewers redesigned to attract their new clientele; and on entertainment, the young 'Pop' movement being largely supported by equally young listeners. Students rioted and protested. Promenaders too now believed – was some of it Sargent's fault? – that they had a right to demand how things should be done.

Colin Davis conducted the Memorial Concert, the *Serenade to Music* (written for Sir Henry Wood), Walton's Viola Concerto, and Elgar's Second Symphony. Promenaders immediately identified themselves with the youngest Chief Conductor of the BBC Symphony Orchestra, calling him 'Colin' and becoming generally familiar. Colin Davis took it in good part, keeping them happy for the next four years. He did not want Sargent's mantle. The BBC Symphony Orchestra and the Proms were not an end for him, but stepping-stones. The Proms were about to stand on their own feet; there would be no further need for a father-figure.

Already known to a small circle through the Chelsea Opera Group, Colin Davis sprang to greater fame in 1959 when at short notice he deputised magnificently for Otto Klemperer in Mozart's *Don Giovanni* at the Royal Festival Hall. Other eligible young men later claimed to have been rung first, but they were out. Conductors are like that. When one gets a big appointment, others always say they turned it down. BBC Symphony Orchestra Chief Conductors traditionally opened the Proms season; Davis did the *Grande Messe des Morts* in 1969 for the centenaries of both Berlioz and Sir Henry Wood, who was born the year the composer died. Naturally William Glock profited by a man with whom Philips were recording all the major works of Berlioz. (Philips recorded the Last Night in 1969 and achieved the remarkable feat of having records on sale by Tuesday morning, less than sixty hours later. The record sleeves were printed in advance. In 1972 they did it again.)

In 1971 Davis opened with Mahler's Eighth Symphony, repeating it during the 1972 season. Though he did not conduct as many concerts in a season as Sargent, he took a share of the staple repertory; his first Beethoven *Choral Symphony* was found 'satisfying and moving'. At the same time Glock was carefully grooming Pierre Boulez, or perhaps grooming British audiences. As a composer he inspired a young *avant-garde*; as an interpreter he brought listeners a step further. When Boulez conducted he convinced. In his hands tough works such as Debussy's *Jeux* and the lesser-known scores of Bartok, Stravinsky, Webern, Berg were a revelation. To Boulez it was all so clearly

23. Sir Colin Davis (*Clive Barda*)

167

music in a great tradition. He was exactly the man to win converts, his own compositions having eased Promenaders into an unfamiliar but obviously brilliantly organised world of sound, its very complexity helping to make Berg and Messiaen sound relatively less inaccessible by comparison.

In 1951 after reading what American critic Virgil Thomson had written of Boulez, Glock invited the Frenchman to contribute an article to *The Score* about Arnold Schoenberg, who had just died. His violent intellectual attack 'Schoenberg is Dead' remains controversial; but the contact between the two men proved ever more fruitful. In 1963 Glock invited Boulez to conduct certain works by Debussy, Berg, Stravinsky and Webern in London, performances which have perhaps not been surpassed. When Colin Davis accepted the musical directorship of the Royal Opera House in 1971 (in which post he was knighted in 1980) it was clear that Glock would wish Boulez to succeed him at the BBC Symphony Orchestra. It was also clear that this might involve some change in the Last Night; 'Land of Hope' could hardly be conducted by a Frenchman.

Colin Davis had already agreed with Glock in 1969 that, the Last Night having been such a personal affair between Sir Malcolm Sargent and the audience, the time seemed ripe for a change. Sir Henry Wood's daughter Tatiana had said a few years earlier, 'My father was all for fun and games as a Last Night treat, but it has now become a shambles'. Sir Henry's centenary was a good moment to restore his *Sea-Songs* complete, without the cuts Sargent had made. Davis disliked 'Land of Hope' as 'smacking a bit of Earl Haigery and sending millions to the slaughter'. The secretary of the Proms Circle objected strongly: 'the last concert is not a musical night. We do not expect it to be' – exactly the problem Davis and Glock wished to overcome. They did omit Elgar's *Pomp and Circumstance March No. 1* from the Last Night; once again there was such an uproar that it had to be played, though only as an encore to his *Cockaigne* Overture which began the second half. Colin Davis announced that a BBC-commissioned work by Malcolm Arnold for the Last Night of 1970 would include both 'Land of Hope' and 'Rule, Britannia'; but the battle was really over. Three such works for audience participation were commissioned, Arnold's *Fantasy*, Williamson's *The Stone Wall* in 1971, and Crosse's *Celebration* in 1972; but on each occasion 'Land of Hope' began the second half (Arnold's *Fantasy* having omitted it after all). By 1973 what Promenaders would regard as their proper rituals had been restored fully, apparently for ever. While not wishing to deny them such end-of-term high jinks, an unfortunate impression is given to millions abroad who have seen only the Last Night on television. They firmly believe that funny hats are worn by the curious British every night of the season. The Danish photographer whose stunning panorama is shown on the cover of this book originally came over to take it on the First Night of 1979. He was nonplussed to find that the audience was not wearing fancy dress for Mahler's Third Symphony.

Glock not only kept on with those strands he had already woven into the fabric, opera, chamber music, more orchestras and conductors, including visitors from abroad; he increased them each season, like a juggler who adds another ball to half a dozen already in the air, and still holds everything in balance.

Having insisted from the first on money for commissioned works, in 1969 he put two into the first part of a concert, a violin concerto by Don Banks and *In alium* by John Tavener, preceded them with Thea Musgrave's *Concerto for Orchestra*, then asked the audience to ballot for which of the three should be played again in the second half. Tavener won, his work using four loudspeakers round the Gallery, pre-recorded tapes, children's voices, and the soloist, June Barton, singing with up to twenty-four superimposed images of her own voice. Some called the ballot a stunt, a 'malodorous innovation . . . the first example of instant concerts'. This was not the case; Newman and Wood tried them even more extensively in 1897. Glock commissioned forty-nine works for the Promenade Concerts, maintaining 'If you are prepared to put a foot anywhere, you must be prepared to put it wrong.' It was not Glock who put his foot in it when the USSR State Orchestra came to play en route to Edinburgh in 1968, but the Russians, who invaded Czechoslovakia the day of their first Prom. After very careful thought the BBC decided not to cancel their concerts. Would-be demonstrators led by Tariq Ali were halted 100 yards short of the Albert Hall. Conductor Evgeny Svetlanov, knowing the way of the world, refused to begin until powerful floodlights installed in the hall by BBC Television News were turned off and the cameras withdrawn. East or West, people tend to put on a show when news cameras are about. There was prolonged applause for a superb orchestra, and for Mstislav Rostropovich, whose performance of Czech composer Dvorak's Cello Concerto could hardly have held more tension. He gave Bach's unaccompanied *Sarabande* for encore 'as if making his own sorrowful protest'. David Oistrakh was conductor and soloist at their third Prom, and Moscow prizewinner John Ogdon played Rachmaninov's Third Piano Concerto in their final concert.

By another irony, Glock's chosen visitors for 1969 were the Czech Philharmonic Orchestra, 'one of the world's finest', under Vaclav Neumann and Zdenek Kosler. The Leningrad Philharmonic under Rozhdestvensky and Evgeny Mravinsky gave four Proms in 1971; the next year there were *two* foreign orchestras. The NHK Symphony Orchestra of Japan turned out to be four years older than the BBC Symphony. Britain was the first country to broadcast, in 1922; the BBC Symphony Orchestra was created in 1930. Japan was not broadcasting until 1925, but formed its orchestra a year later. Six nights later they were followed by the Munich Philharmonic for three Proms under Rudolf Kempe, a renowned conductor who like Boulez and Rozhdestvensky was destined to become Chief Conductor of the BBC Symphony Orchestra.

Glock received his knighthood in 1970; it must have given him some

24. Dame Janet Baker and Sir Adrian Boult (*Godfrey MacDomnic*)

satisfaction. Questions had once been raised about him even in the House of Commons – 'This man will *ruin* the Proms!' He never wavered, keeping his mind always open and alert, and establishing a reputation for frankness and honesty; his answers were always believed. 'In fact', he replied to a questioner, 'there is not one minute more new music in a season now than there was before; it is just different!' Sir Neville Cardus declared that 'highbrows once looked down on the Proms; they are often obliged to look up to them these days.' Glock had shifted the focus of attention back to them. 'It would be hard to devise a series of forty-nine concerts', another critic wrote, 'that better combines the basic symphonic repertoire with a rich selection of works not heard in previous years.' By 1972 Glock had expanded this to fifty-seven concerts, of which more than half were festival 'peaks'.

The season the Chief Conductor did *not* open, 1970, Glock chose to begin with Messiaen's vast *La Transfiguration de notre Seigneur Jésus Christ* with the composer present, and conducted by Serge Baudo who had given the première in Lisbon. It was commissioned for the Gulbenkian centenary. 'Ravel's *Bolero* extended to infinity' was one critic's opinion. Wisely there was no First Night ballot for it; but it *was* a festival event, and there were many of those in William Glock's time, including:

Bach *Christmas Oratorio*	Monteverdi *Il ritorno*	Schoenberg *Gurrelieder*
St Matthew Passion	*d'Ulisse*	*Jacob's*
St John Passion	*Vespers of*	*Ladder*
Beethoven *Leonora*	*1610*	Strauss *Capriccio*
Fidelio	Mozart *The Impresario*	Tchaikovsky *Eugen*
Cavalli *L'Ormindo*	*Zaide*	*Onegin*
La Calisto	Purcell *The Fairy Queen*	Verdi *Don Carlos*
Delius *Requiem*	*King Arthur*	*Sicilian Vespers*
Handel *Semele*	Rameau *Hippolyte et*	Wagner *Das Rheingold*
Messiaen *Turangalîla*	*Aricie*	*Siegfried* Acts I
Symphony		and III

A daunting catalogue perhaps, at one go; but such works were deployed with flair to produce absorbing seasons, varied with air from other planets like the chamber music which ran through these years like a silver thread. Mendelssohn's Octet in 1969 sounded magnificent with the new fibreglass baffles in the Albert Hall roof; instantly nicknamed 'flying saucers' (appropriately enough in the year men first stepped on to the moon), they were considered to be £18,000 well spent on improving acoustics. Sir Henry Wood might have blinked his eyes at a Prom where Schubert's B flat Trio was followed by Act III of Wagner's *Tristan und Isolde*; but he would have blinked them open, not shut. In a Beethoven night the same season (1970) Alfred Brendel played the *Diabelli Variations* before the interval; Colin Davis conducted the *Eroica Symphony* after it. Bach's *Goldberg Variations* were played on a piano by André Tchaikowsky. Roger Woodward filled a Beethoven first half with the *Hammerklavier Sonata*. Who but Sir William Glock would have engaged such pianists in orchestral concerts without giving them a concerto? And done it in a way that made refreshing musical sense?

Promenaders learned with disappointment, and eventually with great and lasting sadness, that Beethoven's *Archduke Trio* could not be played before Schubert's 'Great' C major Symphony in 1971, nor two of his cello sonatas precede the *Choral Symphony* as planned in 1973, due to the indisposition of one of their very favourite soloists of the past decade, Jacqueline du Pré.

There was dancing for the first time at a Prom in 1969 when Deanne Bergsma, Donald Britton, Alexander Grant and Wayne Sleep performed in Stravinsky's Burlesque *Renard*. The same year a generous amount of medieval music took the Proms further back in time than ever before, with works by

Dunstable and Dufay, fifteenth-century dances, Machaut's *Notre Dame* Mass (a great work brought out of the history books into the concert hall with stunning effect), and a whole Monteverdi Prom as well as his 1640 *Magnificat*. David Munrow's first Prom was as a solo recorder player in Bach's Fourth *Brandenburg Concerto*; the next season he appeared with his increasingly popular Early Music Consort, which did so much to recreate medieval works as the vivid entertainment they had once been. As if to strike a balance, the 1969 season also offered a scat singer and jazz trio in *Yeibichai*, commissioned from Wilfrid Mellers; and potentiometers, ring modulators and other electronic wizardry in a Prom which not only had no orchestra but finished with no one there at all. A four-track tape machine now being available, Promenaders finally did hear Stockhausen's *Song of Youth*, which they were denied in 1960.* There was a packed house for the first late-night Prom in 1970 (reminiscent of Glock's Festival Hall 'midnight matinées'). The BBC Symphony Orchestra appeared not just in casual but in fancy dress, as they were playing alongside a Pop group; Alan Civil wore a long blond wig and dark glasses. They divided into three for Tim Souster's BBC-commissioned *Triple Music II*; thinking of *Gruppen*, heard in 1967, critics concluded that 'Souster is no Stockhausen'. They also found forty minutes' improvisation by The Soft Machine (a Progressive Pop group taking its name from a book by William Burroughs) 'self-indulgent' and revealing 'a bankrupt imagination'. It was nevertheless greatly enjoyed, and not just by a strong 'hippie' element among the audience.

Then in 1971 Sir William Glock had an even more breathtakingly simple new idea. Instead of Covent Garden Opera giving concert performances in the Albert Hall, why not move the mountain over to Mahomet and hold a Prom in the Royal Opera House? That way Promenaders would see a complete production staged, lit, and in full costume. Floor seats were removed, and an excellent view of Mussorgsky's *Boris Godunov* from Covent Garden's Stalls could be had by Promenaders for only 50p; there were seats from as little as 80p. Boris Christoff, singing the title role, said he had 'never been so moved by any audience, anywhere'. It only happened once, because Covent Garden was able to continue with its own Opera Proms sponsored by the Midland Bank. Back in Kensington there was a baroque Prom for those unable to get into the much smaller opera house. Two other Proms were given away from the Albert Hall the same season. To perform Beethoven's *Missa*

---

* It was a time of self-indulgent scoring. For Ligeti's *Aventures* and *Nouvelles Aventures* which Boulez conducted in 1971 the composer specified: A large, thick book. A tightly filled cushion. A carpet beater. A small cupboard. A cudgel. A paper bag. A pasteboard suitcase. Tissue paper. Greaseproof paper. A thick carpet. A straw rug-beater. A tin can. A large, flat hammer. A wooden lath. A plastic cup. A balloon. A large toy tin frog. A large bottle. An iron plate. A silk cloth. A metal tray piled high with dishes. A wooden bowl. Marbles. For the second work the percussionist was required to wear shoes with leather soles.

25. Jacqueline du Pré (*Godfrey MacDomnic*)

Solemnis in Westminster Cathedral was an equally brilliant idea, obvious enough once Glock had announced it. The audience there had just enough time to rush back to the Albert Hall for a late-night Prom where Karlheinz Stockhausen talked about his *Mantra* before its performance on two pianos by Alfons and Aloys Kontarsky. This was followed immediately by another innovation, the exquisitely hypnotic sounds of a long late-evening raga improvised before a hushed audience by that great sitar player Imrat Khan, with Latif Ahmed Khan on the tabla. A third outside Prom took place at the Round House, Chalk Farm, chosen as a suitable *endroit* for Pierre Boulez to introduce and conduct contemporary works to a smaller, dedicated audience. (His later Rug Concerts in New York had similar aims.) At the first Round House Prom he heard himself described in George Newson's BBC-commissioned *Arena* as 'the master of orchestral karate', an apt reference to the precise chopping motions he makes with his bare hands when conducting (he never uses a baton).

At another late Prom in 1972 Stockhausen's *Carré* for four conductors and orchestras was played twice, with a talk by the composer in between. A strand of American music also runs through Glock's era. Boulez coupled John Cage's

First *Construction in Metal* with Elliott Carter's *Concerto for Orchestra*. Three evenings later Cage was at the Round House in person to direct his *Hpschd*, which used seven harpsichords, fifty-two tape-recorders, sixteen film projectors, and burbled along quite pleasantly for over an hour. In 1973 London's Brompton Oratory proved a splendid setting for a late-night Liturgical Mass, Palestrina's *Assumpta est Maria* with plainchant and organ solos, directed by John Hoban.

One new idea Sir William Glock thought might continue was the three-part Prom with two intervals. To some extent it has, with at least one each season since the first in 1971, when a staged performance of Stravinsky's *The Soldier's Tale* was the centrepiece. Another innovation which has continued is the idea of having composers, performers and other experts talking about certain works beforehand, first in the Albert Hall's Prince Consort Suite and later in the Royal Colleges of Art and Music nearby. An experiment not so far repeated was the whole of Wagner's *Parsifal* spread over two complete Proms in 1972 (conducted by Pierre Boulez, who became Chief Conductor of the BBC Symphony Orchestra that year). The composer's granddaughter, Friedelinde Wagner, was in the audience, a splendid lady who strikingly resembles her distinguished ancestor.

Far more subtle and probably giving him even greater satisfaction was Sir William Glock's refreshing approach to programme making. Some examples have already been mentioned; a few more may show how he moved away from the conventional overture – concerto – symphony with lasting effect, and not only at the Proms:

> *1969: Four Schubert songs with piano. A Mozart piano concerto. Beethoven Eighth Symphony. INTERVAL. Haydn, Nelson Mass.*

William Glock: *'Far fewer programmes start with an overture, which implies a new kind of concert.'*

> *1970: Four Motets by Byrd. INTERVAL. Elgar, The Dream of Gerontius.*

Hugh Wood: *'We are only just discovering what goes with what.'*

> *1971: Shostakovich, Fourteenth Symphony. INTERVAL. Britten, Spring Symphony. (Two song-cycles with orchestra.)*

> *1972: Sibelius, Fourth Symphony. INTERVAL. Schoenberg, Pierrot Lunaire. INTERVAL. Stravinsky, The Rite of Spring. (Sold out)*

Sir John Barbirolli died before his two 1970 Proms with the Hallé Orchestra. A tribute was played at once, and the first concert a month later was conducted by Charles Groves as a memorial. Sir Adrian Boult conducted a Prom in 1971 for the eightieth birthday of Sir Arthur Bliss, who two years

---

26. Pierre Boulez (*BBC Copyright Photograph*)

before had rescored and conducted his Two-Piano Concerto for Phyllis Sellick and Cyril Smith, who lost the use of one hand due to a stroke. Malcolm Arnold also conducted them in his BBC-commissioned Three-hand Concerto, which had to be encored on the spot. André Previn gave Sir William Walton's Seventieth Anniversary Concert in 1972, and the first of three such events in 1973, a Rachmaninov Centenary Concert including the Proms première of *The Bells*, which was an instant success. Sir Lennox Berkeley (knighted in 1974) was commissioned by the BBC for his Seventieth Birthday Prom and provided a *Sinfonia Concertante* for oboe played by Janet Craxton; the concert included his Third Symphony. Charles Mackerras and Sadler's Wells Opera performed *Gloriana* at Britten's Sixtieth Anniversary Prom the same season.

Such occasions were ever observed; the Victorian Society's excellent idea of a 1969 Prom marking 150 years since the birth of Prince Albert resulted in a concert conducted by Rudolf Schwarz the day after the moon landing, a circumstance which would surely have been appreciated by the Consort after whom the Albert Hall of the Arts and Sciences was named. It was given in the presence of H.R.H. The Duke of Edinburgh, a tribute both to Albert and to the increasing stature of the Proms. H.R.H. Prince Charles went with the Dean of Windsor in 1967 to hear Bach's *St John Passion* conducted by Benjamin Britten. A Promenade Concert was often on the itinerary of distinguished visitors. The Libyan Minister of Culture came in 1968 as guest of the British Council. With many embassy staff they arrived at the last moment from an early dinner and were whisked into their Box. William Glock being at Dartington and his deputy away, the next in seniority had agreed to host an interval reception, Hans Keller, a Viennese musicologist of awesome intellect, who was at the Prom with his wife, a friend, and the friend's wife. The Head of the BBC World Service had also offered help.

There was one long work in the first half. At the interval an interpreter shot out of the Box asking for the Gents. Apparently most of the party had omitted a simple precaution so necessary before sitting through a work like Wagner's *Rheingold*, for example, which has no interval and lasts the whole evening, much of it spent under water. The ministerial entourage was obliged to ascend to the level above and walk half-way round the Albert Hall against a tide of people rushing the other way for an interval drink. En route the procession passed by the open door of the reception room, to the evident astonishment of the Head of the World Service waiting within with his wife. Arriving gratefully at their destination they saw Hans Keller and his party approaching. A BBC man politely held open the double doors to allow the Minister and his staff to enter, then turned to pass the time with the British Council's representative. Both failed to notice that the official party was followed through the double doors by Hans Keller's wife, the friend's wife, the friend, and Hans Keller, all under the impression that inside they would be offered sherry. They came out rather more quickly than they went in, and the expressions on their faces will not easily be forgotten.

27. Karlheinz Stockhausen (*Erich Auerbach*)

When Promenaders looked at the Last Night in the 1973 Prospectus they found that the conductor, not the programme, had been changed. Colin Davis had officiated once more in 1972 after Pierre Boulez became Chief Conductor of the BBC Symphony Orchestra. By then he thought he had done his share. Norman Del Mar in 1973 was first in a new line of conductors to do the Last Night, which henceforth became a concert of British music. As almost his final gift Sir William Glock had given the Proms their complete independence. They were no longer Newman's, nor Wood's nor Sargent's, nor Glock's; they were The Proms. His own association with them ended in 1974 as it had begun in 1940, seated at a grand piano on the platform. After Robert Ponsonby succeeded him as the BBC's music chief, Sir William Glock returned as pianist in Mozart's E flat major Quartet, K493, at a Prom in which the only other work was Mahler's *Resurrection Symphony*, conducted by Pierre Boulez, a programme combination unthinkable before Glock's time. Could anything have been more suitable for a farewell? *The Sunday Times* awarded him its editorial accolade:

TRIUMPHAL MARCH

In a few weeks' time the 79th Concert season opens, with Sir William Glock for the last time playing his role as its organiser. It is all too easy, once something has become an institution, to take it for granted. A word of praise and congratulation about this remarkable musical achievement is therefore timely and more than justified. The Proms provide nothing less than the longest and richest (in musical terms) music festival in the world. The credit for this phenomenon goes right back to the early days of Sir Henry Wood, but above all to the BBC, whose patronage years ago made the Proms a national heritage and, since the coming of television, an international event.

It has been Sir William Glock's special success to have broadened and varied the programmes, taking in more modern works, sometimes moving the concerts themselves outside their traditional home at the Albert Hall to Covent Garden or Westminster Cathedral, and mixing the textures of programmes between orchestral and chamber or instrumental works. He and his predecessors have raised the level and range of musical performance to an extraordinary degree, without losing the popular appeal and informal atmosphere that make the Proms so unique an occasion. London has been for years now the greatest musical centre in the world. The Proms have helped to make it so. Here is a bit of the national heritage of which everyone, musical or not, can and should be proud.

Towards the Eighties

1974–1979

There was bound to be some reaction. 'I have sometimes thought', said Robert Ponsonby with a twinkle in his eye, after he succeeded Sir William Glock, 'that I should like to run the world's *smallest* music festival.' Near his cottage in the Lake District (a sanctuary without telephone) a tiny church in the valley suggests itself as the perfect setting for a week of clavichord recitals. An understandable reaction, after ten years of over-emphatic reference to the Proms as 'the biggest music festival in the world'. It was also confidently expected that it would prove almost impossible to follow Glock. A nice sense of humour and proportion was a desirable qualification for doing so, allied to practical musicianship. Thomas Dunhill taught Robert Ponsonby at Eton; he took a commission in the Brigade of Guards, then went to Trinity College, Oxford, as an organ scholar (his father was organist of Christ Church). He sang opposite Arda Mandikian in the memorable 1950s revival of *The Trojans* and became President of the University Operatic Society. Later he was cast as Masetto in a concert performance of *Don Giovanni* conducted by Colin Davis.

During his time as Director of the Edinburgh International Festival he brought over the opera company of La Scala, Milan, and the Leningrad Symphony Orchestra. 'Beyond the Fringe' flourished under him; but he eventually resigned, protesting that a festival could not be run on safety-first lines. When the BBC appointment was offered he was General Manager of the Scottish National Orchestra. Though he no longer performs publicly, he still plays Schubert's piano sonatas for relaxation and uplift, and frankly admits that he puts works into programmes which are not to his own taste: 'I probably get more pleasure out of chamber music and song recitals than orchestral concerts'.

A further reaction came after Robert Ponsonby had been four years in office. The Composers' Guild attacked the BBC for allowing one person to run the Proms for so long, explaining that 'for many years musicians had been worried that the Controller of Music was responsible to no one for the programmes he selected. It is morally wrong for one individual to dominate until retirement or death, and on public funds too! Mr Ponsonby is not under fire, but the BBC itself, for allowing such control to grow and flourish within its music division, affecting the most important music festival in the world. These concerts are our prize possession and the envy of countries abroad. We ought to take more care of them.'

Now *there* is a breathtaking set of arguments for anyone to consider who has been following the development of the Proms since 1895! Sir Henry Wood dominated the Proms for fifty years. Was that morally wrong? The BBC had absolutely nothing to do with allowing such control to grow and flourish, at least not before 1927, by which time *all* the principles underlying the Promenade Concerts were well established, including that of introducing works by foreign composers.

'Out of our 450 members', said the chairman of The Composers' Guild, 'perhaps fifteen to twenty are regularly represented at the Proms.' There is the real truth of it; and there's the rub as well. The Guild perchance dreams of Proms seasons which would *include* music by its 450 members, and less of that foreign rubbish. What seasons they would be! No longer our prize possession, nor the envy of countries abroad either. The Guild looks back nostalgically to the time when a committee planned the Proms – Sir Malcolm Sargent, Julian Herbage, and George Willoughby, in the decade after 1949, a period universally condemned as the lowest level they ever achieved.*

Robert Ponsonby was not under fire; no indeed he was not. The Composers' Guild was in fact attacking Sir William Glock, which they had not dared do to his face. How they must have hated him! Not only could he tell the difference between good and bad British composers, he could compare them with *foreign* composers as well: 'There must be British music in the Proms, but it must be *good*, not just British'. He had also said quite firmly, 'I think the Proms should be planned by one person, a committee would not do at all'. If the Composers' Guild thought Robert Ponsonby was a seven-stone weakling into whose face sand could with impunity be kicked, they were badly misinformed. Their ill-tempered crusade seems to have failed to achieve any of its ludicrously selfish objectives. Long may it fail.

'I intend to carry on Sir Henry Wood's policy,' said Robert Ponsonby; 'if the programmes became more traditional the vitality of the Proms would collapse. If you accept that the BBC is only in the music business to make money, then there would be no problem in filling the Albert Hall; but I

---

*See pp. 131-132.

28. Bernard Haitink (*Frits van Swoll, courtesy of Phonogram*)

believe the Proms would be dead within two years. Our aim is to offer a balanced series of primarily orchestral programmes to a perceptive and enterprising audience, with some of the masterworks of the past, and some unfamiliar works of the past *and* the present we believe to be important. I take advice from colleagues in the music division; but I think it right that one person should make the final decisions. I don't think a committee system would work. Personal taste cannot enter strongly into the planning – there are works I personally don't enjoy very much.'

The timing of the Composers' Guild's attack considerably weakened the force of its argument. All this took place in 1978, a time when the Proms were becoming so dense with incident that a discerning and adventurous musician could hardly afford to miss a night. The planner may feel in his heart that he has produced a magnificent concert, but two things remain crucial: how many people pay to hear it, and how many critics write about it (and what they write). Box Office takings were considerably up, even allowing for continuing inflation; and practically every concert attracted reviews in several national newspapers.

The usual complaints cropped up: 'Almost every concert is ruined by one hideous modern work' – even after eighty-three years it was still too much to expect people to understand the original purpose of these concerts. 'Modern' also means different things to different people. Bartok's *Concerto for Orchestra*, a popular classic to most music-lovers, may still be a nasty modern score to others, ruining an evening of Sibelius. One man's Tippett is another man's Schoenberg. Elliott Carter's *Variations* and Stockhausen's *Carré* are for the moment extremely hard nuts to crack; but if people resist every unfamiliar name, they may miss music which is both enjoyable and memorable. There must be many who for that reason have never listened to Schoenberg's *Transfigured Night*. Another letter-writer complained in the Press of programmes ruined by the music of Brian Chapple, Iain Hamilton, Webern, Mackeben, and Dostal. Two names do not belong in that sequence, as intelligence tests say; the traps for the unwary are Mackeben and Dostal, composers of 1930s popular light music which might not sound out of place at a Viennese Evening.

The BBC Symphony Orchestra returned in 1974 to a refurnished and redecorated Royal Albert Hall, which always feels like coming home to those involved in the Proms. New maroon-upholstered swivel chairs were appreciated by those among the audience of 7,120 who sat in the Stalls; those they replaced had sometimes clanked or creaked with age. The eightieth season began with Chief Conductor Pierre Boulez directing Haydn's *Harmonie Mass* before the interval, and the orchestra's founder, Sir Adrian Boult, belying his eighty-five years with a 'perennially fresh interpretation of Schubert's "Great" C major Symphony' in which 'the orchestra surpassed themselves'. The Eightieth Anniversary Concert on 10 August was conducted by Charles Mackerras.

The season got under way with the *Gurrelieder* conducted by Boulez on the first Sunday, for the centenary of Schoenberg's birth. On the actual anniversary, Friday 13 September, the Promenaders sang 'Happy Birthday'.* Jessye Norman sang Berg's *Der Wein* 'with complete ease and sumptuous beauty of tone'. Alan Hacker played Mozart's Clarinet Concerto on the basset-clarinet, for which he wrote it. Elisabeth Söderström introduced Malcolm Williamson's BBC-commissioned *Hammarskjöld Portrait*, settings of verse by the late Secretary-General of the United Nations.

Ideas were by no means exhausted. On the third Saturday brass bands played at a Prom for the first time – 'a headline-catching innovation', Robert

---

* Schoenberg became superstitious about 13, predicting that he would survive his last illness if he could get through another Friday the 13th (August 1951); but he died at 13 minutes to midnight.

29. Jessye Norman: an unplanned First Night 1980 *(Horst Maack, courtesy of Phonogram)*

Ponsonby called it. Brass *music* was there from the start, with all those cornet solos; Wood also did Beethoven's *Equali* for four trombones. The Philip Jones Brass Ensemble played right after the brass bands and had often been at the Proms; but Black Dyke Mills and Grimethorpe Colliery were champions in a great British tradition as deep-rooted as choral music. They were conducted by Elgar Howarth, once a member of the Philip Jones Ensemble, and people were amazed at their precision in Holst, Grainger, Elgar, Harrison Birtwistle (*Grimethorpe Aria*), and the following year Gerhard's *Sardana*, Bliss, and Henze's *Ragtimes and Habaneras*, music far removed from the average man's notion of the brass band repertory. In 1975 John Ireland's *Downland Suite* was conducted by the doyen of brass, Harry Mortimer OBE, who had long advocated their participation in the Proms. They have not so far reappeared, though rapturously received; but a kind of apotheosis was achieved in 1979 with Elgar Howarth's arrangement of Mussorgsky's *Pictures from an Exhibition* for the Philip Jones Brass Ensemble, by then already a best-selling record. Choral music found a new home in 1974 with two packed concerts at St Augustine's Church, Kilburn, as well as the Prom in Westminster Cathedral.

There had been mishaps at the Proms, but none like the night André Previn conducted Carl Orff's *Carmina Burana* in 1974. Half-way through, where the bucolic abbot sings 'Wafna!', baritone Thomas Allen staggered, fell back, bravely tried to recover, and collapsed in a dead faint from the intense heat. The performance was not only being broadcast, it was being recorded by BBC television as well. André Previn quickly moved on to the tavern scene 'In taberna quando sumus'. Solo singers are customarily covered by a stand-in from the chorus; he expected things to sort themselves out. Later in the week when he had fully recovered, Thomas Allen generously allowed the TV programme to go out exactly as it happened, the producer having kept his head and his cameras filming. Only the other soloists' eyes betrayed their astonishment when a complete stranger moved through the orchestra to stand beside them, Thomas Allen having been taken to hospital. Neither they nor André Previn had any idea what was going on.

Patrick McCarthy, an ex-student of the London Opera Centre and a great admirer of Thomas Allen, had been standing in the Arena following the performance with a vocal score; he had sung the baritone solos himself in Birmingham some months previously. When Allen fell, McCarthy went backstage and offered to deputise. Someone produced a dinner-jacket and black tie, and on he went, to make a confident first entry at the lovely line 'Dies nox et omnia'. André Previn made no attempt to hide his obvious relief that whoever this was, at least he could sing. But whatever happened to the chorus stand-in? Thomas Allen's understudy was Dr Christopher Hood, whose first duty was to his Hippocratic oath; he had attended the stricken baritone and gone with him to St George's Hospital. Patrick McCarthy's mother, listening at home, recognised his voice and burst into tears. The incident prompted a pre-concert shout from the crowded Arena a few nights later – 'A Promenader has fainted; would one of the soloists please take his place?' – one of their better efforts.

Promenaders encountered four top American orchestras, the first to play at the Proms. In 1974, while the London Symphony Orchestra was at the Hollywood Bowl, Zubin Mehta brought the Los Angeles Philharmonic to the Albert Hall during a two-month tour of Europe. They were taken aback by the Prommers' habit of 'tuning flat' with orchestras, but soon caught the spirit of the thing. At the 1975 Proms Pierre Boulez conducted his 'other' orchestra, the New York Philharmonic, in Mahler's Ninth Symphony and Elliott Carter's *Concerto for Orchestra*, 'which made every section sweat'. That same year the Cleveland, 'the string quartet of American orchestras – down to the last desk they are all equals', gave 'the most precise performance of Bartok's *Miraculous Mandarin* ever heard'. However, some found Lorin Maazel's way with Beethoven's *Eroica* Symphony 'a pompous, retouched and bumped-up interpretation'. Sir Georg Solti told the Chicago Symphony Orchestra in 1978, 'You wait till we get to the Proms; I will show you an audience!' They were bowled over, not only by their reception, but also by the physical nearness of people – 'At the Hollywood Bowl you can hardly see them,' said one of the players. They gave two Proms and four symphonies. Sir Michael Tippett was present for the British première of his Fourth Symphony, written for them, 'a virtuoso birth-to-death piece which is both moving and deeply satisfying'. As an encore they did a fizzing *Barber of Seville* Overture the first night, 'to show our appreciation', as Solti said. Next night 'the clean, hard-edged Chicago sound' was heard to advantage in Bruckner's Fourth Symphony, 'an imposing, even daunting reading'. Prommers also heard the Sydney Symphony Orchestra in 1974, the Cologne Radio and Rotterdam Philharmonic Orchestras in 1977, and Zubin Mehta again in 1979, on that occasion to give two Proms with the Israel Philharmonic Orchestra.

Rudolf Kempe gave a splendid Strauss *Heldenleben* with his Royal Philharmonic Orchestra at a 1974 Prom, and prophetically conducted the BBC Symphony Orchestra for the first time; he was to succeed Pierre Boulez as Chief Conductor a month after his two further Proms with them in August 1975. He should have begun the 1976 season with Beethoven's *Missa Solemnis* but tragically died before it opened, 'an incalculable loss'. The audience stood in silence before Colin Davis conducted the Beethoven Mass in Kempe's memory. For his six Proms, and for two in the same season which were to have been given by the Early Music Consort under David Munrow, who had also died, deputies were urgently found.

Pierre Boulez would eventually give up the New York Philharmonic as well and return to Paris, perhaps to embark on his life's work. A suspicion was emerging – Boulez had voiced it himself – that composers were searching for something which had not yet been found. As with parallel trends in Art, an *avant-garde* presupposed a Movement to follow. Either none had appeared, or it could not yet be discerned. The French were spending millions on the

30. Kyung-Wha Chung (*Clive Barda*)

research institute IRCAM,* underground at the Pompidou Centre, to bring
their most distinguished musician back to Paris. There, working with
colleagues from all over the world, Boulez hoped that the way forward might
be discovered. Some critics felt that, among the widely divergent styles of
modern composition, only Boulez had created 'an original, unmistakable
idiom' as in *Pli selon pli*, with which he took his leave at the 1975 Proms.
(Some who remembered an earlier performance were disappointed that an
enjoyable incident was not repeated; an electrical fault in 1969 had caused the
fountain to start when the vibraphone was switched on.) 'What the players
have learned from Boulez' a critic wrote, 'is not only to play the right notes at

---

*Institut de Recherche et Coordination Acoustique/Musique. By May 1980 it had moved from
trying to map music's future, to become an electronic music studio perhaps without equal.

31. Jill Gomez (*Erich Auerbach*)

the right time, but to play them with as much attention to quality as if they were by Schubert.'

Robert Ponsonby was quietly making his presence felt through variety, innovation and tradition. Two hours before a Prom in 1974 he handed to Hans Haselböck two themes chosen by Deryck Cooke from Bruckner's *Mass in E minor*, which was sung the same evening. The Austrian organist used both in the first exhibition of the noble art of organ extemporisation to be witnessed at the Proms. Bruckner himself had overdone that art 100 years earlier in six inaugural recitals on the same organ. Dame Janet Baker sang *Savitri* in the first Proms performance of Holst's opera, one of the many operatic roles she sang so unforgettably at these concerts. There was now no shortage of opera. Ravel's *L'Heure Espagnole* and Janacek's *Katya Kabanova* were given in 1974. A disappointing audience for the latter did not quell Robert Ponsonby's enthusiasm for Janacek; in 1979 the Czechs awarded him the Janacek Medal.

In June 1975, a month before the Proms, the Henry Wood Hall in Southwark officially opened for rehearsal and recording. Basil Cameron died the same month at the age of ninety. The BBC Symphony Orchestra, not long back from Japan, dedicated a Prom conducted by Haitink on 12 August to the memory of Dmitri Shostakovich. The International Youth Orchestra, of young musicians from many countries, played a testing programme of Stravinsky, Berg and Strauss under Claudio Abbado; Kyung-Wha Chung's performance with them of Tchaikovsky's Violin Concerto was televised. The future of the BBC's own young Training Orchestra in Bristol was in question; the BBC could no longer afford to maintain it alone, and eventually it had to be disbanded.

Sir Michael Tippett at seventy conducted for Paul Crossley in his Piano Concerto, 'probably the best of all British piano concertos'. Edward Cowie's BBC-commissioned *Leviathan* was considered 'overgrown, rather than monstrous; a heap of musical blubber'. (His Piano Concerto in 1978 fared much better.) Sir Lennox Berkeley's *Voices of the Night* received a performance of great sympathy from Sir Adrian Boult, 'a bit frail, and walking with a stick, but what authority!' John Tavener's *Ultimos Ritos* sounded even better in Westminster Cathedral than when John Poole and the BBC Singers gave the première in Holland (seen here on television).

There was a jazz-oriented Prom by the Nash Ensemble (Milhaud, Richard Rodney Bennett, Lambert and Weill) – except for Bartok's *Contrasts*, 'written for Benny Goodman, but hardly jazz'. In five Proms soprano Jill Gomez ranged over five centuries, singing Early Music in Westminster Cathedral, Beethoven's *Choral Symphony* and Stravinsky's *The Rake's Progress* at the Albert Hall, and (from memory) John McCabe's *Notturni ed Alba* which she had recently recorded. Stephen Bishop, 'the most intellectual and intuitive of this generation of pianists', took the daring and possibly unique step of hyphenating his real surname Kovacevich to his adopted surname Bishop, henceforth wishing to be known as Stephen Bishop-Kovacevich.

Before the 1976 season Robert Ponsonby caused a stir by making a distinction between very popular and very great music. 'Some popular works which are not indisputably great, and can easily be heard outside the Proms, should no longer earn a place.' There were a few mild protests; yet a critic the previous year had written that 'the final full-orchestra blaring of the F major flute melody in Grieg's Piano Concerto is one of the most awful experiences the concert hall has to offer'. Did he perhaps repent in 1979 when Emil Gilels chose to play it with Colin Davis, a performance critics called 'a revelation'?

Opera performances spanned 700 years, from the thirteenth-century musical drama *The Play of Daniel* in St Augustine's Church, to Bartok's *Duke Bluebeard's Castle* conducted by Boulez. Haitink's performance of Britten's *War Requiem* five nights later was simultaneously broadcast on BBC television and Radio 3 in stereo, an increasing trend. There was a short Weber first half, for the 150th anniversary of his death. People complained that there was no Gilbert and Sullivan night; the whole of *Patience* from English National Opera under Charles Mackerras must have been too big for them to see!

Critics complained that foreign music had a poor showing that season, compared with British works ('the Second Viennese School has a thin time'). Next year they complained of exactly the opposite. Two works by Elisabeth Lutyens were performed in 1976, her seventieth year. Heinz Holliger played at two Proms and was declared 'a Pop star of the oboe, who can make it do almost anything'. There was an American Prom for the Bicentennial Year; and Australian composer Richard Meale failed to finish an advertised Piano Concerto for Roger Woodward, presenting a problem to Proms planners. French pianist Claude Helffer agreed to play Elliott Carter's Concerto instead, if the score could be sent to him in Paris. It failed to arrive, so he declined. In the end, Ralph Holmes played Samuel Barber's Violin Concerto.

The Silver Jubilee of Her Majesty Queen Elizabeth II in 1977 brought a silver programme for a First Night of British works, conducted by Andrew Davis in the presence of Their Royal Highnesses The Duke and Duchess of Kent and broadcast for the first time in quadraphony. Two more concerts of British music followed, with the first of three Jubilee commissions in the fiftieth season to be organised by the BBC. Andrew Davis, conducting as many Proms as anyone this year, said he used to Promenade fourteen or fifteen times a season when he was a boy. 'I've always loved the Proms. It's a superb audience. Once the music starts, the quietest, most attentive in London.'

'His current Prospectus is a marvel,' wrote *The Sunday Times* of Robert Ponsonby's 1977 season. Four Contemporary Masterworks concerts were offered for the price of three. (A similar scheme had been half-heartedly tried in 1959, without the bargain price.) First *The Raft of the Medusa*, a revolutionary parable dedicated to Che Guevara by Hans Werner Henze (whose equally political *El Cimarrón* had been done at the Round House two years before). It proved an extraordinarily intense and moving experience, with John Shirley-Quirk magnificent as the mulatto Jean-Charles who so nearly survives, and those who died on the raft (as in Géricault's painting) symbolised by singers moving across the stage to form an increasing chorus of the dead. How to tell people? The chance to experience it has gone, perhaps for a long time. The other Masterworks were a splendid performance of Tippett's *The Midsummer Marriage* by the Welsh National Opera; Messiaen's *Turangalîla Symphony* conducted by Andrew Davis; and the Cologne Radio Choir and Symphony Orchestra in Berio's *Coro*, 'a work of grand moments which held the attention of the audience', introduced and conducted by its composer.

The Martyrdom of St Magnus, a chamber opera about the twelfth-century Earl of Orkney murdered for his pacifism, was commissioned for the Jubilee, recorded in St Magnus Cathedral, and first performed publicly at the Round

House with composer Peter Maxwell Davies conducting. BBC Symphony Orchestra men wore boaters and blazers when Sir Charles Groves conducted the parody Foxtrot *St Thomas Wake* a fortnight later. His Orkney-inspired *Stone Litany* was heard at a Prom in 1975, *Dark Angels* and a staged performance of *Eight Songs for a Mad King* in 1976, and his Symphony was to come in 1978. Richard Rodney Bennett's new *Actaeon* (savagely killed because he saw a goddess bathing) used 'every trick in the horn book, and some new ones'. It was written for Barry Tuckwell, who learned it whilst touring his native Australia; in 1978 he played Thea Musgrave's Concerto, in which 'seven other horns brayed from all round the hall'.

The young Italian Riccardo Muti had rapidly become a Proms favourite since his debut in 1976. Sir Adrian Boult surpassed himself in 1977, with magnificent Brahms and Elgar, his choice of music by two other Masters of the King's and Queen's Musick, Bliss and Malcolm Williamson (soloist in his own Organ Concerto written round Boult's initials A–C–B), and a noble reading of *Job* dedicated to him forty-six years earlier by Vaughan Williams. So he bowed out of the Proms, though none knew it then, nor could have suspected it so soon after he had cheekily given Eric Coates's *Dambusters March* as an encore to Holst's *Planets*. Leopold Stokowski would be seen no more either; he had died in his ninety-fifth year.

The New Zealand Dorian Choir, a BBC *Let the Peoples Sing* winner, sang Palestrina in St Augustine's Church. 'For emotional response', a critic decided that Boulez stood well above other composers in the London Sinfonietta's Round House Prom the same evening; though *Phlegra*, which they commissioned, was 'the first work by Xenakis I have not found unbearable'. There was a concert *for* Benjamin Britten, of his own works and Schubert favourites, including the 'Trout' Quintet, by Clifford Curzon and the Amadeus Quartet. Ida Haendel played the Brahms Concerto with which years before she had made her Proms debut aged ten. Murray Perahia played two Mozart concertos, conducting from the piano; and at Scots-born James Loughran's first Last Night he persuaded the whole audience to link arms for 'Auld Lang Syne' (except H.R.H. Princess Margaret, as someone observed).

'A vintage year,' declared critics of the 1978 Proms; 'Mr Ponsonby seems to have struck the essential balance between idealism and opportunism; to have the measure of audience and Albert Hall; and to have given a fair deal to both concert-goers and radio listeners.' BBC Symphony Orchestra players who had looked forward to unbuttoned playing under Kempe were equally delighted with Rozhdestvensky, conducting his first Prom as their new Chief. 'The BBC has achieved a miracle in capturing the finest Russian conductor of our time'; it was the result of long and patient negotiation. Gennadi Christmas-man (as his name translates) would dart among his players at rehearsals, listening intently, good-humoured, galvanic, and awesomely expert. His wife Victoria Postnikova played Britten's left-hand *Diversions*, and he conducted the Fourth Symphony Shostakovich had withdrawn for forty

32. Young artists: soprano Emma Kirkby (*Clive Barda*)

years. 'Rarely has such playing been heard from this orchestra.'

Bass Gwynne Howell, opening the 1978 season in Verdi's *Requiem*, conducted by Andrew Davis, spoke for many soloists when he said that 'performing at a Prom is like giving a concert in the Underground at rushhour. People are standing practically under your feet'. Verdi's opera *Macbeth* followed later, also Rameau's last opera *Les Boréades* and Schoenberg's music drama *The Lucky Hand*; but why, with 365 days in the year, did Southern

33. Young artists: Simon Rattle (*Alan Wood*)

Television choose to show their Glyndebourne recording of *Don Giovanni* on the same evening as Glyndebourne did Mozart's *Così fan tutte* at the Royal Albert Hall?

Youth was everywhere in evidence; H.R.H. Prince Charles, President of the Jeunesses Musicales World Orchestra, attended their Prom with Sir Robert Mayer, the centenarian whose love for young people helped to create it. Simon Rattle, at twenty-one the youngest Proms conductor in 1976, was something of a conductor of the season in 1978, directing three different orchestras. One of the best young German conductors, Hans Zender, also distinguished himself in a Beethoven-Schumann Prom, and modern works at the Round House. Christopher Hogwood conducted the largest baroque orchestra assembled since the eighteenth century in Handel's *Water Music*.

Liszt's oratorio *Christus* was sung under Brian Wright, who had earlier done it at the first six-week London Liszt Festival, and John Poole conducted Rachmaninov's unaccompanied Vespers in Westminster Cathedral, 'the devotional note of the music truly struck and sustained'. Messiaen's *Quartet for the End of Time* and Stockhausen's *Kontakte* were performed at Riverside Studios, Hammersmith, a new venue tried and abandoned the same season.

Andrzej Panufnik was 'rehabilitated at the Proms' in 1978 after an unexplained twenty-year ban on his music. Politics? Possibly; he was an early refugee from behind the Iron Curtain. Other Poles did freely perform in the West, Witold Lutoslawski conducting at two Proms in 1979 and meeting Panufnik again for the first time in many years. Critics found Panufnik's *Sinfonia di Sfere* 'hypnotic and fascinating; he virtually creates a new sort of orchestra, with textures as clean as Britten's, and he conducts like a true composer'. (He was conductor of the Cracow and Warsaw Philharmonic orchestras before leaving Poland.) Sir Lennox Berkeley's three-movement Fourth Symphony had been performed for his seventy-fifth birthday by Sir Charles Groves and the Royal Philharmonic Orchestra, who repeated it at the Proms; and Yehudi Menuhin played Priaulx Rainier's Violin Concerto as he had at the previous year's Edinburgh Festival.

The 1979 Proms were presented in the finest Prospectus yet designed. Slightly larger, it allowed room for several good feature articles, pertinent points printed below individual programmes, many illustrations, and a musical crossword (tickets to the Last Night for the first correct solution opened). It also read like one of the finest seasons, a fusion of all that is best in these concerts. More than three-quarters of the music was from a now familiar repertoire. There were two BBC commissions, and several other important first performances; three operas; and three major choral works including a 'never-to-be-forgotten' *Messiah*. The twenty-eight orchestras and ensembles included the Israel Philharmonic, and for the first time three of these were commercially sponsored. There was one sensational novelty, music and dancing by the Sasono Mulio Gamelan Orchestra of Surakarta. However modestly Robert Ponsonby offered the first big ethnic group to play at these concerts, they were received as 'the most significant and stimulating of this year's Proms'. Adroitly juxtaposed with composers influenced by their exotic sounds – Maxwell Davies, Ravel and Messiaen the same evening, Britten and Boulez elsewhere – they stayed long in the memory for 'the magic, the ritual force of their ancient tradition'.

There were four concerts half-way through by Gennadi Rozhdestvensky and the BBC Symphony Orchestra, just back from the Edinburgh Festival. Two Russian nights, a British night, and the Proms première of a vast early work by Sibelius, *Kullervo*, derived from the Kalevala legends of Finland. The Ensemble InterContemporain from IRCAM under Peter Eötvös played one icily deterring late-night programme (Marcland, Berio, Birtwistle) to 'a strong contender for the worst attended concert in Proms history', which contained music of considerable lyric beauty and some superb playing. Their

34. Walter Susskind, Peter Maxwell Davies, Robert Ponsonby, Sir Charles Groves, Rudolf Schwarz, Yehudi Menuhin and James Loughran, oblivious of an unknown passer-by who joined them, much to the amusement of his friends (*The Times*)

full Prom under Boulez two nights later was a quite brilliant evening of folk settings by Bartok and Stravinsky, two pieces by Varèse, and three by Schoenberg, whose Piano Concerto Roger Woodward had played to an almost full Saturday-night audience a month before.

Young Oliver Knussen's BBC-commissioned Third Symphony was not finished until the morning of its first rehearsal, although begun in 1973.

'That's nothing to the players,' said the BBC Symphony Orchestra's General Manager, 'provided a nice readable copy is put in front of them.' It was conducted at the same short notice by its dedicatee, Boston's young Michael Tilson Thomas. Stravinsky's *Les Noces* had to be cancelled because of that symbol of the times, failure to reach agreement over pay. Moura Lympany celebrated fifty years as a soloist by joining Malcolm Williamson to play his Two-piano Concerto. *The Sea*, which Frank Bridge so often used to direct himself at the Proms, was performed the same evening. Daniel Barenboim conducted Mozart's Piano Concerto, K595, one night for Sir Clifford Curzon; then both of them played the Concerto for Two Pianos, K365. The Royal Albert Hall organ had been heard in concertos and solos at least twice during every season since 1974.

Why was 'Rule, Britannia' going to be omitted in the Queen's Jubilee Year? someone wrote in 1977. Why was Trinidad-born Sandra Browne going to sing it this year? Why, when the Last Night had come and gone, had no one sung it at all? The public always gets this wrong. 'Rule, Britannia' at the end of Sir Henry Wood's original *Sea-Songs* is for orchestra alone. The soloist sings in Sargent's own arrangement which he used to tack on instead.

On the Last Night of 1979 the first BBC videogram recording at a Prom was made. Philips plan to issue it just before the 1981 season as a videodisc, the first to be marketed in the United Kingdom, and the first video programme produced by BBC Enterprises. A curious request came from Russia during the 1979 season, for a full text of 'Land of Hope and Glory'. The Estonian Symphony Orchestra wanted to perform it in Tallinn at an October concert.

There would be no more First Night telegrams bringing good wishes from Lady Jessie Wood, nor bouquets of flowers to her each season from the BBC Symphony Orchestra. She had died, 'aged about ninety-seven', at her home in Sussex.

'Summer would not be summer without the Proms'

istory repeated itself at the beginning of 1980. In mid-January
Gennadi Rozhdestvensky stood where Sir Henry Wood used to stand,
on the rostrum in the Duke's Hall of the Royal Academy of Music.
Honoured that morning by Wood's old alma mater, he rehearsed its youthful
symphony orchestra in the First Symphony of Shostakovich, as Sir Henry
used to rehearse eighty-five years before. The question quivering in the air
was whether Rozhdestvensky would be in London to conduct Elgar's
Oratorio *The Apostles* at the opening night of the 1980 Proms season on 18
July. Russian troops had recently moved into Afghanistan. There were those
who felt sport should be above politics; but many countries were proposing to
boycott the Olympic Games in Moscow. Could music escape? The Russians
refused to let some of their artists perform abroad. Western orchestras
cancelled tours of the Soviet Union. Against a background of international
tension, the BBC increased its broadcasts to Russia. Rozhdestvensky did
arrive, on 15 July, only to find that BBC Symphony Orchestra musicians and
their colleagues had been on strike against the BBC since 1 June, manning
picket lines in front of Broadcasting House in London, and elsewhere.
Whatever had gone wrong?

In 1980 the BBC had reached a point where £130 million had to be cut from
its expenditure over the next two years. These unprecedented economies were
the result of successive governments having been unable, or unwilling, to
increase the BBC's revenue – via television licence fees – by a sufficient
amount to meet its needs. A promise, made in 1969, that the BBC's obligation
to maintain house orchestras, 'beyond the strict needs of broadcasting', would
be taken into account was never honoured, though it was obviously the BBC's
own choice whether its orchestras broadcast full-time or not. The BBC's long-

term intentions were sound. They wished to create one orchestra of world class; to reinforce certain other orchestras, and to obtain more flexibility in light music. Outside the BBC there was some sympathy with all these aims, though perhaps not always among players. The independent Annan Report on the future of broadcasting, in 1977, expressed 'strong doubts', on financial and artistic grounds, about the BBC having to maintain all its thirteen 'musical bodies', or being tied to existing musical structures. But it would not have 'wished to see a national orchestra in Scotland or Wales abandoned'. The BBC's mistake was to believe that unavoidable economies provided a heaven-sent opportunity to achieve more than one of its objectives, without the blame being attributable to the BBC for any redundancies.

In February 1980 the BBC announced that it would have to reduce by £500,000 the £6½ million currently spent on musicians. Half a million pounds may seem only a drop in the ocean of £130 million cuts overall; but the BBC was proposing to disband five of its eleven orchestras in order to save it, and eventually sent dismissal notices to 172 of its players. These affairs gathered momentum in the first months of 1980, the BBC sticking by its action and the Musicians' Union warning that this would lead to a strike. The BBC made a public statement at – of all places – a Press Conference on 29 May to announce the 1980 Proms. The BBC Scottish Symphony Orchestra, one of the five to be disbanded, was due to play at the seventh concert. The other four under notice were the Midland and Northern Radio Orchestras, the Northern Ireland Orchestra, and the London Studio Players. The BBC Scottish had been under threat once before, in Sir William Glock's day. An uproar then had soon scotched that idea. Might not the same happen again? Or might the BBC immovably resist being routed a second time? That could become dangerous; but why had a symphony orchestra been lumped in with four light orchestras in the first place? It is open to question whether the whole music profession would have manned the barricades over the London Studio Players and their like.

At that Proms Press Conference, the BBC's position was presented in such an uncompromisingly belligerent statement that people of standing in the wider musical world outside went away wondering what on earth the BBC thought it was doing. It immediately lost them most of whatever sympathy there had been for the real financial problems, and got the BBC's case off firmly on the wrong foot. Two days later, on Sunday 1 June, not only BBC players but the entire 41,000 membership of the Musicians' Union came out on strike against the BBC.

Pickets covered BBC premises throughout the country. It quickly became clear that no performer would make music inside while the strike continued. They would make music outside, though; the insolent strains of 'Colonel Bogey' brought worshippers out of All Souls' Church that Sunday morning. There were to be many such impromptu entertainments, either as a show of support, or – like those outside the Royal Festival Hall – to keep faith with

35. Sir Charles Groves, Sir Lennox Berkeley, Lady Barbirolli and Sir Geraint Evans supporting the pickets (*The Times*)

people who turned up not knowing that the BBC's International Festival of Light Music was cancelled. It quickly became clear also that beyond these outposts lay the threatened fortress of the Promenade Concerts, just six weeks away.

'The greatest examples of Music and Art are world possessions and unassailable even by the prejudices and passions of the hour,' the directors of Queen's Hall had stated in 1914. 'Six weeks is a long time in an industrial dispute,' said the BBC in 1980. 'During our talks with the Musicians' Union, not one constructive suggestion has come from their side.' 'Utterly pessimistic' about the outcome of such talks, the MU claimed 'we have had to put up with the BBC's petulant arrogance throughout. They have broken agreements and refused to negotiate.' Contact between the two sides ended in deadlock; but a clearer evaluation was beginning to take shape elsewhere.

In Geneva, an emergency motion by the International Federation of

36. BBC Symphony Orchestra players, Chairman Colin Bradbury (*centre*), give an impromptu concert outside All Souls' Church during the strike (*Gerald Manning*)

Musicians condemned the BBC's proposals, and pledged support for the British Musicians' Union. The English National Opera's orchestra in London refused to play if a broadcast of Beethoven's *Fidelio* went ahead. The BBC released the company from its contract, so that the Coliseum audience should not be disappointed. In Leeds, English National Opera North's orchestra allowed Delius's *A Village Romeo and Juliet* to be broadcast only after the BBC accepted some extraordinary preconditions. Foreign orchestras in London and abroad withheld permission for the BBC to broadcast their concerts. A representative of the Toronto Mendelssohn Choir (due to sing at the Proms) said that Canadian musicians were appalled; whilst in America it was rumoured that within ten years the BBC planned to get out of orchestral management entirely. Surely they would not disband the BBC Symphony Orchestra! In June 1980, what guarantee was there? The West German Orchestral Union was deeply concerned that the BBC could not keep just 500 musicians in a total of 25,000 employees, when German radio stations, with a similar total, supported sixteen orchestras, 1,130 players altogether. No member of the Incorporated Society of Musicians would perform for the BBC; public concerts were lost, and radio presenters such as Jack Brymer withdrew. The Musicians' Benevolent Fund let it be known that it would help in cases of hardship. Other London orchestras played outside Broadcasting House in support of their colleagues; and students from the schools of music joined picket lines. There were no pickets outside the BBC's Music Division building. None were needed; there was total support inside for those on strike, and considerable sympathy throughout the rest of the BBC. Many of its staff chatted openly with pickets, respected colleagues and well-known musicians, wishing them well. If anyone passing through the lines saw in their inexhaustible good humour and politeness any lack of guts or fighting spirit, they were badly mistaken. 'Please do not underestimate our resolve,' they told the BBC's Governors; 'we remain convinced of the rightness of our cause.'

'Keep Music Live,' their badges proclaimed. Records and 'live' broadcasting being balanced through 'needle-time' agreements,* it could hardly be otherwise. The slogan conveyed a flavour of danger. The Association of Broadcasting Staff having forbidden 'live' transmissions, or repeats of earlier broadcasts, the BBC was putting on far more records than usual, fast using up that 'needle-time'. The danger was that many people do not seem to mind listening to records. There were also some skirmishes and fouls. BBC Scotland rattled a sabre at its Symphony Orchestra for proposing to play in Perth, but climbed down when it went ahead. The BBC's Welsh Orchestra played at the Llangollen Eisteddfod only after assurances that they would not be broadcast or televised. The BBC held back holiday payments from many of its players. The MU swiftly reminded them that, even if the strike ended close to the Proms, the BBC Symphony Orchestra was entitled to, and would take, the usual month's holiday. Players confided privately that if only it did end they would willingly resume work at once, to get the Proms under way. 'Summer would not be summer without the Proms' – that one opinion voiced the fears of many. The BBC said that final preparations were going ahead 'in the confident expectation that the Proms will take place'. But behind the scenes meetings were held to make plans for the abandonment of an entire season, for the first time in Proms history. 'The BBC is prepared to sacrifice the Proms rather than drop the plan to disband five house orchestras. If the MU chooses not to allow broadcasting of the Proms, there will be no Proms.' The BBC also said that *they* were not on strike; the musicians were – a plausible remark. In any dispute, only one party is on strike. This does not mean that the other side is blameless. 'If it comes to a choice between saving

---

*Phonographic Performance Ltd licenses the BBC to broadcast records for so many hours per week. The Musicians' Union ensures that this does not unacceptably reduce 'live' broadcasting.

£500,000 and saving the Proms, the Proms must lose.' For a strong impression that Culture stood at the gates of Broadcasting House, while the barbarians were inside, the BBC had only itself to blame. The shadow of Caliban lurked about its corridors. That role was not played by Robert Ponsonby, a pained and silent witness to the folly of others, standing aloof from the main conflict, but forced to unpick the delicate tapestry of his intricately worked 1980 Proms season, thread by thread.

All disputes have their natural span. There was confidence that a solution would be found to this one, saving face on both sides. The Proms had never yet failed to start on time. In the midst of all this brouhaha, the dignified presence of Sir Adrian Boult made itself felt through a letter to *The Times*, suggesting that the Proms go ahead in public, and be recorded, for broadcast only after the strike ended. Was this the hoped-for compromise? The BBC Symphony Orchestra would have had to break the strike in order to play. The Musicians' Union rejected it as the ramshackle contrivance it now appears, however well meant. That same day Lady Barbirolli, Sir Lennox Berkeley, Sir Geraint Evans and Sir Charles Groves stood with the pickets in front of Broadcasting House; and the next day André Previn, listening to the London Symphony Orchestra's brass playing outside. How long could the BBC disregard such mounting condemnation? For much longer, apparently, than might have been expected. The Advisory, Conciliation and Arbitration Service (ACAS) invited both sides separately for discussions, but concluded there was 'not enough common ground to attempt a settlement'. There was also an unprecedented 3½-hour debate in the House of Commons, not primarily about the Proms but about the disbandment by the BBC of five house orchestras. While it was taking place, an orchestra conducted by Antony Hopkins repeated history by playing Handel's *Water Music* from a barge on the Thames, 'the only decent music that we have heard from the Terrace in recent years', as one Hon. Member put it. The debate united both sides of the House in disapproval, and even 'achieved the impossible' – among Scottish MPs – 'by uniting Scotland on one issue'.

Hansard makes unusually lively reading. Although there was considerable understanding of the BBC's funding problems – 'the real responsibility rests with Governments to make certain that a sensible licence fee is charged' – the final consensus was that 'the BBC should, and must, reconsider its proposals'. The Musicians' Union would 'continue the dispute until, in the view of all intelligent, humane and right-thinking people, it has won a dispute that it did not seek, that it did not embark upon, and that was entirely provoked by the incompetence of the BBC management'. For the BBC to save the Proms, it would have to go back to the MU and say: 'We are in trouble. We think that there have to be cuts. Can we sit down and negotiate about them?' That would have needed a man big enough to say 'sorry'; but there was none around. The BBC showed no outward sign of being affected by MPs' unanimous disapproval. Sneers were made privately that few had attended the debate, which seems a wilful misunderstanding of how Parliament debates specialised issues; MPs not directly involved always leave the Chamber to those who are.

It gradually came to be recognised that since the last Proms crisis, even since Sir William Glock retired, top management at the BBC had become a different breed. As the eloquent Bryan Magee MP put it, during that long debate: '. . . nearly all of them reach the top via a concern with current affairs broadcasting, journalism, politics, or management itself, and not through an involvement with the arts and artistic broadcasting'. The belief that new BBC men were apparently no longer upholders of cultural traditions (particularly if inconveniently expensive) came as a great shock to those here and abroad who had always quoted the BBC with praise and envy.

Of those men, the one who initiated the fateful steps leading to the strike, and then bore the main retaliatory onslaught against the BBC, was radio's Managing Director, Aubrey Singer, whose roly-poly bonhomie screens the tough, obstinate Yorkshireman beneath. Justly or unjustly, he will be recalled as the man who stopped the Proms in 1980, the first time in eighty-six years they did not start as planned, a disaster even the blitz failed to achieve.

Aubrey Singer brought to BBC radio a revitalising influence, and an abundance of fresh ideas. Music, however, is a territory where many air their views, but which very few really understand. A bond unites performers, in a way that those who have not made music can perhaps never fully comprehend. The first BBC man in all this publicly to declare a passionate love of music was George Howard, of Castle Howard, appointed to be the next Chairman of the Board of Governors, at what could have been a crucial meeting on 3 July. It was the last one before the Proms at which they might have intervened. That morning pianist Cristina Ortiz and conductor Norman Del Mar handed in to the Governors a petition with over half a million signatures. But instead of saying 'sorry', they opted to go back to ACAS for further discussions. George Howard, a big man in the finest sense, was not due to take office until 1 August, too late to save the Proms. One even more obvious mediator had so far been silent. Lord Goodman, conciliator extraordinary and prominent music-lover, devised a scheme whereby the Arts Council (of which he had been a notable chairman) would run the Proms, and his Association for Business Sponsorship of the Arts guarantee any deficit. This was acceptable to the MU, but – with only twelve days to the First Night – the BBC brusquely rejected it.

Seventeen BBC music producers petitioned their Director-General, Sir Ian Trethowan, to halt the 'irreparable damage' being done, and to restore the BBC's 'reputation and dignity'. One of the most distinguished, Dr Robert Simpson, resigned a few days afterwards, out of 'growing disquiet' and 'dwindling respect', writing to *The Times*: 'I can no longer work for the BBC without a profound sense of betrayal of most of the values I and many others believe in; and its management includes elements whose authority I cannot accept without shame.' Nothing could more eloquently have articulated widespread feelings, or put such fresh heart into many colleagues. MU pickets were handing out new button badges to bemused passers-by. The legend 'SAXINGA' looked at first like some obscure instrument. 'I don't like the way this dispute has become personalised', said Aubrey Singer; 'I am a servant of the BBC Board of Governors'. Figaro, the Barber of Seville, might well have made a similar claim. Talks between the BBC and the MU at ACAS again broke down, before nightfall on 11 July. According to some people, 'Saxinga' was beginning to sound like the only way out.

A grotesque fate swiftly overtook the MU's announcement that members of the BBC Symphony Orchestra would stage an alternative First Night of their own at Alexandra Palace. That old north London landmark burned to the ground the same day, forcing a move to Wembley Conference Centre. The Royal Opera House Orchestra ran a Late Night Concert for the MU's hardship fund. Jessye Norman, José Carreras, Sir Geraint Evans and many others gave their services. Although the Proms already looked doomed, on 11 July the BBC presented revised proposals in a good statement, made much too late, which also suggested disbanding a sixth orchestra, the Scottish Radio, making matters worse, despite the promise to create a new BBC Scottish Sinfonia. Sir Ian Trethowan officially announced the cancellation of the First Night, adding: 'The road to the Albert Hall lies past the negotiating table. We are there, and we would like to see the Musicians' Union join us to discuss our proposals'. 'The simple fact', wrote the MU to *The Times*, 'is that the BBC is not at the negotiating table, nor has been since February.' Nor would they 'consider any modification of their intentions, contenting themselves with the continuously repeated claim that they had decided upon the best way to serve "the interests of the listener".' Aubrey Singer warned that BBC radio could 'carry on . . . until this time next year with no problem whatsoever', which was sheer bluff. Radio 3 had already discovered that it could carry on for only seven more weeks. While Sir Colin Davis rehearsed for the Wembley First Night (with scores and parts freely lent by the London Symphony Orchestra), the BBC, MU, Arts Council and Lord Goodman went before the House of Commons Select Committee on Education, Science and the Arts, the first such body to intervene in an industrial dispute. A bit of concession on both sides brought the first glimmer of hope, and a recommendation that Lord Goodman chair a meeting of the other three parties. If that started the Proms, then Lord Goodman might also try to resolve the strike.

On 18 July there were two First Nights simultaneously. The Proms as planned by the BBC became broadcasts only, as they had in 1944; but this time there were not even the proper performers. Listeners heard Elgar's *The Apostles* from gramophone records. The Wembley First Night, organised by BBC Symphony Orchestra members, and given to keep faith with Proms audiences, took place on a cold, grey evening at the worst start to a summer since 1912. Sir Adrian Boult sent a telegram, wishing he could be there to shake everyone's hand. Dame Janet Baker and many other eminent musicians sat in the audience. The Master of the Queen's Music, Malcolm Williamson, attended all the Wembley Proms, and said that feeling was running equally high in other areas he had visited. Promenaders sang 'Happy Birthday' to the fifty-year-old BBC Symphony Orchestra (many wearing 'Keep Music Live' badges), and greeted Sir Colin Davis and Cristina Ortiz with 'Remember, there is no Singer in tonight's concert!' Rarely can the well-worn tunes of Tchaikovsky's First Piano Concerto have held such emotional charge. Was this a brave beginning, or a turning-point in history? Might the Proms perhaps never start again? Audience and performers drew closer together, outcast but united. People were not ashamed to have tears in their eyes; and many felt bitter towards the BBC for bringing things to such a pass. Both parties to the dispute held back from the brink over this concert. The BBC did not try to stop its orchestra playing; and the orchestra resisted any temptation to be broadcast by independent radio or television. Either would have given great provocation to the other side.

The first steps away from catastrophe had already been taken that same afternoon. Sir Ian Trethowan's view, that the strike had to be settled before trying to re-start the Proms, had prevailed. In Lord Goodman's words, 'Events happened at great speed', when he met both sides separately, following the House of Commons Select Committee's recommendations, 'but there was pretty unanimous agreement that the sensible thing was to seek to resolve the strike issue; that the Prom problem would not be solved until the major question had been disposed of'. So the parties returned to ACAS with the added benefit of Lord Goodman's presence, but without Aubrey Singer, who dropped out of the picture. This time they hammered it out for three whole days, emerging after midnight on the third, to announce that a formula had been worked out which might end the strike. At Lord Goodman's insistence, no details were disclosed until the Musicians' Union and the BBC's orchestras had studied them and agreed to hold a ballot. He thought it 'inconceivable that the proposals should not be accepted'; though in fact they meant some players voting themselves out of a job. The BBC continued to broadcast approximate Proms from records. Their Symphony Orchestra announced sixteen alternative Proms, to be given at Wembley; and gave the second on 24 July, with Sir Charles Groves and John Shirley-Quirk. The Royal Philharmonic Orchestra donated £6,000 to the MU hardship fund, the proceeds of a concert by Paul Tortelier and Antal Dorati. MU pickets remained at their posts, 'still in good heart'; and Robert Ponsonby said he felt 'incredibly happy' that the Proms might soon be starting. The formula, 'fair and satisfactory to both sides', kept the BBC Scottish Symphony Orchestra, the BBC Northern Ireland Orchestra (to be enlarged as soon as possible), and the London Studio Players in revised form. The BBC Scottish Radio Orchestra, never part of the original proposals, and the Northern and Midland Radio Orchestras, would be disbanded; but in March 1981, not

August 1980 as formerly proposed. Any voting against this by Scottish musicians was felt unlikely to affect the final outcome. The BBC would guarantee, in freelance work, two-thirds of the salaries of dismissed players for five years, rather than an earlier promise to 'plough back' money saved by disbanding orchestras. There was more than a touch of sophistry in the way the BBC disclosed these terms, but there is a time to be magnanimous; they were having to climb down a very long way.

If the players affected voted to approve all this, work could be resumed on Monday 4 August - Wagner Night at the Albert Hall; what more appropriate start, unless it could have been 10 August? Then it was realised that a rehearsal on the day would not be enough; and in the prevailing circumstances, no one felt like asking the BBC Symphony Orchestra to come in one day beforehand. What a pity. The tentatively revised programme for that evening would have ended with the Suite from *Die Meistersinger*. There was a Viennese Prom at Wembley on 25 July. Apart from the First Night, these alternative Proms were not yet full, lacking funds for extensive advertising, or access to radio and television. Word was spreading, though; people had begun to ring Broadcasting House, asking for details of 'the BBC's alternative Proms' at Wembley!

As it turned out, the fourth Wembley Prom on 1 August was also the last. At midday the result of that secret ballot was made public by the General Secretary of the Musicians' Union, John Morton, an adversary the BBC had almost certainly underestimated; an imposing man who speaks with authority, every word carefully considered. His members had approved the formula for ending the dispute by 393 in favour, to only 80 against, a majority much larger than expected. A light orchestral ensemble played from the top of an open bus outside Broadcasting House, officially closing the picket lines. Within minutes Sir Ian Trethowan welcomed the outcome, thanking Lord Goodman for his great help in achieving it, and hoping the Albert Hall Proms might start on 7 August. In the afternoon Robert Ponsonby confirmed that they would, and proposed to offer two tickets for the price of one, as an immediate incentive to get things going. In the evening Simon Rattle conducted the BBC Symphony Orchestra for the first time, at the Wembley Prom. To their credit, neither the orchestra nor its union did a lap of honour; the orchestra's chairman, Colin Bradbury, spoke with dignity about the settlement of the longest strike in MU history. After the concert there was special praise for John Morton, who had master-minded their campaign and calmly and firmly put their case before ACAS, before Parliament and to the Press, who were as unstinting in their appreciation of his accessibility as they had been convinced of the justice of his cause. He 'never put a foot wrong', according to Colin Bradbury, who described how the crisis had brought symphony players and their union closer than ever before. It was also an important factor in uniting, just one month later, the Musicians' Union (the players) and the Incorporated Society of Musicians (the soloists) into one formidable body, which will certainly watch broadcasting organisations very closely in future. John Morton viewed the result with mixed emotions: 'It is a matter of profound regret that such a strike should ever have been necessary, and we can only hope that the BBC management will have learned from the virtually unanimous condemnation of their behaviour'. Later, BBC Chairman George Howard, stressing that neither side had 'won', was 'absolutely delighted that common sense has prevailed'. If neither side had 'won', the BBC had lost something infinitely precious. How long would it take to restore its damaged image? How long to rebuild confidence and trust in its integrity? And how would it ensure that such things could never happen again?

'Let us look forward, rather than back,' said Robert Ponsonby when the BBC Symphony Orchestra reassembled for the first rehearsals. 'In my part of the world,' John Pritchard announced from the rostrum, 'when there is something to celebrate, we play a really horrible chord.' So they played a loud raspberry, and then a second, even louder – the orchestral equivalent of 'Merde!', with which soloists are often wished good luck, 'Bonne chance!' being considered fatal. Gennadi Rozhdestvensky came to support the orchestra, his wife Victoria Postnikova already back in Moscow, her earlier Prom cancelled by the strike. The third First Night of the 1980 season was given at the Albert Hall in real Proms weather, sweltering hot. Everyone tried hard, but it was hardly the authentic send-off, nor did the season ever completely recover afterwards. That was not the fault of soprano Jessye Norman, radiant in Mahler's Fourth Symphony and Messiaen's *Poèmes pour Mi*, nor of the Promenaders, back on form and loudly reading from a smuggled television announcer's script, just as Michael Berkeley was about to speak it before the cameras – 'Try keeping a straight face when *that* happens to you!' A feeling of anticlimax was perhaps inescapable; peace, after all, is less riveting than war.

'We've had four weeks of Proms, and it feels like a four-week season,' was how Promenaders assessed their own reaction to a most unusual year. It generally takes that long for things to get into their stride. 'If any orchestra sounds more beautiful in the Royal Albert Hall than the Amsterdam Concertgebouw,' wrote one critic, 'I have yet to hear it.' Their Bruckner Fifth Symphony under Bernard Haitink – 'one of the wonders of the musical world' – helped considerably to restore authentic Proms fever. Alas, the public's understandably long-delayed return to the Box Office narrowly denied them the expected full house. 'I am saddened and disappointed at the bookings for some concerts,' said Robert Ponsonby, whose long labours had deserved a better reward. Except for a brief period in the 1950s, the Proms have always needed financial backing. In the 1960s the BBC hoped to take in cash

37. Gennadi Rozhdestvensky with his wife, Victoria Postnikova
(BBC Copyright Photograph)

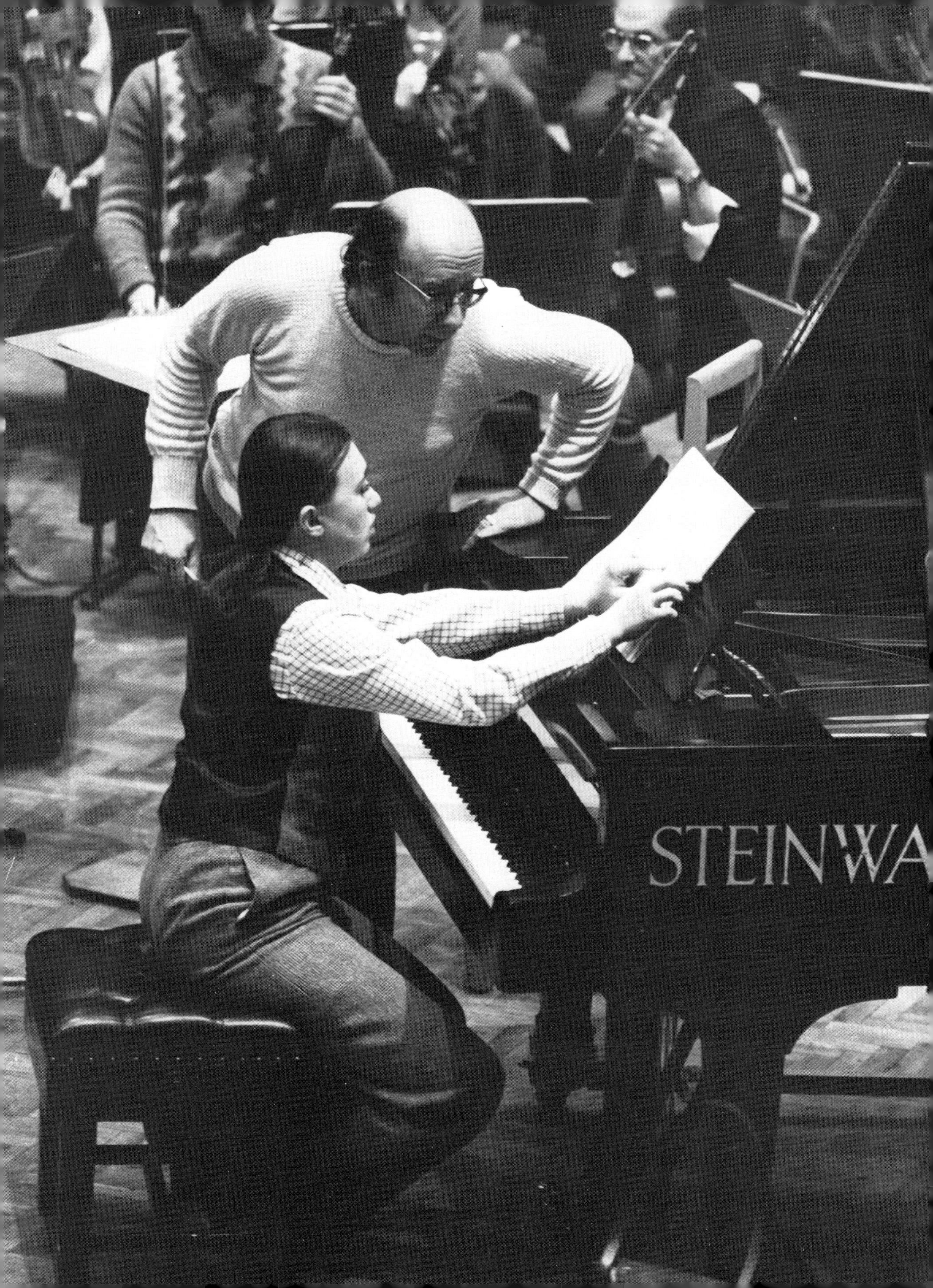
STEINWA

sufficient to cover what they had to pay out, in performers' fees and so on; to break even, because their own orchestras' and staff salaries come from a different BBC 'purse'. More recently, with inflation pushing up the cost of everything (but not ticket prices in proportion) a BBC subsidy of £40,000 on a season had not been unusual. Tragic losses in 1980 were the result of tragic events. May they never be repeated.

There was no lack of variety in the truncated season. Audiences heard John Lill in 'the kind of performance Brahms would have liked to give' of his Second Piano Concerto; and Sir Clifford Curzon playing Beethoven's *Emperor* Concerto for the 200th time in a long career. Penderecki conducted his Violin Concerto; Elliott Carter heard Charles Rosen, 'superhuman' in his dauntingly complex Piano Concerto; and Kiri Te Kanawa gave 'seductive performances' of five early songs by Strauss. Rozhdestvensky set the place ablaze with Schubert's 'Great' C major and Britten's 'Spring' symphonies; and Claudio Abbado raised the roof with Tchaikovsky's Fourth.

A much-trumpeted new work, *Ringed by the flat horizon*, by student composer George Benjamin sounded much like the mixture as before; almost anyone from Messiaen to George Crumb might have written it. Edmund Rubbra's short Eleventh Symphony (the sole 1980 BBC commission) sounded like the mixture as before 1950; his time may come again. 'I *think* Tippett's still alive,' said a woman in the Stalls rather loudly to her companion. Sir Michael, sitting right behind them, looked pleased with the splendid première of his Triple Concerto. It may well prove a masterpiece; a suspicion reinforced when seen on BBC television a few nights later, the undoubted jewel of the 1980 season. Not everyone buys a programme. On another evening, those who had not, found Tippett's *Ritual Dances* rather pleasant for Stockhausen, whose JUBILEE they thought it was. Stockhausen's piece had been taken out at the last moment, due to the illness of Andrew Davis.

Promenaders were once more outside the Royal Albert Hall with their sleeping bags by the start of the last week, those on one side hoping for returned tickets to the Last Night, those on the other side preparing for the annual rush across the Arena to be first at the barrier behind the conductor's rostrum, with a chance of being seen on television during the second half. One in the queue did a brisk trade in unsold 'Wembley Proms 80' T-shirts from a carton beside him. This rumbustious crowd furled its flags during Delius's *Sea Drift*, proving that there is music on the Last Night, and they know it; you could also have heard a pin drop in Grainger's unaccompanied *Brigg Fair*. Few in the huge audience would have known that Dame Eva Turner sat with them in the Stalls, just below Sir Henry Wood's old Box; and next to her, Lady Jessie Wood's grandson Henry, with his own small son, Edward. Just before the televised second half, the camera trained on announcer Richard Baker broke down, forcing him to face another, in a Box too far away for him to read from a tele-prompt. Like the true professional he is, he introduced all the items from memory.

Australian conductor Sir Charles Mackerras made a suitably antipodean speech at the end of his first Last Night, tiptoeing through the minefield of things unmentionable. For once, it would have been inappropriate to ask three cheers for the BBC; instead, he spoke of its Symphony Orchestra's fifty glorious years, all of them shared by Sidonie Goossens OBE, still at her harp on the platform beside him, taking part in her sixtieth Last Night. Sir Charles made only oblique references to the strike, but they were not lost on his audience: 'It's *intended* to start next year's Proms on July the 17th' brought a deafening roar of approval. He also led into 'Auld Lang Syne' by recalling that his professional career had begun as an oboe player in the BBC Scottish Symphony Orchestra.

The next day Promenaders duly arrived at the Church of the Holy Sepulchre to lay the laurel wreath on Sir Henry Wood's tomb. Some time afterwards, the woman whose ideas led to that church accumulating such special associations was acknowledged there by a framed inscription:

> The Council of Friends of the Musicians' Chapel was formed at the inspiration of Lady Jessie Wood (Jessie Goldsack) 1883-1979, who will be remembered by countless musicians for her kindness and encouragement.

Nothing much else left to do. Sunday morning after the Last Night feels strange and hollow, like the sad ending of a lovely long holiday. Off with the motley, then, and into the cupboard with it until next season; when like summer's flowers the glorious Proms will once more burst into blossom, all over again.

❧

Promenade

Season after season Robert Ponsonby pays tribute to a panel of music producers and other members of his staff, brought together for the wide range of their interests. 'In making the programmes I have had much help and sound advice from the group of colleagues within the BBC who have a special concern for the Proms. I hope that they have enjoyed their involvement.' He also meets representatives of the Promenaders each year, to let them put forward their views, regarding this as a valuable and positive contribution, very different from gossip and rumour. They discuss programmes, likes and dislikes, successes and failures, improving conditions in the Promenade, even the doors that sometimes squeak.

Promenaders are what these concerts are about. The 2,500 young people standing to listen make them different from every other kind of concert. Come into the Arena and hear what some of them have to say.

'Most of us are students; when summer is over, it's over, apart from one or two reunions at Covent Garden Proms or the Festival Hall.'

'You'd quickly become a wreck if you tried to catch every Prom. Only about a dozen people do.'

'We don't like some of the prearranged shouting. "Heave!" when the piano lid is lifted was a nice tradition. "Ho!" from upstairs spoils it.'

'The T-shirts and boaters were a great idea. There ought to be at least a badge every season, otherwise we just update the old gear.'

'A lot of us sense the public is definitely hostile to what now goes on at the Viennese Evening and the Last Night, or any Prom being televised. We are fed up with the behaviour of a few people. Verdi's *Requiem* or Mahler's Third Symphony are *not* the place for prearranged shouting between Arena and Gallery.'

38. Proms are about Promenaders! (*Godfrey MacDomnic*)

'Older people do watch us on TV and think well, not *all* youngsters are delinquents or drug addicts.'

'It would be nice to have Beethoven and Tchaikovsky nights like they used to; or at least the basic classical repertoire.'

'Some people get ready to shout before a work like the *Tallis Fantasia* or *Les Noces* is over. It can *ruin* the end of *The Planets*. And that shout before the *Eroica* started was definitely planned. It nearly threw Andrew Davis.'

'There's no substitute for the real thing, and it's cheap.'

'I should think all that electronic gear will one day lie around like a heap of old junk.'

'We can tell good playing from bad, you know!'

'The public here and abroad gets the wrong image of the Proms. We would like to have the *whole* of the Last Night televised, not just the second half.'

'My money's on Henze and Michael Tippett; and perhaps Hugh Wood and John McCabe. One of the women composers could survive as well.'

'People *are* still moved by music; it creeps up on you. One time it suddenly sounds different. That's when you buy the record!'

'If people cry, why should they not laugh?' said Richard Strauss of his *Don Quixote*. What gives music, or drama, or literature this power to transmit emotion? 'Is it not strange that sheeps' guts should hale souls out of men's bodies?' wrote Shakespeare. But how do the tears and laughter get in? The composer was not laughing or crying; he was wrestling with form. Nor is the performer; he is concentrating on technique. With a poet's insight, Peter Porter approaches the heart of it: 'When there is no technique, emotion comes out as embarrassment. When there is technique, it comes out as the original emotion.'

We may never get closer than that.

39. Promenaders waiting for the doors to open (1980) *(Godfrey MacDomnic)*

❧

Continuity . . .

A nyone who has been to Promenade Concerts at the Royal Albert Hall will have noticed certain activity going on before and behind two glass-partitioned Boxes (called Loggias) to the left of the platform, at the top of the steps. Behind each window there is a small BBC control cubicle in which sits a Studio Manager responsible for the overall balance of sound when a concert is being broadcast. All are now broadcast in stereo (some have been broadcast in quadraphony).

The left-hand cubicle is for the BBC's national networks; the right-hand one for broadcasts overseas. In front of each sit the announcers, usually one on the left for BBC Radio 3, 4 or 2; sometimes more than one on the right for the various BBC external services, or foreign stations taking a live relay of the concert. Announcers use lip microphones held close to the mouth, for they are in the auditorium with the audience and have to speak quietly. Notes on the programme lie illuminated on a small lectern in front of them; but what they tell listeners about goings-on at the hall is unscripted.

High up and outside the auditorium is a much more complex control studio, where a senior Studio Manager balances the concert for broadcasting. He may adjust the volume of sound from any microphone in the hall, exercising musical judgment and following the performance with a full score. Both this control room and the small control cubicle are connected by telephone with the central nervous system at Broadcasting House, Langham Place.

The producer of a BBC television broadcast from the Proms sits in one of several highly equipped television vans outside the Albert Hall. Before him is a bank of TV screens, one monitoring each of his cameras in the hall, and a master screen showing which of the various pictures is being transmitted at a given moment. A red light on the camera itself indicates the same thing. Cameras can be spotted in various parts of the hall. The greater illumination

40. Richard Baker interviews Promenaders from the 'moat' on the Last Night (1975) (*BBC Copyright Photograph*)

they require is provided by many floodlights, which raise the temperature inside the auditorium, sometimes uncomfortably so for performers on a hot summer's evening.

The television announcer may be seen talking to a TV camera in one of the Grand Tier Boxes. Richard Baker has also for many years gone into the 'moat' between platform and Arena to interview Promenaders on the Last

Night. Viewers have wondered how, under a ballot system, so many of the same faces may be seen year after year along that front barrier. It is because a season ticket to the Arena (there is no other) includes the First and Last Nights and avoids the ballot. The purchaser has only to make sure of an early place in the queue to be among the first at the barrier. Some camp outside the Albert Hall for a week like bargain hunters at sale time. Some buy a season ticket and go to nothing but the Last Night, considering this excellent value for £20, as it was in 1979. Promenade Concerts have their fanatical devotees just like Frank Sinatra or any Pop group.

Each of the television cameramen reads from a 'shooting script' clipped to his camera, carefully worked out by the producer, who can speak to each cameraman via a tiny earpiece. The radio teams transmit the sound of a concert as it is; the television producer has also to provide pictures which will continuously interest people watching their TV screens at home. As there is usually little movement at concerts, this calls for some ingenuity.

In Broadcasting House and Television Centre there is always another announcer who keeps things going between one programme and the next. This link is spoken from an appropriately named Continuity Studio. As the hands of the studio clocks approach 7.30 p.m. on the day of a Promenade Concert, a continuity announcer waits to come in at the end of the preceding programme . . .

'That was *The Waste Land* by T. S. Eliot. It was broadcast from a gramophone record, and read by Eliot himself.'

(*There is a moment's pause, like a fresh thought.*)

'You are listening to Radio 3. And now for this evening's concert we join my colleague Patricia Hughes at the Royal Albert Hall.'

(*A new background fills the stereo receiver like a deep breath. There is a basic low murmuring of many conversations, splashed here and there by notes from high and low instruments; rustling, movement, coughing; the tangible sounds of a great concourse.*)

'Good evening, and welcome to tonight's Henry Wood Promenade Concert, which is being given by the BBC Symphony Orchestra.

'The concert is one of five during the present season at which all Sir Michael Tippett's symphonies are being played in celebration of his eightieth birthday. The main work in tonight's programme is his Fourth Symphony, which will be played after the interval. The concert will begin in a few moments with the first performance in this country of . . .'

Acknowledgments

Many people have contributed, directly or indirectly, to this book, not least the performers and the Promenaders. So many photographs have been offered that I abdicated the impossible task of selection to the publisher; nevertheless, many have had to be left out which deserved inclusion.

If any name has been omitted from those who have so kindly spoken or written to me, or otherwise helped, I hope to be forgiven. Amongst those to whom I am indebted are:

Miss M. Alexander
John Amis
Miss M. Andersen
Felix Aprahamian
Dame Isobel Baillie
Paul Beard
Jean Bettesworth
Alan Blackwood
Harry Blech OBE
Pierre Boulez
Charles Bye
BBC Information Division
   Music Division
   Radio and tv programmes
   Radio Times
   Hulton Picture Library
   Reference Library
   Written Archives Centre
John Coldstream
Uvadale Corbett
Christopher Cristodoulou
Lilian Davies

Peter Maxwell Davies
Sir Colin Davis
Harry Ellis
Mrs Elizabeth Entwistle
Anne Fairholme
Mrs H. W. Fairholme JP
Megan Foster
Miss C. Fowke
Max Gilbert
Sir William Glock
Sidonie Goossens OBE
Kenneth Gosling
H. J. H. Greenacre
Rodney Greenberg
Sidney Griller
Jennifer Hall
Nicholas Hall
Arthur Hammond
Stephen Hearst CBE
Peter Heyworth
Antony Hopkins CBE
Paul Huband

Mrs Jonathan Huntingford
Niel Resdahl Jensen
Edgar Johnson
Geoffrey Last
J. H. Lawrie
Sir Anthony Lewis CBE
Mrs I. Loynes
Mr W. Loynes
Geoffrey Manuel
Denis Matthews CBE
Peter Mereweather
Alan H. Morriss
Harry Mortimer OBE
Ralph Nicholson
Robert Ponsonby
Peter Porter
Mrs Audrey Powell
John Pritchard CBE
Christopher Regan
Arthur Reckless
C. B. Rees
William Relton

Cormac Rigby
Miss M. E. Rudgley
Gordon T. Sanders
Dr William Sargant
Mrs Elvira Selsby
Mrs G. N. Simmonds
Dr Robert Simpson
Dr Peter Skeggs
Pamela Smith
Fritz Spiegl
Paul Strang
David Stripp
Eric Thompson OBE
Dame Eva Turner
Rev Richard Tydeman
Anita Webber
David Webster
Avril Wood
Dorothy Wood OBE
Lady Jessie Wood
C. L. Wykes

Index of Events

This is a book intended for reading, rather than for looking things up in. Nevertheless, page references to the main events may be found useful. These are given in the first index, and a roster of performers mentioned in the text in the second. A third index lists only those works which occur in the text – a complete list of everything performed at the Proms would run to perhaps twenty thousand entries.

EIGHTEEN NINETY-FIVE
The Proms are planned 24. Robert Newman, Henry Wood, Dr George Cathcart 24. Wagner and low pitch 24. The concerts take shape 29. The opening night 32.

THE VANISHING BAND
Classical Night 36. One-composer nights 37. Wagner on Monday, Beethoven on Friday 38. A different orchestra (the Deputies System) 38.

'THIS BRAT WOOD'
Training 42. Discipline 43. Wood's mother's death 46. Marriage to Princess Olga Ourousoff 47. Plebiscite Concerts 47. By Royal Command 48. Two-composer nights 49.

IN THE MIDST OF LIFE
Operatic Selections dismantled 51. Bankruptcy 52. Sir Edgar Speyer's syndicate 52. Jessie Goldsack 54. Wood's illness 54. His father's death 54. Beethoven's *Choral Symphony* 54. His Septet 55. Wood's *New Fantasia on British Sea-Songs* 56. Death of Olga 56.

THE GREAT WAR
Wood remarries 60. Schoenberg's *Five Orchestral Pieces* and Stravinsky's *Firebird* 61. The Great War 59, 62. Consequent changes 62. New Queen's Hall Orchestra 62. Tuesday Russian Night 63. First woman Leader 64. Chappell & Co sponsor the Proms 64. British composer-conductors include Malcolm Sargent 65. British Broadcasting Company 67. King George V and Queen Mary; first visit 67. Single-opera Wagner Nights, Madrigals, and organ solos 68. Death of Robert Newman 69.

DIFFERENT DRUMMERS
BBC sponsorship 71. Sir Henry Wood and his Symphony Orchestra 71. New Prospectus 72. Five microphones in Queen's Hall; and Broadcasting House next door 76. British Composers' Concerts 76. Wood and Bach (Klenovsky) 78. BBC National Chorus 79. Listeners abroad 80. Wagner cancelled 80.

DIARY OF A YOUNG MAN
Leader Laurance Turner 88. Composers conducting, Elgar, Vaughan Williams, Quilter, Lambert, Bax, Bliss, Walton, Ireland 88-92, 97, 98. An interruption 95. With Boyd Neel and Leslie Woodgate 97.

SIR HENRY WOOD'S JUBILEE
Marriage breakdown 100. Lady Jessie Wood 101. Marie Wilson, Paul Beard, Leaders 101, 102. More broadcasts abroad 102. Coronation, King George VI 102. Wood's Jubilee 104. His bust

in Queen's Hall 104. The Second World War 106. BBC Symphony Orchestra evacuated 106. Wood's 'farewell season' under Royal Philharmonic Society 107. Basil Cameron, Associate Conductor 107.

BEYOND THE CALL OF DUTY
All-night Proms 108. Destruction of Queen's Hall 110.

JUBILEE OF THE PROMS
To the Royal Albert Hall 112. Back to the BBC 113. Sir Henry's stroke 114. Wagner losing ground, Bach gaining ground 114. First Sunday Prom (unplanned) 114. Three orchestras for the Jubilee 115. Wood honoured 116. BBC accepts 'Henry Wood Promenade Concerts' 116. Government again suspends Proms 117. BBC Symphony Orchestra evacuated again 117. Wood's last Prom; his death and memorial 118, 119.

THE KING IS DEAD
BBC Symphony Orchestra and London Symphony Orchestra 121. Basil Cameron, Sir Adrian Boult, joint conductors 122. Constant Lambert, Associate Conductor 122. Sir Henry's bust salvaged 122. Single-opera Wagner Nights again 125. Problems of succession 125, 126. Cameron, Boult, and Dr Malcolm Sargent, with three orchestras 126. All Proms broadcast 126. First television 127, 132. Sir Malcolm Sargent and Basil Cameron in charge 127. Inquest on the Last Night 128.

SARGENT: THE GOLDEN YEARS
Sir Malcolm, BBC Chief Conductor 126. Questions of repertoire and behaviour 131. *Sea-Songs* dropped 133. Royal Festival Hall 136. Auditions short-lived 137. Immediate second performance 137. Coronation Concert, Queen Elizabeth II 139. Sir John Barbirolli and the Hallé Orchestra 139. Diamond Jubilee Year; Sir Thomas Beecham 140. Sargent brings back Gilbert and Sullivan 140. Three centenaries 142. First soloist on two instruments 143. A new way with Bach 144. Sargent 'Chief Conductor of the Proms' 145.

CHECKMATE: SIR WILLIAM GLOCK
Glock in control at the BBC 148. Thursday Invitation Concerts and Midnight Matinées 148, 149. The foreign conductors question 149. New music and music from the past 150. Glyndebourne Festival Opera 151. Bruckner and Mahler 153. Paul Beard retires 154. Foreign conductors at last 154. The Amadeus String Quartet and other chamber music 154. Covent Garden Opera 156. Basil Cameron's eightieth birthday and last season 156. Sargent's seventieth birthday concert 156. Dorati, Boulez, Rozhdestvensky, Loughran 156. Sir John Barbirolli given Mahler Medal 157. First foreign orchestras 158. First Sunday Prom (planned) 158. Leopold Stokowski 158. Sargent unable to conduct 1967 season 159. His last appearance 162. Death of Sir Malcolm Sargent 164.

'THIS MAN WILL RUIN THE PROMS'
Sargent Memorial Prom; new Friday start 165. Colin Davis, BBC Symphony Orchestra's youngest conductor 167. A Last Night record 167. Pierre Boulez 168. 'Land of Hope and Glory' dropped 168. BBC commissions 169. Audience ballot at Prom 169. USSR State Orchestra's Proms 169. Some 'festival' events 171. Improved acoustics 171. Dancing, Dufay, and The Soft Machine 172. Proms go to the Royal Opera House, Westminster Cathedral, the Round House and Brompton Oratory 172-175. Late-night Proms 174, 175. Three-part Proms 175. Programme making 175, 176. Sir John Barbirolli Memorial Prom 176. Rachmaninov Centenary 176. Anniversary Proms: Sir Adrian Boult, Sir William Walton, Sir Lennox Berkeley, Benjamin Britten 176. The Duke of Edinburgh, and Prince Charles, at Proms 176. British conductors and British works on the Last Night 178. Sir William Glock's farewell Prom 178.

TOWARDS THE EIGHTIES

Robert Ponsonby succeeds Sir William Glock 179. The Composers' Guild 180. Ponsonby's policy 180, 181. Pierre Boulez, Chief Conductor, BBC Symphony Orchestra, opens 1974 season 182. Brass Bands 182, 184. Mishap in *Carmina Burana* 184. Four American orchestras 185. Death of Rudolf Kempe 185. Boulez and IRCAM, Paris 186. Organ extemporisation 187. Henry Wood Hall opened 188. Death of Basil Cameron 188. American Bicentenary Year Prom 189. Silver Jubilee of H. M. The Queen 189. Proms in quadraphony 189. Four Contemporary Masterworks concerts 189. Sir Adrian Boult's last Prom 190. Death of Leopold Stokowski 190. Proms go to St Augustine's Church 190; and to Riverside Studios 193. 'Auld Lang Syne' 190. Gennadi Rozhdestvensky, Chief Conductor, BBC Symphony Orchestra 190. Simon Rattle, the youngest Proms conductor 192. The first crossword 193. A Gamelan Orchestra 193. *Les Noces* cancelled 195. The first BBC videogram 195. Death of Lady Jessie Wood 195.

'SUMMER WOULD NOT BE SUMMER WITHOUT THE PROMS'

Musicians on strike 196. Events leading to the strike 196-201. A compromise solution? 201. The House of Commons debate 201, 202. Alternative Proms 203-205. BBC cancels First Night 203. A glimmer of hope 203. Simultaneous First Nights 203, 204. A formula to end the strike 204. The last Wembley Prom 205. The third First Night 206. Proms finances 206, 208. The 1980 Last Night 208, 209.

Index of Performers Mentioned

Abbado, Claudio 188, 208
Adler, Larry 137, 138
Alcock, G. W. 68, 85
Alexandra Quartet 60
Allen, Thomas 184
Allin, Norman 92
Alwyn, William 156
Amadeus String Quartet 150, 154, 190
Amsterdam Concertgebouw 61, 158, 206
Anda, Geza 153
Anderson, George 125
Anderson, Marian 80

Ansermet, Ernest 85
Arnold, Malcolm 138, 139, 176
Ashkenazy, Vladimir 156
Austin, Frederick 65
Austral, Florence 67, 92
Avis, Marjorie 136

Bachauer, Gina 133, 137
Backhaus, Wilhelm 53, 54, 84, 101
Baillie, Dame Isobel (Bella) 66, 79, 119
Bairstow, Edward G. 68

Baker, Dame Janet 150, 158, 187, 204
Ball, George Thalben 68, 85, 118, 145
Barbirolli, Sir John 139-142, 157, 176
Barenboim, Daniel 195
Barjansky, Alexandre 93
Bartlett, Ethel and Robertson, Rae 67, 92
Barton, June 169
Baudo, Serge 171
Beard, Paul 85, 99, 102, 119, 139, 154, 158

Beecham, Sir Thomas 63, 86, 87, 99, 140
Benjamin, Arthur 68
Berganza, Teresa 153
Bergsma, Deanne 172
Berkeley, Sir Lennox 107, 176, 201
Bishop-Kovacevich, Stephen 153, 188
Black Dyke Mills Band 184
Bliss, Sir Arthur 65
Bloch, Ernest 85, 86
Blyth, May 94
Booth, Webster 140
Borg, Kim 143
Boughton, Rutland 65
Boulez, Pierre 156, 162, 167-169, 174, 175, 177, 178, 182, 185, 186, 188, 190, 194
Boult, Sir Adrian 64, 66, 114, 115, 117, 118, 121, 122, 126-129, 136, 143, 153, 156, 176, 182, 188, 190
Bowden, Pamela 150
Boyd Neel Orchestra 86
Bradbury, Colin 205
Brain, Aubrey 67, 95
Brain, Dennis 139
Brainin, Norbert 150
Brannigan, Owen 124
Braun, Helena 137
Bravington, Eric 128
Bream, Julian 143
Brendel, Alfred 171
Bridge, Frank 65, 67
Britten, Benjamin 162, 176
Britton, Donald 172
Brosa, Antonio 96
Browne, Sandra 195
Brymer, Jack 142, 200
Bunting, Christopher 132
Busch, Adolf and Hermann 101
Bush, Alan 86
Busoni, Ferruccio 43
Butler, Antonia 108
Butt, Dame Clara 48

Cambridge University Madrigal Society 141
Cameron, Basil 107-109, 113-115, 121, 122-128, 130, 138, 139, 156, 188
Cammaerts, Tita 64
Carewe, John 153, 156
Carreras, José 203
Casals, Pablo 53
Caskel, Christoph 150
Cassadò, Gaspar 86
Catterall, Arthur 61, 73, 76, 108
Cherkassky, Shura 32, 143
Chicago Symphony Orchestra 185
Christoff, Boris 174
Chung, Kyung-Wha 188
Civil, Alan 172
Cleveland Symphony Orchestra 185
Coates, Eric 64, 65
Cohen, Harriet ('Tania') 68, 75, 86, 88, 91, 96, 97, 136
Cohen, Raymond 142
Cole, Maurice 118
Cologne Radio Symphony Orchestra and Choir 185, 89
Colonne, Eduard 58, 149
Copland, Aaron 114, 132
Cortot, Alfred 85
Covent Garden Opera 154, 156, 172
Cranmer, Arthur 94
Crossley, Paul 188
Cunningham, G. D. 68, 85, 98
Curzon, Sir Clifford 68, 75, 95, 116, 142, 190, 195, 208
Custard, Reginald Goss 68
Czech Army Choir 114
Czech Philharmonic Orchestra 169
Czyz, Henryk 162

Darke, Harold 68
Davies, Fanny 53
Davies, Meredith 154
Davis, Andrew 189, 208, 212
Davis, Sir Colin 104, 136, 150, 153, 160, 162, 165, 167, 168, 171, 177, 179, 185, 188, 203, 204
Dawson, Peter 54
De Greef, Artur 32, 63

Del Mar, Norman 120, 153, 177, 202
Desmond, Astra 66
Dods, Marcus 162
Dolmetsch, Carl 144
Dorati, Antal 153, 156, 204
Dupré, Marcel 88, 96, 102, 140
Dushkin, Alexander 84, 91

Early Music Consort 172, 185
Eisdell, Hubert 66
Eisenberg, Maurice 85
Elgar, Sir Edward 65, 67, 76, 85, 94
Elwes, Gervase 53
English Singers 68
Ensemble Intercontemporain 193
Eötvös, Peter 193
Evans, Sir Geraint 151, 201, 203

Falkner, Sir Keith 98
Felderer, Ingeborg 156
Ferrier, Kathleen 119, 124, 126
Feuermann, Emmanuel 101
Flagstad, Kirsten 142
Fogg, Eric 65
Foldes, Andor 143
Fournier, Pierre 128
Francescatti, Zino 137
Freni, Mirella 151
Furtwängler, Wilhelm 101, 121

Gabarain, Marina de 153
Garland, Dora 64
Gerhardt, Elena 62, 101
German, Edward 65
Gertler, André 142
Gibbs, Armstrong 65
Gilels, Emil 188
Gillegin, Ernest 79
Giulini, Carlo Maria 154, 156
Glazunov, Elena 101
Glock, Sir William 107, 178
Glossop, Peter 153
Glyndebourne Festival Opera 58, 151, 153-156, 192
Glynne, Walter 63
Godow, Louis 97

Goldsack, Jessie 54
Goldsmiths' Choral Union 139
Gomez, Jill 188
Goodall, Reginald 87
Goodson, Katharine 89, 99
Goossens, Eugene 65; Léon 105, 124, 143; Marie 143; Sidonie 87, 102, 143, 209
Grainger, Percy 53
Grant, Alexander 172
Greenbaum, Kyla 124
Grier, Arnold 85
Griller Quartet 116
Grimethorpe Colliery Band 184
Groves, Sir Charles 156, 176, 190, 193, 201, 204
Grumiaux, Arthur 124

Hacker, Alan 182
Haebler, Ingrid 150
Haendel, Ida 112, 119, 150, 190
Haitink, Bernard 162, 188, 206
Halifax Madrigal Society 68
Hallé Orchestra 139-142, 157
Hambourg, Mark 53, 140
Hammond, Joan 105, 118
Harper, Heather 143
Harrison, Beatrice 73, 93
Harrison, Julius 65
Harty, Sir Hamilton 63, 84, 86
Harvard Glee Club 141
Harvey, Jean 143
Harvey, Trevor 120, 136
Haselböck, Hans 187
Helffer, Claude 189
Hely-Hutchinson, Victor 75
Henderson, Roy 95
Henschel, Sir George 27, 60
Heseltine, Philip (Peter Warlock) 80
Hess, Dame Myra 46, 54, 66, 73, 91, 97, 98, 106, 117, 142, 150
Heyner, Herbert 63
Hindemith, Paul 78, 84
Hoban, John 175
Hogwood, Christopher 192
Holliger, Heinz 189
Hollingsworth, John 120, 132, 136, 144, 156
Hollweg, Ilse 142
Holmes, Ralph 189

Holst, Gustav 65
Holst, Henry 140
Hood, Dr Christopher 184
Hopkins, Antony 114, 201
Horenstein, Jascha 158
Howarth, Elgar 184
Howell, Gwynne 191
Howells, Herbert 65
Hubermann, Bronislaw 87
Humby, Betty 68
Hurst, George 161

International Youth Orchestra 188
Ireland, John 85, 97
Israel Philharmonic Orchestra 185, 193
Iturbi, José 67

Jacob, Gordon 65
Jarred, Mary 95
Jeans, Susi 126
Jeunesses Musicales World Orchestra 192
Joachim, Joseph 21, 53, 56, 86
Jones, Kathleen 143
Jones, Trefor 98
Joyce, Eileen 99, 128
Jullien, Louis 21
Jurinac, Sena 143

Kanawa, Kiri Te 208
Karajan, Herbert von 32
Katin, Peter 137
Kempe, Rudolf 156, 169, 185, 190
Kennedy, Daisy 75, 76
Kentner, Louis 112
Kersey, Eda 117
Khan, Imrat and Latif Ahmed 174
Klemperer, Otto 46, 167
Kodaly, Zoltan 78, 127
Kohler, Irene 94
König, Heinz 150
Kontarsky, Alfons and Aloys 150, 174
Köstler, Zdenek 169
Koussevitsky, Serge 84
Krenz, Jan 162

Kreisler, Fritz 84, 124
Kurtz, Edmund 143

Labbette, Dora (Lisa Perli) 63, 68, 88, 95
Lambert, Constant 122, 124-126
Lamond, Frederic 96
Langdon, Michael 151
Lara, Adelina de 27
Laszlo, Magda 141
Leicester Symphony Orchestra 66, 111
Leningrad Philharmonic Orchestra 169
Levi, Hermann 27
Lewis, Richard 141, 142, 151
Ligabue, Ilva 151
Lill, John 208
Linko, Liisa 142
Lloyd, Marie 20
London Philharmonic Choir 138
London Philharmonic Orchestra 99, 111, 114, 125, 126, 139
London Symphony Orchestra 34, 38, 39, 45, 86, 107, 108, 112, 115, 121, 126, 139, 156, 185, 203
Los Angeles Philharmonic Orchestra 185
Los Angeles, Victoria de 136
Loughran, James 157, 190
Lunn, Kirkby 53
Lush, Ernest 136
Lutoslawski, Witold 193
Luxon, Benjamin 31
Lympany, Moura 112, 118, 137, 195
Lysy, Alberto 153

Mackenzie, Sir Alexander 65
Maclean, Quentin 78
McCarthy, Patrick 184
Maazel, Lorin 185
Mackerras, Sir Charles 176, 182, 189, 209
Mackintosh, Jack 77
Mahler, Gustav 27
Malcolm, George 144

Malcuzynski, Witold 124
Mandikian, Arda 179
Marchant, Sir Stanley 68
Mason, Berkeley 108
Matthews, Denis 105, 142
Mehta, Zubin 185
Melba, Dame Nellie 21, 119
Melchior, Lauritz 66
Melis, György 151
Melsa, Daniel 63
Menges, Isolde 75
Menuhin, Yehudi 76, 124, 153, 193
Meredith, Burgess 114
Merrick, Frank 86
Mewton-Wood, Noel 128
Meyer, Kerstin 143
Mitchell, Ena 136
Moiseiwitsch, Benno 63, 66, 73, 75, 88, 92, 95, 105, 108, 117, 133, 142
Monreale, Leonardo 151
Monteux, Pierre 156
Moore, Gerald 107, 108
Mortimer, Harry 184
Moscow Radio Orchestra 158
Mottl, Felix 27, 34
Mravinsky, Evgeny 169
Muck, Carl 24, 27, 64
Mullings, Frank 60
Munich Philharmonic Orchestra 63, 169
Munrow, David 172, 185
Muti, Riccardo 190

Nash, Heddle 89, 97
National Youth Orchestra 143
Navarra, André 137
Neel, Boyd 97
Neumann, Vaclav 169
Neveu, Ginette 124
Newman, Robert 142
New Music Ensemble 153
New Symphony Orchestra 58
New York Philharmonic Orchestra 55, 107, 185
New Zealand Dorian Choir 190
NHK Symphony Orchestra 169
Nicholls, Agnes 34
Nicholson, Ralph 109
Nikisch, Artur 43, 61; Mitja 67

Norman, Jessye 182, 203, 206

Ogdon, John 143, 169
Oistrakh, David 169
Ord, Boris 141, 144
Ortiz, Cristina 202, 204
Ouroussoff, Princess Olga (Mrs Henry J. Wood) 47, 56, 60, 63

Panufnik, Andrzej 142, 193
Parikian, Manoug 137
Park Sisters 46, 49
Parker, W. Frye 39, 40
Patti, Adelina 63
Payne, Arthur 39, 40, 48, 54
Pears, Sir Peter 124, 139, 150
Perahia, Murray 190
Perkin, Helen 80
Perlemuter, Vlado 153
Peterkin, W. A. 21-23, 35, 36, 40, 54, 56, 117
Petri, Egon 54, 101
Philharmonia Orchestra and Chorus 62, 154
Philip Jones Brass Ensemble 184
Phillips, Montague F. 68
Piatigorsky, Gregor 101
Pini, Carl 99
Pitt, Percy 54, 71, 75
Polish Army Choir 114
Polish Radio Symphony Orchestra 162
Poole, John 188, 193
Postnikova, Victoria 190, 206
Pouishnoff, Leff 89, 102
Poulenc, Francis 80, 85
Pré, Jacqueline du 153, 156, 172
Previn, André 31, 176, 184, 201
Prey, Hermann 153
Primrose, William 124, 139
Pritchard, John 58, 149, 151, 162, 206

Queen's Hall Orchestra (New) 43, 48, 52, 58, 60-62, 64, 67, 71, 72, 75, 76
Quilter, Roger 89

Rachmaninov, Sergei 84, 104, 105, 114, 176
Randegger, Alberto 40
Rascher, Sigurd 104
Rattle, Simon 192, 205
Rawsthorne, Alan 84, 126
Reckless, Arthur 108
Reeves, Sims 38, 40, 53, 66
Reiss, Thelma 102, 105
Reizenstein, Franz 143
Reszke, Jean de 63
Reynolds, Howard 30, 40, 46, 50
Richter, Hans 45
Richter-Haaser, Hans 143
Riddle, Frederick 142
Rignold, Hugo 143
Robinson, Stanford 79, 126-28
Ronald, Sir Landon 71, 87
Rosen, Charles 208
Rosenthal, Moritz 86
Rosing, Vladimir 63
Rostal, Max 124, 128
Rostropovich, Mstislav 156, 169
Rothwell, Evelyn (Lady Barbirolli) 139, 201
Rotterdam Philharmonic Orchestra 185
Roujitzky, Wolodia 49
Royal Academy Orchestra 46, 118, 196
Royal Choral Society 140
Royal Liverpool Philharmonic Orchestra 156
Royal Philharmonic Orchestra 70, 151, 193, 204
Rozhdestvensky, Gennadi 156, 158, 169, 190, 193, 196, 206, 208
Rubbra, Edmund 113
Rubinstein, Arthur 101

Sadler's Wells Opera 149, 176
Sammons, Albert 73, 92, 97, 99
Sanzogno, Nino 149
Sarasate, Pablo 56
Sargent, Sir Malcolm 16, 41, 58, 60, 65, 80, 93, 110, 119, 125, 126, 128-133, 136, 137, 139-142, 145, 149, 150, 153-

156, 158, 162, 164, 165, 167, 168, 180

Sasono Mulio Gamelan Orchestra 193

Sauer, Emil 27, 52

Scharrer, Irene 63

Scheyrer, Gerda 151

Schidlof, Peter 150

Schiller, Allan 143

Schnabel, Artur 146

Schoenberg, Arnold 61, 84

Schumann, Clara 27, 53, 86

Schumann, Elisabeth 101, 122

Schwarz, Rudolf 145, 153, 176

Schwarzkopf, Elisabeth 139

Scott, Cyril 65

Scott, Margaretta 107, 128

Scriabin, Alexander 95

Sevcik, Ottokar 43, 75

Shirley-Quirk, John 189, 204

Shuard, Amy 133

Sitwell, Dame Edith 122

Sleep, Wayne 172

Slobodskaya, Oda 96

Smith,Cyril and Sellick, Phyllis 73, 113, 119, 158, 176

Smyth, Dame Ethel 61, 65, 80, 91

Söderström, Elisabeth 150, 182

Soft Machine 172

Solomon (Cutner) 63, 73, 84, 94, 105

Solomon, John 125

Solti, Sir Georg 154, 185

Spoorenberg, Erna 142

Stadlen, Peter 147

Stanford, Sir Charles Villiers 21, 56

Starker, Janos 143

Steindel, Bruno 48

Stern, Isaac 26

Stewart, Charles 111

Stokowski, Leopold 78, 154, 158, 190

Stosch, Madame von (Lady Speyer) 52, 53, 62

Stratton, George 108, 124

Strauss, Eduard 32

Stravinsky, Igor 84; Soulima 101

Suddaby, Elsie 96

Suggia, Guilhermina 128

Susskind, Walter 143

Sutherland, Dame Joan 137, 150

Svanholm, Set 137

Svetlanov, Evgeny 169

Swingle Singers 31

Sydney Symphony Orchestra 185

Szeryng, Henryk 150, 153

Szigeti, Josef 84, 86, 89, 101, 124

Tauber, Richard 101

Tausky, Vilem 141

Taylor, Richard 144

Tchaikovsky, Peter Ilyich 53

Tchaikowsky, André 171

Tear, Robert 31

Tertis, Lionel 53, 80, 94, 99, 117

Teyte, Dame Maggie 46, 66, 94, 119

Théméli, George 136

Thomas, Michael Tilson 195

Thompson, W. W. 75

Thurston, Frederick 139

Tippett, Sir Michael 188, 212

Titterton, Frank 67, 95

Toch, Ernst 95

Toronto Mendelssohn Choir 199

Torquay Municipal Orchestra 121

Tortelier, Paul 204

Toscanini, Arturo 101

Tovey, Sir Donald Francis 54

Ts'Ong, Fou 161

Tubbs, Carrie 61

Tuckwell, Barry 190

Tureck, Rosalyn 142, 144

Turner, Dame Eva 56, 73, 100, 104, 107, 108, 119, 137, 140, 159, 208

Turner, Laurance 88

USSR State Orchestra 169

Varga, Tibor 153

Varviso, Silvio 154

Vienna Philharmonic Orchestra 61

Vogel, Edith 137

Wagner, Richard 27; Siegfried 27, 77

Walker, Norman 67

Walter, Bruno 85

Walters, Jess 137

Walton, Sir William 92, 102

Warlock, Peter (Philip Heseltine) 80

Waterman, Fanny 114

Wearing, Stephen 98

Webern, Anton 84

Weir, Gillian 158

Weisgall, Hugo 114

Weldon, George 141

Welsh National Opera 189

Whittaker, Douglas 139

Widdop, Walter 67

Widor, Charles Marie 92, 93

Willcocks, Sir David 115, 156

Williams, Harold 67

Williams, Ralph Vaughan 65, 84, 89, 98, 104, 114, 138, 142

Williamson, Malcolm 143, 190, 195

Wilson, Marie 88, 98, 101

Wilson, Sir Steuart 75, 122

Wittgenstein, Paul 80, 137

Wood, Sir Henry J. 16, 22-31, 35-39, 42-49, 51, 52, 54-56, 58, 59, 61-66, 67, 69, 71, 72, 75-77, 79-81, 84, 86, 88, 89, 91, 94-96, 98-101, 104-109, 112-115, 117, 118, 120-122, 124-128, 131, 137, 140-142, 156, 159, 164, 167, 169, 171, 180, 196, 208, 209

Woodgate, Leslie 97, 98, 124, 144

Woodhouse, Charles 69, 76, 88, 91, 94, 95, 101

Woodward, Roger 171, 189, 194

Woytowicz, Stefania 162

Wright, Brian 192

Wykes, Christopher 111

Wyss, Sophie 86, 92

Ysaÿe, Eugène 43, 52

Zabaleta, Nicanor 143

Zender, Hans 192

Index of Works

Allitsen, Frances *Song of Thanksgiving* 47

Alwyn, William *Harp Concerto* 143; *Concerto Grosso* 156

Arne, Thomas *Keyboard Concerto* 78; *Rule, Britannia* 49, 81, 133, 168, 195

Arnold, Malcolm *Harmonica Concerto* 138; *English Dances* 139; *Fantasy* 168; *Three-hand Concerto* 176

Auber, Daniel *Ovt. The Bronze Horse* 29

Bach, J. S. *Amore Traditore* 55; *Brandenburg Concertos* 55, 77, 78, 98, 139, 144, 172; *Chaconne* 55; *Christmas Oratorio* 171; *Chorale Prelude* 88; *Concerto for two keyboards* 67, 98; *Concerto for four keyboards* 105; *Double Concerto (violins)* 108; *Goldberg Variations* 171; *Ich will den Kreuzstab* 55; *Jesu, Priceless Treasure* 144; *Keyboard Concerto in D minor* 144; *Magnificat* 141, 144; *Mass in B minor* 21, 43, 55, 60; *Partita in E* 94; *Prelude and Fugue in D (orch. Respighi)* 98; *Sarabande (solo cello)* 169; *St John Passion* 162, 171, 176; *St Matthew Passion* 60, 171; *Suites* 55, 98, 117; *Toccata and Fugue in D minor* 55, 78, 145; *Toccata in F* 78, 95. Bach- Gounod *Ave Maria* 77

Ballads *Gold o' the World* 66; *Homing* 75; *I Love the Moon* 66; *Love Went A-Riding* 95; *My Heart has a Quiet Sadness* 66; *She Wandered Down the Mountainside* 28; *Sing, Joyous Bird* 68; *The Fishermen of England* 68; *Thou'rt Passing Hence* 54

Banks, Don *Violin Concerto* 169

Bantock, Sir Granville *Omar Khayyam* 82

Barber, Samuel *Violin Concerto* 117, 189

Bartok, Bela *Bluebeard's Castle* 188; *Concerto for Orchestra* 138, 182; *Contrasts* 188; *Dance Suite* 98; *Miraculous Mandarin* 91, 185; *Sonata for Two Pianos and Percussion* 150; *Violin Concerto* 124

Bax, Sir Arnold *Cello Concerto* 86; *Concerto for Left Hand* 136; *Happy Forest* 96; *London Pageant* 102; *November Woods* 86; *Phantasy for Viola* 94; *Piano Sonata No. 4* 86; *Quintet for Strings* 86; *Symphonic Variations* 68; *Symphony No. 3* 91, 97; *No. 6* 139; *Tale the Pine-trees Knew* 87, 98; *Tintagel* 86; *Violin Concerto* 117; *Violin Sonata No. 2* 86

Beethoven, Ludwig van *Ah, perfido* 118; *An die ferne Geliebte* 75; *Archduke Trio* 171; *Battle Symphony* 46; *Choral Fantasia* 105; *Choral Symphony* 34, 54, 68, 79, 104, 105, 114, 125, 127, 136, 151, 158, 167, 171, 188; *Diabelli Variations* 171; *Equali* 184; *Eroica Symphony* 84, 171, 185, 212; *Fidelio* 56, 171; *Hammerklavier Sonata* 171; *Leonora* 125, 171; *Missa Solemnis* 150, 165, 172, 185; *Piano Concerto No. 2* 63; *No. 3* 49, 53, 101; *No. 4* 46, 53, 137; *No. 5 (Emperor)* 73, 208; *Septet* 55, 154; *Symphony No. 5* 47; *No. 7* 118; *No. 8* 175; *Violin Concerto* 46, 75, 101, 153

Benjamin, Arthur *Concertino* 68; *Harmonica Concerto* 138, 139; *Jamaican Rumba* 68; *Violin Concerto* 97

Benjamin, George *Ringed by the flat horizon* 208

Bennett, Richard Rodney *Actaeon* 190; *Aubade* 156

Berg, Alban *Altenberg Songs* 150; *Der Wein* 182; *Lyric Suite* 84; *Wozzeck* 94

Berio, Luciano *Coro* 189; *Perspectives* 150

Berkeley, Sir Lennox *Colonus' Praise* 128; *Flute Concerto* 139; *Introduction and Allegro for Two Pianos* 107, 146; *Sinfonia Concertante* 176; *Symphony No. 1* 113; *No. 3* 176; *No. 4* 193; *Voices of the Night* 188

Berlioz, Hector *Damnation of Faust* 60, 153; *Grande Messe des Morts* 149, 167; *Ovt. The Corsair* 84; *Te Deum* 114; *The Trojans* 179

Birtwistle, Harrison *Grimethorpe Aria* 184

Blacher, Boris *Variations on a Theme of Paganini* 150

Bliss, Sir Arthur *Colour Symphony* 102, 153; *Introduction and Allegro* 91; *Piano Concerto* 105; *Two-piano Concerto* 105

Bloch, Ernest *Concerto Grosso* 86; *Concerto Symphonique* 128; *Helvetia* 85; *Schelomo* 68, 85; *Suite Symphonique* 124

Borodin, Alexander *Prince Igor* 56; *Second String Quartet* 126

Boughton, Rutland *Oboe Concerto* 105

Boulez, Pierre *Le Marteau Sans Maître* 146; *Pli selon pli* 186

Brahms, Johannes *Double Concerto* 101; *Four Serious Songs* 126; *Four Songs* 60; *Liebeslieder*

Waltzes 136, 139; *Lullaby* 101; *Paganini Variations* 53, 54; *Piano Concerto No. 2* 73, 97, 208; *Symphony No. 2* 114; *No. 4* 85; *Violin Concerto* 75, 89, 101, 190

Brian, Havergal *New English Suite* 55; *New Overture, For Valour* 55; *Symphony No. 12* 158

Bridge, Frank *The Sea* 61, 65, 195

Britten, Benjamin *A Young Person's Guide* 126, 153; *Burning Fiery Furnace* 162; *Cantata Misericordium* 154; *Concerto for Left Hand* 137; *Diversions* 190; *Gloriana* 176; *Les Illuminations* 105, 124, 162; *Nocturne* 150; *Oboe Quartet* 86; *Peter Grimes* 124; *Piano Concerto* 104; *Serenade* 139; *Sinfonia da Requiem* 113; *Spring Symphony* 141, 175, 208; *Variations on a Theme of Frank Bridge* 104; *War Requiem* 96, 154, 188

Bruch, Max *Violin Concerto No. 1* 143

Bruckner, Anton *Mass in E minor* 187; *Symphony No. 4* 185; *No. 5* 206; *No. 7* 55; *No. 9* 153

Bush, Alan *Symphony in C* 113; *Violin Concerto* 128

Busoni, Ferruccio *Indian Fantasy* 99

Butterworth, George *A Shropshire Lad* 64, 89; *The Banks of Green Willow* 64

Cage, John *First Construction in Metal* 175; *Hpschd* 175

Carter, Elliott *Concerto for Orchestra* 175, 185; *Piano Concerto* 189, 208; *Variations* 158, 182

Casella, Alfredo *Le Couvent sur L'Eau* 65

Castelnuovo-Tedesco, Mario *Oboe Concerto* 139

Cavalli, Pietro *La Calisto* 171; *L'Ormindo* 171; *Messa Concertata* 158

Chabrier, Emmanuel *Espana* 139

Chopin, Frédéric *Ballade in F* 94; *Funeral March* 56; *Piano Concerto No. 1* 53, 86, 112; *No. 2* 85, 86, 112

Coates, Eric *Dambusters March* 190; *Miniature Suite* 60

Coleridge-Taylor, Samuel *Hiawatha* 140; *Violin Concerto* 61

Converse, Frederick *Californian Sketches* 97

Cooke, Arnold *Concert Overture No. 1* 96

Coward, J. M. *Vocal Waltz* 49

Cowie, Edward *Leviathan* 188; *Piano Concerto* 188

Crosse, Gordon *Celebration* 168

Davies, Peter Maxwell *Dark Angels* 190; *Eight Songs for a Mad King* 190; *Fantasia on an In Nomine* 153; *Stone Litany* 190; *St Thomas Wake* 190; *Symphony* 148, 190; *The Martyrdom of St Magnus* 189

Davies, Walford *Solemn Melody* 139

Debussy, Claude *Children's Corner* 60; *Fêtes* 97; *Ibéria* 61; *Images* 55; *Jeux* 150, 167; *La Mer* 55, 94; *Le Martyre de St Sébastien* 55; *L'Enfant Prodigue* 82; *Nocturnes* 92; *Prélude à l'après-midi d'un Faune* 55

Delius, Frederick *A Mass of Life* 141, 158; *Appalachia* 87; *A Song of Summer* 76; *A Song of the High Hills* 76, 84; *A Village Romeo and Juliet* 89, 93, 99, 199; *Brigg Fair* 95; *Cello Concerto* 93; *Cello Sonata* 93; *Dance Rhapsody* 98; *Double Concerto* 95, 99; *Eventyr* 99; *Idyll* 92, 93, 95; *In a Summer Garden* 93; *Irmelin* 140; *On Hearing the First Cuckoo* 127; *Over the Hills and Far Away* 99; *Paris* 87, 93; *Piano Concerto* 55, 95, 99, 117; *Requiem* 171; *Sea Drift* 208

Dohnanyi, Ernst von *New Suite* 61; *Variations on a Nursery Song* 66

Dukas, Paul *The Sorcerer's Apprentice* 91

Dupré, Marcel *Carillon* 88

Dvorak, Anton *Cello Concerto* 60, 169; *New World Symphony* 46, 104; *Slavonic (Sclavic) Dances* 29, 37; *Te Deum* 141

Elgar, Sir Edward *Cello Concerto* 73, 128, 156; *(arr. Tertis)* 80; *Chant, Belges, Chant* 64; *Coronation Ode* 54; *Enigma Variations* 54, 87; *Falstaff* 65, 89, 96; *Introduction and Allegro* 49, 55; *New Symphony in A flat (No. 1)* 54, 97; *Nursery Suite* 76; *Organ Sonata* 85; *Ovt. Cockaigne* 72, 88, 94, 168; *Pomp and Circumstance March No. 1 (Land of Hope and Glory)* 15, 54, 55, 168; *Symphony No. 2* 55, 85, 88, 121, 136, 156, 167; *The Apostles* 196, 203; *The Dream of Gerontius* 60, 110, 133, 142, 175; *The Kingdom* 94, 96; *Violin Concerto* 73, 76, 92, 124

Enesco, Georges *Rumanian Rhapsody No. 1* 60, 89

Falla, Manuel de *El Amor Brujo* 153; *Nights in the Gardens of Spain* 88; *Seven Popular Spanish Songs* 153; *Three-Cornered Hat* 95

Fauré, Gabriel *Fantaisie* 65; *Masques et Bergamasques* 65; *Requiem* 141

Franck, César *Symphonic Variations* 94, 104; *Symphony* 105

Foulds, John *A World Requiem* 96, 154

Gade, Niels *Symphony No. 4* 29

Gerhard, Roberto *Catalan Songs* 92; *Symphony No. 1* 153; *Sardana* 184; *Violin Concerto* 150

Gibson, Henry *Gaelic Pipe March* 97

Gilbert and Sullivan *Gondoliers* 28; *Iolanthe* 28; *Ivanhoe* 43, 46; *Mikado* 28; *Patience* 189

Glazunov, Alexander *Piano Concerto* 61, 98

Gluck, Christoph Willibald *Alceste* 56

Godfrey, Frederick *Reminiscences of England* 49

Goossens, Sir Eugene *Concert Piece* 143; *Symphony No. 1* 114; *Kaleidoscope* 88; *Scherzo: Tam O'Shanter* 65; *Sinfonietta* 95

Grainger, Percy *Brigg Fair* 208; *Handel in the Strand* 53, 91; *Molly on the Shore* 53; *Shepherd's Hey* 95

Grieg, Edvard *Bergliot* 107; *Peer Gynt* 47; *Piano Concerto* 53, 63, 89, 98, 161, 188

Halvorsen, Johan *Boyards' March* 40

Handel, George Frideric *Alexander's Feast* 124, 154; *Cello Sonata* 108; *Israel in Egypt* 126, 153; *Judas Maccabaeus* 95; *Messiah* 60, 69, 193; *Organ Concertos* 88, 96, 98, 118, 140; *Semele* 171; *Water Music* 192, 201; *Zadok the Priest* 139

Harty, Sir Hamilton *Sea-Wrack* 95; *Violin Concerto* 102; *With the Wild Geese* 63

Hawley, Stanley *The Bells* 40

Haydn, Joseph *Drum Roll Symphony* 94; *Emperor Quartet* 49, 154; *Farewell Symphony* 108; *Harmonie Mass* 182; *Nelson Mass* 175; *Piano Concerto* 96; *Symphony No. 99* 140; *The Creation* 96, 142, 154; *The Seasons* 94, 141

Henze, Hans Werner *Ode to the West Wind* 132; *Raft of the Medusa* 189; *Ragtimes and Habaneras* 184

Hérold, Ferdinand *Ovt. Zampa* 51, 78

Hindemith, Paul *Conzertmusik* 84; *Cupid and Psyche* 116, 124; *Mathis der Maler* 84; *News of the Day* 91, 98; *Organ Concerto* 78; *Philharmonic Concerto* 88; *Unaufhörliche* 84

Holst, Gustav *Savitri* 187; *Somerset Rhapsody* 98; *The Planets* 64, 65, 88, 94, 145, 190, 212

Honegger, Arthur *Chant de Joie* 94; *King David* 142; *Liturgical Symphony* 128; *Third Symphonic Movement* 91

Howells, Herbert *Birthday Suite* 125; *Procession* 98

Hübler, Heinrich *Concertstück for Four Horns* 49

Ibert, Jacques *Diane de Poitiers* 139

Ireland, John *Downland Suite* 184; *Legend* 96; *London Overture* 142; *Mai-Dun* 97; *Piano Concerto* 80, 98, 101, 128; *Soldier's Return* 85; *These Things Shall Be* 125

Ives, Charles *Three Places in New England* 150

Jacob, Gordon *Festal March* 125; *Violin Concerto* 139

Janacek, Leos *Katya Kabanova* 187

Jullien, Louis *British Army Quadrilles* 32, 38

Khachaturyan, Aram *Ode to Stalin* 118; *Piano Concerto* 118

Knussen, Oliver *Symphony No. 3* 194

Kodaly, Zoltan *Dances of Galanta* 97; *Hary Janos* 78, 97, 105, 127, 140; *Peacock Variations* 132; *Psalmus Hungaricus* 96

Koenig, H. *The Post Horn Galop* 37, 40, 46

Lambert, Constant *Horoscope* 104; *Music for Orchestra* 89; *The Rio Grande* 84, 97, 122

Larsson, Lars-Erik *Saxophone Concerto* 104

Leoncavallo, Ruggiero *Pagliacci* 66

Lewis, Sir Anthony *Overture for Unaccompanied Chorus* 104

Ligeti, György *Aventures; Nouvelles Aventures* 172

Liszt, Franz *Christus* 192; *Dante Symphony* 55; *Faust Symphony* 89, 97; *Hungarian Fantasia* 53, 140; *Kennst du das Land* 94; *Orpheus* 92; *Piano Concerto No. 1* 53, 54, 89, 97, 143; *St Francis Preaching to the Birds* 89

Litolff, Henry *Scherzo* 143

Loeffler, Charles *The Death of Tintagiles* 64

Lutyens, Elisabeth *Viola Concerto* 131

MacCunn, Hamish *Land of the Mountain and the Flood* 37

Mackenzie, Sir Alexander *Eugene Aram* 40

McCabe, John *Notturni ed Alba* 188

Machaut, Guillaume de *Notre Dame Mass* 172

Maconchy, Elizabeth *Variazioni Concertanti* 157

Mahler, Gustav *Kindertotenlieder* 158; *Resurrection Symphony* 154, 162, 178; *Symphony No. 1* 55, 79; *No. 3* 79, 153, 168, 210; *No. 4* 56, 206; *No. 5* 91; *No. 6* 157; *No. 8* 156, 165, 167; *No. 9* 158, 185; *No. 10* 153, 156

Martin, Frank *Petite Symphonie Concertante* 148

Martinu, Bohuslav *Memorial to Lidice* 122; *Piano Concerto No. 2* 139

Massenet, Jules *Last Sleep of the Virgin* 140; *Ovt. Phèdre* 40

Meale, Richard *Piano Concerto* 189

Mellers, Wilfrid *Yeibichai* 172

Mendelssohn, Felix *Hymn of Praise* 46, 55; *Italian Symphony* 29; *Octet* 154, 171; *Piano Concerto in G minor* 29, 37, 53; *Reformation Symphony* 151; *Spring Song* 28; *Violin Concerto* 38, 40, 47, 91, 108, 153

Messiaen, Olivier *Et Exspecto Resurrectionem Mortuorum* 162; *La Nativité du Seigneur* 158; *La Transfiguration de notre Seigneur Jésus Christ* 171; *Oiseaux Exotiques* 153; *Poèmes pour Mi* 206; *Quartet for the End of Time* 193; *Turangalîla Symphony* 171, 189

Milhaud, Darius *Two Marches* 124

Moeran, E. J. *Farrago* 97

Moniuszko, Stanislav *The Haunted Castle* 114

Monteverdi, Claudio *Il ritorno d'Ulisse* 171; *Magnificat* 172; *Vespers* 171

Mozart, Wolfgang Amadeus *Clarinet Concerto* 139, 182; *Così fan tutte* 153, 192; *Don Giovanni* 151, 153, 167, 179, 192; *Horn Concerto* 67; *Idomeneo* 156; *Impresario* 171; *Marriage of Figaro* 56, 94, 109, 154; *Piano Concerto in A, K488* 118; *in C, K503* 150; *in E flat, K543* 96; *in B flat, K595* 195; *Quartet in E flat* 178; *Requiem* 153; *Sinfonia Concertante* 53, 142, 150; *Two-piano Concerto* 94, 195; *Zaïde* 171

Murrill, Herbert *Three Hornpipes* 98

Musgrave, Thea *Concerto for Orchestra* 169; *Horn Concerto* 190

Mussorgsky, Modest *Boris Godunov* 172; *Pictures from an Exhibition* 63, 184

Newson, George *Arena* 175

Nono, Luigi *Songs of Life and Love* 154

Orff, Carl *Carmina Burana* 141, 184

Paganini, Niccolò *Violin Concerto* 137

Palestrina, Giovanni *Mass, Assumpta est Maria* 175

Panufnik, Andrzej *Rhapsody* 142; *Sinfonia di Sfere* 193

Parry, Sir Hubert *Jerusalem* 133; *Job* 142; *The Birds of Aristophanes* 66

Penderecki, Krzysztof *St Luke Passion* 162; *Violin Concerto* 208

Pfitzner, Hans *Three Preludes from Palestrina* 66

Phillips, Montague F. *Piano Concerto No. 2* 68

Pitt, Percy *Coronation March* 46; *New Suite in Four Movements* 37

Pizzetti, Ildebrando *La Pisanella* 65

Play of Daniel, The 188

Poulenc, Francis *Aubade* 80; *C* 113; *Two-piano Concerto* 91; *Organ Concerto* 158

Prokofiev, Serge *Piano Concerto No. 1* 65; *Symphony No. 5* 124; *Symphony No. 7* 142; *Violin Concerto* 96, 124

Puccini, Giacomo *La Bohème* 88, 94, 97; *Tosca* 142; *Turandot* 73

Purcell, Henry *Abdelazer* 153; *Dido and Aeneas* 156; *King Arthur* 171; *The Fairy Queen* 171; *The Indian Queen* 158; *The King Shall Rejoice* 139

Rachmaninov, Sergei *Corelli Variations* 84; *Isle of the Dead* 63; *Paganini Variations* 105; *Piano Concerto No. 1* 54; *No. 2* 66, 73, 89, 105; *No. 3* 68, 95, 169; *Symphony No. 3* 105; *The Bells* 176; *Vespers* 193

Rainier, Priaulx *Violin Concerto* 193

Rameau, Jean Philippe *Hippolyte et Aricie* 171; *Les Boréades* 191

Ravel, Maurice *Bolero* 88, 171; *Concerto for Left Hand* 80, 137; *Daphnis and Chloë* 88, 121; *La Valse* 88, 97; *L'Heure Espagnole* 187; *Pavane* 60; *Piano Concerto* 88; *Rapsodie Espagnole* 55; *Valses Nobles et Sentimentales* 61

Rawsthorne, Alan *Ovt. Cortèges* 124; *Ovt. Street Corner* 124

Reger, Max *Serenade* 55

Reizenstein, Franz *Concerto Popolare* 143

Rimsky-Korsakov, Nicolai *Capriccio Espagnol* 51; *Chant Indou* 98; *Scheherazade* 99, 104

Rodrigo, Joaquin *Concierto d'Aranjuez* 143

Rossini, Gioacchino *The Barber of Seville* 77, 185

Rubbra, Edmund *Sinfonia Concertante* 113; *Symphony No. 4* 113; *No. 11* 208; *Viola Concerto* 139

Rubinstein, Anton *Piano Concerto No. 4* 53

Saint-Saëns, Camille *Cello Concerto* 102; *Le Carnaval des Animaux* 67, 104, 113; *Phaëton* 102; *Piano Concerto No. 4* 53, 102; *Rondo Capriccioso* 52; *Samson and Delilah* 53, 142; *Symphony No. 3* 102

Sargent, Sir Malcolm *An Impression on a Windy Day* 65, 140; *Nocturne and Scherzo* 66; *Valsette in A minor* 66. Arrangements: *Rule, Britannia (Arne)* 133; *Four Serious Songs (Brahms)* 126; *String Quartet No. 2 (Borodin)* 126

Scharwenka, Xavier *Operatic Prelude, Mataswintha* 40

Schloesser, Adolf *Les Enfants de la Garde* 30

Schmitt, Florent *New Suite, Reflets d'Allemagne* 60

Schoenberg, Arnold *De Profundis* 150; *Erwartung* 156; *Five Orchestral Pieces* 61, 97, 143, 150; *Gurrelieder* 84, 171, 182; *Jacob's Ladder* 171; *Moses and Aaron* 158; *Piano Concerto* 124, 194; *Pierrot Lunaire* 176; *The Lucky Hand* 191; *Transfigured Night* 84, 182; *Variations* 84, 149; *Violin Concerto* 153

Schubert, Franz *Great C major Symphony* 37, 91, 121, 136, 153, 171, 182, 208; *Lieder* 101; *Octet* 162; *Symphony No. 5* 140; *Trio in B flat* 171; *Trout Quintet* 190; *Unfinished Symphony* 29, 37, 46, 104; *Wanderer Fantasia* 75

Schuman, William *Free Song* 123-124

Schumann, Robert *Concertstück for Four Horns* 49; *Piano Concerto* 46, 53, 73, 84, 91, 136; *Piano Quintet* 109; *Symphony No. 4* 46

Scott, Cyril *Britain's War March* 63; *Festival Overture* 96

Shostakovich, Dmitri *Concerto for Piano and Trumpet* 128; *Leningrad Symphony* 113; *Piano Concerto* 142; *Symphony No. 1* 196; *No. 4* 154, 190; *No. 5* 124; *No. 8* 116, 117, 156; *No. 9* 124; *No. 10* 142; *No. 11* 142; *No. 12* 154; *No. 14* 175; *The Nose* 85

Sibelius, Jan *En Saga* 54, 140; *Kullervo* 193; *Luonnotar* 142; *Swan of Tuonela* 92; *Swan White* 54; *Symphony No. 1* 87, 142; *No. 2* 84; *No. 4* 176; *No. 5* 84, 140, 156; *No. 6* 78,

140; *No. 7* 84, 140; *Tapiola* 78, 87; *Violin Concerto* 54, 140

Smetana, Bedrich *Ovt. Bartered Bride* 126

Smyth, Dame Ethel *Concerto for Violin and Horn* 80; *The Prison* 87; *The Wreckers* 61, 91

Souster, Tim *Triple Music II* 172

Starakadomsky, Mikhail *Concerto for Orchestra* 126

Stockhausen, Karlheinz *Carré* 174, 182; *Gruppen* 162, 172; *JUBILEE* 208; *Kontakte* 40, 193; *Mantra* 174; *Song of Youth* 150, 172

Strauss, Richard *Also sprach Zarathustra* 31; *Burlesque* 67, 96; *Capriccio* 171; *Don Juan* 51, 65, 96; *Don Quixote* 65, 96, 212; *Duet Concertino* 128; *Ein Heldenleben* 99, 102, 185; *Oboe Concerto* 124; *Operatic Prelude, Guntram* 40; *Parergon* 80; *Rosenkavalier Waltzes* 60; *Salome* 61, 96; *Symphonia Domestica* 55; *Till Eulenspiegel* 51, 65, 94; *Tod und Verklärung* 65, 89

Stravinsky, Igor *Capriccio* 84; *Firebird Suite* 61, 104; *Four Norwegian Moods* 116; *Les Noces* 153, 195, 212; *Octet* 154; *Oedipus Rex* 150; *Renard* 171; *Symphony in Three Movements* 149; *Symphony of Psalms* 61, 138; *The Rake's Progress* 188; *The Rite of Spring* 40, 84, 126, 176; *The Soldier's Tale* 175; *Violin Concerto* 91

Sullivan, Sir Arthur *The Lost Chord* 46; *Thou'rt Passing Hence* 54 (See also Gilbert and Sullivan)

Tailleferre, Germaine *Concerto for Two Pianos* 102; *Harp Concerto* 102

Tallis, Thomas *Spem in Alium* 153

Tapp, Frank *Metropolis* 96

Tate, Phyllis *London Waits* 92

Tavener, John *In Alium* 169; *Ultimos Ritos* 188

Taylor, Deems *Circus Suite* 99

Tchaikovsky, Peter Ilyich *Capriccio Espagnol* 94; *Casse-Noisette* 104; *Cossack Dance* 117; *Eugen Onegin* 56, 66, 133, 171; *Manfred Symphony* 153; *Marche Solennelle* 40; *Ovt. 1812* 133; *Piano Concerto No. 1* 53, 84, 88, 204; *Queen of Spades* 63, 137; *Rococo Variations* 105; *Swan Lake* 117, 139; *Symphonie Pathétique* 84; *Symphony No. 4* 53, 208; *No. 5* 158; *Violin Concerto* 87, 113, 188

Tchérépnin, Nikolai *Piano Concerto* 64

Tippett, Sir Michael *Birthday Suite* 125; *Con-*

certo for Double String Orchestra 124; *Piano Concerto* 188; *Symphony No. 4* 185, 216; *The Midsummer Marriage* 189, 208; *Triple Concerto* 208

Toch, Ernst *Symphony No. 2* 95

Touschmalov, Mikhail Orch. *Pictures from an Exhibition (Ravel)* 63

Turina, Joaquin *Procession del Rocio* 95

Varèse, Edgar *Déserts* 158; *Ecuatorial* 158

Verdi, Giuseppe *Aida* 49, 56; *Don Carlos* 171; *Iago's Credo* 63; *Il Trovatore* 49; *Macbeth* 191; *Otello* 156; *Requiem* 141, 154, 165, 191, 210; *Sicilian Vespers* 171

Villa-Lobos, Heitor *Choros 8* 80

Vivaldi, Antonio *Concerto for Four Violins* 105; *Flute Concerto* 150

Wagner, Richard *Die Meistersinger* 68, 142, 205; *Lohengrin* 66, 68; *Parsifal* 68, 98, 175; *Rienzi* 27, 35, 140; *Tannhäuser* 47, 56, 66, 96; *The Flying Dutchman* 24; *The Ring of the Nibelungs* 27, 60, 68, 97; *Das Rheingold* 68, 171, 176; *Die Walküre* 27, 156; *Siegfried* 55, 60, 66, 91, 171; *Götterdämmerung* 63, 77, 92, 107, 154; *Tristan und Isolde* 27, 45, 56, 66, 68, 92, 141, 171

Walton, Sir William *Belshazzar's Feast* 80, 86, 96, 141, 156, 162; *Coronation Te Deum* 139, 156; *Crown Imperial March* 102; *Façade* 92, 104, 122; *Orb and Sceptre March* 139; *Sinfonia Concertante* 97; *Troilus and Cressida* 141; *Viola Concerto* 78, 124, 167;

Where Does the Uttered Music Go? 124

Warlock, Peter (Philip Heseltine) *Capriol Suite* 80

Weber, Carl Maria von *Concertstück* 37; *Invitation to the Waltz* 51; *Ovt. Turandot* 94

Webern, Anton *Five Orchestral Pieces* 153; *Six Pieces* 149

Weisgall, Hugo *American Comedy 1943* 114

Widor, Charles Marie *Fifth Symphony* 65, 93; *Sinfonia Sacra* 65

Williams, Ralph Vaughan *Fantasia on English Folk Songs* 55; *Greensleeves* 98; *Job* 190; *London Symphony* 98, 124; *Norfolk Rhapsody* 55; *Pastoral Symphony* 65, 89, 96, 104; *Piano Concerto* 88; *Romance for Harmonica* 137; *Serenade to Music* 13, 104, 140, 156; *Sinfonia Antartica* 139; *Songs of Travel* 98; *Suite, The Wasps* 61; *Symphony No. 5* 114, 137; *No. 9* 142; *Tallis Fantasia* 65, 84, 98, 142, 212; *The Lark Ascending* 98; *The Running Set* 98; *The Story of a Flemish Farm* 124

Williamson, Malcolm *Hammarskjöld Portrait* 182; *Organ Concerto* 190; *Piano Concerto* 143; *The Stone Wall* 168; *Two-piano Concerto* 193

Wood, Sir Henry J. *Fantasia on British Sea-Songs* 49, 56, 67, 78, 80, 128, 133, 136, 143, 168, 195; *Fantasia on Scottish Melodies* 56; *Fantasia on Welsh Melodies* 56. Orch. *Pictures from an Exhibition (Ravel)* 63 As 'Paul Klenovsky', arranged *Toccata and Fugue in D minor (Bach)* 78, 140, 156

Xenakis, Yannis *Phlegra* 190